T0301498

REMAKING THE REAL ECONOMY

Escaping Destruction by Organised Money

Gordon Pearson

First published in Great Britain in 2020 by

Policy Press, an imprint of
Bristol University Press
University of Bristol
1-9 Old Park Hill
Bristol
BS2 8BB
UK
t: +44 (0)117 954 5940
e: bup-info@bristol.ac.uk

Details of international sales and distribution partners are available at
policy.bristoluniversitypress.co.uk

British Library Cataloguing in Publication Data
A catalogue record for this book is available from the British Library

ISBN 978-1-4473-5658-5 hardcover
ISBN 978-1-4473-5659-2 paperback
ISBN 978-1-4473-5661-5 ePub
ISBN 978-1-4473-5660-8 ePdf

Cover design: blu inc, Bristol
Front cover image: Will Pearson
Bristol University Press and Policy Press use environmentally
responsible print partners.
Printed in Great Britain by CMP, Poole

For Olive, Edie, Martha, Stanley, Florence, Angus and Rowan who will inherit this world and will take so much better care of it than we have.

Contents

List of abbreviations   vi
Preface   vii

PART I   Where are we now?   **1**
1   The 'witchcraft' and 'institutional truths' of 21st   3
         century neoclassical belief
2   'Old enemies of peace': constituents of organised money   23
3   Resulting profound wrongs, destructions, inequalities   41
         and frauds

PART II   Where do we want to get to?   **57**
4   Democratic commitments to sustainable progression   59

PART III   How do we get there?   **77**
5   Real people: engines of enterprise   79
6   Organisational systems and their coordination   91
7   Organisational systems interactions with the real economy   107

PART IV   Action   **123**
8   Systemic action for progression without destruction   125

PART V   How are we doing?   **147**
9   Measures of real progression   149

Practitioner notes on real organisational systems   165
References   207
Index   219

List of abbreviations

CECP	Chief Executives for Corporate Purpose
CEO	Chief Executive Officer
EMH	efficient market hypothesis
EU	European Union
GDP	Gross Domestic Product
GDPR	General Data Protection Regulation
IMF	International Monetary Fund
IPCC	Intergovernmental Panel on Climate Change
LLP	limited liability partnership
MDGs	Millennium Development Goals
MIT	Massachusetts Institute of Technology
M&MC	Monopolies and Mergers Commission
MST	maximising shareholder take
MV	Quantity of Money per time period x Velocity of its circulation
NASA	National Aeronautics and Space Administration
NHS	National Health Service
OFT	Office of Fair Trading
OPEC	Organisation of Petroleum Exporting Countries
PPE	Philosophy, Politics and Economics
PSD	Primary Standard Data
PT	Prices x number of Transactions per time period
QE	quantitative easing
R&D	Research and Development
RAF	Royal Air Force
SDGs	Sustainable Development Goals
SMEs	small and medium sized enterprises
UNESCO	United Nations Educational, Scientific and Cultural Organisation
WW2	Second World War

Preface

The Big Bang brought the universe into existence almost 14 billion years ago, with the solar system including planet Earth, forming around 4.5 billion years ago. DNA studies have identified Homo sapiens as having emerged as a distinct species around 195,000 years ago, the last few minutes of the Big Bang day.[1] In the last few seconds, humans have created systems which could sustainably satisfy all peoples' needs, wants and most of our desires, but are instead heading us for oblivion, simply in order to satisfy the predatory gain of a few at huge cost to the whole human race.

The story of Easter Island is sometimes presented as a parable for Earth. The first settlers discovered an island paradise with plentiful food supplies of fish, birds and vegetation, as well as trees providing raw materials for shelter, clothing and boat construction. The islanders prospered, and they carved their giant religion-based *Moai* statues which remain today, remnants of their particular system of beliefs, but serving no practical purpose.

As the population grew, so did the inevitable consumption and waste of all the island's limited resources. The islanders failed to recognise their interdependence with the island's other species. Eventually they were all consumed, and inevitably population collapsed. It has been said the last survivors, at below subsistence level, even resorted to cannibalism – surely the ultimate inequality. That obvious interdependence of biological species is even more important in today's recognisably fragile world.

Global population remained a few hundred million for thousands of years, limited by recurrent famine and plague. That stagnation was ended by the 18th century revolution in agriculture which produced a reliable food surplus for the first time; this was a major contributor to enabling the subsequent industrial revolution, which changed everything. World population had grown to an estimated 1 billion by 1800, and has since exploded to around 7.75 billion today, forecast to be 9.5 billion by 2050 with some forecasts of over 11 billion by 2100.[2] Moreover, average real income per head in the advanced economies is now estimated at around 1000 per cent higher than before the first industrial revolution.[3]

While those increases of population and affluence clearly present the problems exampled by Easter Island, they were achieved through human enterprise, inventiveness and industry, in which the Easter Islanders were more limited. We are still achieving extraordinary gains from new technologies with their newly globalised reach. The opportunities are there to change fundamentally the ways we develop, improving the richness of life on Earth and at the same time making it permanently sustainable. But we are being led to our own destruction by an economic ideology which, despite having been shown many times to be utterly false since it was invented in the mid-19th century, has only increased its power and influence, especially over the past few decades.

This text provides a broad analysis based on the practical realities of how the world works. Driven by human enterprise, working in a wide variety of organisational systems, generating new technologies, processes, employment and progressions, remaking the real economy appears to be the route to permanent sustainability. That solution appears still to be available but seems unlikely to remain so for long.

The text is structured along the lines of a simple business strategy model:[4]

> Where are we now?
> Where do we want to get to?
> How do we get there?
> Action
> How are we doing?

The main focus is on the advanced economies of the world, the lead exemplar being the UK which, together with the US, appears to be leading the race to the bottom. But the 'we' referred to here has to include the whole human race, both present and future, because, at the end of the sustainable day, we will truly all be in it together. Beyond that, the argument is also raised that 'we' must include all forms of biological life because it is becoming clear that they are all interdependent, and all vulnerable, as what seems likely to be a decisive tipping point is approached. A whole lot of things appear to be wrong, and not just slightly wrong, but wrong to such an extent that survival itself appears threatened.

Where are we now?

We are being controlled by an economic ideology, based on false assumptions and theorising. That ideology is exercised, supported and promoted by its prime beneficiaries, the self-perpetuating 'organised money' establishment. The result is we are enabling social and ecological destructions, untenable inequalities and criminality, which are well known but largely ignored by those with the power to rule. While there are signs of potentially fundamental change, actual achievement falls far short of what is required, despite the necessary action responses to the COVID-19 pandemic.

Where do we want to get to?

This has long been defined by democratic institutions and largely agreed internationally, and mostly granted legal foundation. It has been expressed many times in the form of commitments to environmental stewardship, human rights, equal opportunities and with some social balance to promise a better future. Politicians make heroic statements about their aims for the people whose interests they are supposed to represent. But their fine words have rarely been supported by adequate action.

How do we get there?

This is what really matters. It will clearly be driven by human beings, working together in various forms of organisation which are the key to progression. That systems approach is based on observation of reality. We know so much more about humanity than the simplistic and false 'greed is good' assumptions of microeconomic theorising. And we also know so much more about how real organisational systems work.

Quality specialists Deming,[5] Juran[6] and others,[7] applied the necessary knowledge and understanding to how organisations of all kinds work most effectively in the real world. An overview is provided of the various alternative formats for such organisational systems which could all contribute to achieving sustainable progression by the development and application of the necessary technologies to all three very different layers of the real economy.

Action

Initiatives are outlined for remaking the real economy. That is to be achieved by rebuilding the social–infrastructural economy, re-establishing the progressive–competitive economy and refocusing the technological–revolutionary economy. That way democratically expressed commitments to social and ecological sustainability might be fulfilled simultaneously with genuine economic progression rather than simple growth. But that will only be achieved by restraint (in an ideal world: self-restraint) of the organised money establishment. The key to achieving that will depend on the complete displacement of the 21st century version of neoclassical belief.

How are we doing?

This is measured by assessing real progression towards fulfilment of the democratically agreed commitments, rather than the simplistic, fixable and ideologically motivated metrics of GDP and its growth.

In January 2020 there are increasing indications that influential bodies across the globe are recognising the destructions wreaked by false economic dogma. They appear to be espousing revised agendas. In the US, the Business Roundtable is redefining the purpose of the corporation, asserting that the 'long-term success of these companies and the US economy depends on businesses investing in the economic security of their employees and the communities in which they operate'.[8] Similar moderation is being promoted by the *Financial Times'* New Agenda,[9] based more on the observation of economic realities. That new direction could result in genuinely sustainable progression. But the reality of such commitments has yet to be demonstrated. The massive relearning experience provided by Covid-19 could make the new direction more fully operational.

Practitioner notes on real organisational systems

Moral philosopher Adam Smith commenced his enquiry into the nature and causes of the wealth of nations, by observing human enterprise in the 'trade of the pin-maker'. The Practitioner notes aim to follow that example. Observation of practical realities, in many different situations, still provides knowledge and understanding of human enterprise and how organisational systems work, taking account of the social and ecological macro-systems with which they interact. That reality seems to be a more reliable foundation for decision making than the ivory tower economic theorising which is driving us all to destruction.

Brief accounts are included of different processes of value creation by people collaborating with each other, in manufacturing, in distribution and in services. They also include examples of value extraction by the predatory financial sector. The effective working of all organisational systems, whether public not-for-profit or private for-profit, is dependent on whether a system and its active components are properly focused on fulfilling the system's existential purpose to create value in some form or other; or whether it is diverted into value extraction and destruction.

Practitioner notes outline industrial innovation, compliant with Deming's systems approach; initiatives are identified for remaking the real economy and ending destructions by organised money while being supportive of both social and ecological macro-systems.

A satisfactory resolution may still be within this generation's reach. But it seems unlikely to remain so for long. Action with urgency appears now to be essential for survival.

Gordon Pearson
April 2020

PART I

Where are we now?

These opening three chapters identify what appear to be the critical dimensions of our current position and direction of travel. We are not in a good place and we are not headed in the right direction.

We are allowing ourselves to be guided by misconceived and unrealistic neoclassical microeconomic theory which bears little relation to economic realities. Despite having been shown many times to be utterly false, the theory remains, even in 2020, dominant as a belief system which influences behaviour.

The prime beneficiaries of that system have established themselves as an apparently self-perpetuating establishment, which continues to extend its control across an ever increasing proportion of the global economy.

The result has been all manner of ecological destructions, inequalities, frauds and criminality which, unless controlled and reversed, will in the end make planet earth uninhabitable.[1]

That's where we are.

We don't need to be here – there is an alternative.

1

The 'witchcraft' and 'institutional truths' of 21st century neoclassical belief

Introduction

After thousands of years of virtual stagnation, the real economy took off in the 18th century, supporting huge rises in population and standards of living. It was a real revolution of invention and innovation, involving the development of a transport infrastructure to carry the raw materials to the new mills and factories, initially by canal, later by rail. At first the new machinery was driven by waterpower and later by steam, creating whole new industries in textiles, iron and chemicals. All were developed without recourse to economic theory, the prime requirement being for human creativity and industry to improve and progress.

However, it was a revolution which needed to be properly understood if the best political-economic decisions were to be taken as to its control and direction. Moral philosopher Adam Smith sought that understanding with his *Inquiry into the Nature and Causes of the Wealth of Nations*, which was published in 1776, the year Richard Arkwright's first water-powered cotton mill commenced production and the American colonies declared their independence.

Smith opened his inquiry with observations of the processes of pin manufacture. From that practical account of the work and its outcomes, he drew some conclusions as to the creation of wealth. As moral philosopher, he developed ideas as to how that wealth might best be accumulated, employed and distributed among 'ranks of people' as well as allocated to state provision of defence, justice, education and public works and institutions 'which may be in the highest degree advantageous to a great society'.[1]

That approach to understanding was fundamentally based on the observation of real operations, processes and systems, and their apparent outcomes. An alternative approach was to theorise ideas and models which were not based on empirical observation, but more according to an internal logic. Jean-Baptiste Say conjectured

3

Say's Law, an early example of such theorising. It stated that supply creates its own demand, because production earns the money that is spent on other productions. There is obviously some truth in that idea, but absolutely no possibility of mathematical precision. It is also dependent on the assumption of economic equilibrium: that prices will adjust to equate supply with demand through the processes of competitive supply. It therefore excludes the possibility of excess supply causing gluts and consequently recessions. Real world experience has repeatedly demonstrated that to be false, but it nevertheless survived as a theory, even a law, that successive generations of students of economics were taught.

Smith also conjectured, as moral philosopher, that the value of anything depended on the amount of labour involved in its production. That theoretical concept, the labour theory of value, was picked up later and argued with greater precision by David Ricardo.[2] It was this theorised analysis of the political economy which attracted many others to the development of what Marx later referred to as 'classical political economy'.[3]

Thus, two distinct strands of explanatory analysis developed from the industrial revolution: on the one hand, the observation of real organisations, processes and systems; and, on the other, theoretical modelling based on some internal logic with limited reference to reality.

Understanding by observation

Smith's introduction to the *Wealth of Nations* reported the processes involved in pin manufacture:

> One man draws out the wire, another straightens it, a third cuts it, a fourth points it, a fifth grinds it at the top for receiving the head; to make the head requires two or three distinct operations; to put it on, is a peculiar business, to whiten the pins is another; it is even a trade by itself to put them into the paper; and the important business of making a pin is, in this manner, divided into about eighteen distinct operations.[4]

By specialising in these different stages of production, ten people, working in collaboration with each other, could produce 'upwards of 48,000 pins in a day' whereas a single individual could perhaps make one a day and 'certainly could not make twenty' – a truly revolutionary productivity gain of at least 240 times.

Such improvements, though no doubt mostly more modest in scale, were achieved in cotton and wool textile production, coal and iron ore extraction, iron founding, transportation and all the activities and processes which made up the first industrial revolution that changed the world forever.

Smith argued that the efforts of those many individuals working primarily for their own interest in the new industries emerging in the late 18th century were robust foundations for economic development. The pin factory exampled the potential productivity gains available from work being divided into different specialised functions and tasks, with people working in collaboration with each other to achieve the organisation's overall purpose.

Smith was also specific regarding the role of markets free from government interference. The productivity gains from specialisation would be of no real value if the additional pins produced could not be sold. At that time, the mercantilist system of tariffs and subsidies was widely used by governments to protect their own national markets from overseas invasion. But that limited the overall size of markets and so also limited the potential gains that might be made by people specialising and applying the new industrial 'technologies'.

That was the context in which Smith argued the case for the 'invisible hand' of market forces; that is, not regulated by interfering governments. However, market forces only work if the market is truly competitive. But the natural process of competitive markets, as they develop, is to be led by the most successful providers which, in due course, achieve a dominant market power, or tend to collude with others to form cartels of varying degrees of formality. Either way they would achieve control of prices and quantities traded in order to serve their own best interests. It was therefore important for markets to be regulated so as to protect competition.

That was the thread of Smith's work, based on observation of reality, to provide the knowledge and understanding of the operation and behaviour of real organisations and the working of their human components. It suggested how organisations might best be coordinated so as to achieve long-term benefits in terms of reduced cost and increased output, as well as the huge potential gains in living standards for society at large.

Smith also recognised the ill effects of such industrial processes which required the endless repetition of actions. He warned that such specialisation of work could lead to the 'mental mutilation' of workers, a problem he described in some detail.

His proposal was to counterbalance those ill effects by providing for the free education of workers, paid for by the wealthy through

5

a progressive system of taxation. He suggested that it was 'not very unreasonable that the rich should contribute to the public expense, not only in proportion to their revenue, but something more than in that proportion.'[5] That way everyone gained. It is an assertion made in Book V, Chapter 2, Part 2, *Of taxes,* a section widely excluded from modern editions including the currently available Oxford Classics Edition referred to in this text. The reason for its exclusion is not explained though its inclusion would clearly be inconvenient to some economic theory.

Industrial practitioners tended to follow that reality based model, though often without Smith's moral restraint. Their excesses made it increasingly necessary to regulate hours and conditions of working by law, such as the UK's Factory Acts, which set some limits on the exploitation and abuse of employees.

That reality based strand of Smith's work was later developed as part of the management curriculum in the early American business schools.[6] Empirical studies of human behaviour and organisation increased understanding of that reality and led to what Drucker later referred to as the management revolution.[7]

It was that systematic observation of productive processes which initially had a profound influence on political decision making of the time, as was acknowledged by Pitt the Younger:

> [Smith's] extensive knowledge of detail and depth of philosophical research will, I believe, furnish the best solution to every question connected with the history of commerce and with the question of political economy.[8]

It was the knowledge of detail, derived from observation of reality, that defined the best solutions. It was not the application of theoretical models of economic agents and their imagined functioning.

But that reality based strand of Smith's work was largely set aside by succeeding generations of theoreticians.[9] They picked up on Smith's theoretical conjecturing about such as the nature of value, and developed it further so that it came to dominate political-economic decision making as outlined in the following sections.

The 'science' of neoclassical theorising

Smith's 'inquiry' focused on what is here referred to as the real economy: those activities which provide the essentials of life for all, and for its development and progression, employing people as well as providing the basics of a progressing society. Initially, it was enabled by a supportive financial sector, raising the funds for the required investment.

Smith's conjectures about the labour theory of value, developed further by Ricardo, Say and others, led to the development of classical economics, based around assumptions regarding self-interested individuals and similarly self-interest driven competitive business organisations.

Bentham and his student, J.S. Mill, offered a more enlightened version, accepting that individuals and the organisations they ran might be motivated by broader more generous motivations than pure self-interest. Marx later further politicised the debate by presenting the labour theory of value as the capitalist justification for exploiting the working class[10] whose condition had been reported by Engels.[11]

Political-economics has since included a focus on the pursuit of macroeconomic theory to explain the economics of everything from differing perspectives, broadly defined along the single dimension between capitalism and socialism. Each is based on selective summations of microeconomic theories, rather than the practicalities of what actually happened at the coal face or on the pin factory shop floor.

By the mid-19th century, attempts were being made to develop an overtly scientific, or at least mathematical, approach to economic theorising. Economic agents and processes were modelled mathematically. They were based on the idea of economic man, which fitted mathematical expression by being driven to maximise its own self-interest. Similarly, economic production was modelled as existing solely to maximise profits. All manner of impossible assumptions were made simply in order for the mathematical models to be internally consistent. The maths was then solved and the results inflicted on the real world by indoctrinated decision makers. That was what became known as neoclassical economics.

Such mathematical models could take no account of time, nor of the evolution of markets and technologies. Nor could they make any accommodation with any defined and agreed democratic purpose or moral value such as fairness or integrity, including any such relating to the common good. The more enlightened but non-quantitative J.S. Mill assumptions could not be modelled. The mathematics was incapable of representing real businesses, real markets, real products and services, or any of the roles fulfilled by real human beings. Moreover, most of the quantities it dealt with were actually immeasurable, and it could take no account of any social effects or consequences which might be critical to a civil society and for which government was required to be responsible. And, of course, it could take no account of the global ecosystems on which it has had such profound destructive effect.

Ruskin likened it to 'witchcraft', pointing out that though it might have had a 'plausible idea at the root of it', it nevertheless lacked 'applicability'.[12] Being based on abstruse theorising rather than the study and experience of real systems, applicability was one of the things it certainly lacked.

Alfred Marshall, author of the first standard economics textbook which led economics to mathematical definition, pointed out the unreality of assumptions which the mathematics required. Labour was necessarily treated as 'a commodity', which it clearly was not; the laws of supply and demand, 'a much more mechanical and regular action than is to be found in real life'; and their so-called 'laws' regarding 'profits and wages that did not hold even for England in their own time'.[13]

Successive generations of dedicated researchers have since been led to the development and elaboration of economic theorising, in pursuit of its acceptance as a 'science'. In so doing, they have added huge depth and breadth to its coverage. The result has been a labyrinthine web of theoretical concepts, hypotheses, so-called laws and mathematical models, based on all manner of false and impossible assumptions, which bear no relation to the real world we live in. At root, all these models are based on the fictitious ideas of greed dominated economic man and the individual enterprise which exists only to maximise profits and therefore to minimise costs including wages. That was the neoclassical model which was dominant up until the 1929 Wall Street Crash and subsequent austerity driven Great Depression.

The so-called efficient market hypothesis (EMH) is an example of such modelling, which is an extension of market equilibrium theorising. EMH holds that in a free market, prices fully reflect all available information as to true values. It is therefore held that such markets, free from government and central bank interference, would end the volatility of business cycles, booms and busts. That view was still held in early 21st century, a period referred to as 'the great moderation' for which both politicians and economists at the time took credit. According to the EMH, such events as the 1929 and 2008 crashes could not happen.

Another maths-based item of pretend science was the formula, devised by joint Nobel Memorial prize winners, Scholes and Merton, which the Long-Term Capital Management (LTCM) hedge fund used to manage investment in financial derivatives. LTCM should not, according to the theory, have been able to fail, since high, risk-free returns were guaranteed. But after less than four years, LTCM had to be bailed out by 16 global banks providing over US$3.5 billion support.

It was closed down two years later. The maths was immaculate; all it lacked, as Ruskin would have pointed out, was applicability.

These were attempts to develop economics as a science, and to apply that science to the real world. The list of such failures is endless. Robert Lucas's 1995 Nobel Memorial Prize lecture on monetary neutrality is an elegant example of the necessary abstruse academic theorising in the detail of neoclassical economics. The following extract illustrates the unreality on which the maths was based:

> Assume simply that old and young engage in some kind of trading game, to which the old bring the cash m obtained in the previous period's trading. Either before, or perhaps during, the play of this game, the old receive a proportional transfer that totals x. Let each young person and each old person select a trading strategy. Notice that the strategy of a young person can depend on m, and the strategy of an old person can depend on m and x. On the basis of these choices, suppose a Nash equilibrium is reached under which each young person supplies some amount of labor and ends up with some amount of cash. I will restrict attention to symmetric equilibria, so that in equilibrium each young person ends up with mx dollars. Each young person also ends up supplying $f(m, x)$ units of labor, and this quantity is also the equilibrium consumption of each old person, where the notation is chosen to emphasize that m and x are the only state variables in this model. Different specifications of the trading game will have different implications for this outcome function f.[14]

Lucas provided pages of such microeconomic theorising, ignoring the simple fact that equilibrium does not exist in the real world. He noted with sympathy his illustrious predecessors, 'without any of the equipment of modern mathematical economics … were simply not able to work out the predictions of their own theories'.[15] The simple truth was that those earlier economists were fortunate not to have been seduced by the availability of computer based mathematics and therefore had to depend, at least to some extent, on common sense and observed reality. That freedom is no longer available; the deep technicalities of the theoretical subject area are left to the experts in computerised calculation and have lost all connection with reality.

Many leading economists do, of course, reject the pretend science. Routh identified more than a score who were critical of the economic mainstream, adding his own more comprehensive assessment of the ideology as it was in 1975:

> Economics ... ignores facts as irrelevant, bases its constructs on axioms arrived at *a priori*, or 'plucked from the air', from which deductions are made and an imaginary edifice created. ... Man and society are stripped of their attributes, as if they could exist without psychological, political, legal, historical or moral dimension. Thus verification is both impossible and regarded as unnecessary. In effect, then, orthodox economics becomes a matter of faith and, ipso facto, immune to criticism.[16]

Neoclassical economics is clearly not concerned with reality and is certainly no science. In science, a theory does not impact on reality. If a theory says the sun goes round the Earth, it remains a theory, until it is shown to be false, after which it is discarded. In microeconomics, a theory can remain, despite being frequently shown to be false. But it is hardly a theory, more a matter of blind belief. As such it can have a profound impact on reality by influencing human behaviour.

In 1989, J.K. Galbraith delivered the commencement address to women graduates of Smith College, Massachusetts, recommending them to the pursuit of 'simple truth'. He warned of the dangers posed by 'institutional truths'. They were not truths at all, but falsehoods that individuals would be persuaded to buy into in order to progress in the relevant institution in which they might be seeking to develop their careers.[17]

Such were the essential untruths of neoclassical microeconomics, including its depiction of humanity as self-interest maximising economic man, the firm as a profit maximising production unit, real products and services as undifferentiated commodities, and markets as automatically competitive when freed from government regulation. All are profoundly wrong. Nevertheless, neoclassical economics has been given sufficient support and promotion for it to remain the dominant set of economic beliefs, influencing both the reality of human behaviour and the operation of economic units such as for-profit businesses.[18]

The Mont Pelerin influence

Neoclassical was the version of microeconomic theory that was 'lying around', as Milton Friedman put it,[19] when in the late 1970s, the post-war application of Keynesian economics appeared to be failing with the improbable, according to Keynes, coincidence of economic stagnation and high rates of inflation. A more credible explanation was provided by Piatier:[20] 'stagflation' was the combination of stagnation arising from the maturing of second industrial revolution industries and the inflation arising from, among other things, OPEC's (Organisation of Petroleum Exporting Countries) 400 per cent rise in oil prices.

The Keynesian approach to economic decision making had emerged following the 1929 Wall Street Crash and subsequent Great Depression. It was based on limiting the overweening power of international finance and encouraging the global development of economic growth and social democracy. For several decades, it was successful.

Neoclassical microeconomic theory had, however, not just been 'lying around'. It had been developed and promoted by those attending the Mont Pelerin Society meetings since 1947.[21] They were reacting against the Marxist ideology which, after the Russian revolution, had mutated from the socialist utopia into the real world centrally planned totalitarian communist dictatorship.

The Mont Pelerins, including von Mises, Hayek and Friedman, argued the case for a free market system 'based on profit and competition' and 'private ownership of the means of production'[22] to provide the best conditions for economic and social progress.[23] They were driven to defeat the Marxist ideology which, following the Russian example, posed a powerful threat to Western capitalism, for which freedom, as opposed to totalitarian dictatorship, was the key, whether applied to individuals or markets. The politics of capital, rather more than the 'science' of economics, resolved the political–economic debate into the simplistic dichotomy between socialism and capitalism.

Hayek defined socialism as not merely 'espousing the ideals of social justice, greater equality and security' but also encompassing the particular means by which those ideals might be achieved:

> ... socialism means the abolition of private property, of private ownership of the means of production, and the creation of a system of 'planned economy' in which the entrepreneur working for profit is replaced by a central planning body.[24]

For Hayek, those means, and the ends to which they were dedicated, were inseparable. Even the espousal of social justice, or the aim of greater equality, was forecast by Hayek and colleagues to lead inevitably to full-on centrally planned, socialist dictatorship. The potential communist threat even led to fear of any moves towards a more socially equitable economy,[25] such as the UK's state interventions and nationalisations that had initiated and supported economic regeneration following the Second World War (WW2).

The stated prime aim of the free market economists was to guarantee man's personal freedom, which they defined as the absence of coercion. Hayek asserted that 'To follow socialist morality would destroy much of present humankind and impoverish much of the rest.'[26] Von Mises had similarly argued that if we wished to save the world from 'barbarism' we would have first to 'conquer Socialism'.[27] Government intervention of any kind was recognised as the prime evil. That ignored the fact that, among many essential interventions, the gold standard was itself an intervention of unequalled scale and importance.

Von Mises had argued that the programme of liberalism, 'if condensed into a single word, would have to read: property, that is, private ownership of the means of production'.[28] Thus, even for the Austrian School's version of laissez faire, government would be required to protect property rights. But, in their idealised world, government would be needed for precious little else.

An early 20th century idea, the quantity theory of money, had expressed the economy with the equation $MV = PT$, where M is the quantity of money in the economy, V the velocity of its circulation, P the level of prices and T the number of transactions in a specified time period. While the equation is a truism and identifies macroeconomic quantities, their content is largely immeasurable and its various interpretations susceptible to simplistic political debate.

Nevertheless, successive governments, guided by neoclassical theory, have concentrated their attention on M, the quantity of money, rather than V the velocity of its circulation. That ignored the lessons from the 1930s, when the Great Depression was prolonged by the focus on M and the resulting emphasis on austerity. It was only ended by Roosevelt's refocusing on V with the publicly funded New Deal job creation schemes aimed at relieving the poor and putting money into their hands. They had no option but to spend it immediately, thus increasing V and so generating economic growth to help bring the Great Depression to an end.

Those lessons were largely set aside, as was clear following the 2008 crash. Economic stimulation by public spending paid for out of taxation, was largely replaced by the focus on control of M, with austerity driving spending policies, their impacts multiplied by reducing taxation. Even leading quantity advocate Friedman admitted the theory had largely failed its post Keynesian applications.[29]

According to the theory, the potential gains from tax reduction would be decided by 'the market', which would, of course, allocate them to the most efficient and effective applications. Even since the relearning experience of the 2008 crash, the avowed policy focus remained fixed on M rather than V, though after more than a decade of austerity, that may now be waning just as it did after the 1930s Great Depression.[30]

An exception was made, post 2008, for the financial sector, which had risked its survival by reckless and fraudulent dealing in sub-prime securities. The sector must have been encouraged by the widely held understanding that, if it all went wrong, the financial sector was too important to be allowed to fail and would be bailed out by their allies in central banks and government. In the year following Lehman's bankruptcy, the 'US spent 4.5 per cent of GDP recapitalising its banks' while the 'UK spent 8.8 per cent of GDP' and 'total sovereign support for the banking sector worldwide was estimated at some $14trillion'.[31]

Such quantitative easing (QE) was intended to relieve stressed balance sheets enabling resumption of high return, high risk trading, with little benefit to the real economy and the common good. QE has no doubt reinforced the financial sector's confidence of receiving similar support when the next financial crash occurs. However, the COVID-19 pandemic is providing a further massive relearning experience. It is forcing governments across the globe to set aside neoclassical predispositions for austerity, and make funds available for a 21st century New Deal to address the pandemic's impacts. Such a people's New Deal has the potential to substantially assist the remaking of the real economy and to escape some destructions by organised money.

Neoclassical economics has also made a backward grab for academic credibility by claiming their roots in the work of Adam Smith who, as 'father of economics', had the answer to the economic problem. The Adam Smith portrayed by today's politically motivated theorists, think tanks and lobbyists is a misrepresentation, claiming Smith support for all the necessary free market credentials, advocating profit maximisation as the driving force of industrial development. Such a portrayal is often justified by reference to the following much-cited quotation:

> It is not from the benevolence of the butcher, the brewer, or the baker, that we expect our dinner, but from their regard for their own interest. We address ourselves not to their humanity but to their self-love.[32]

Smith, of course, recognised the need for self-interest, especially when survival was threatened, but his observations on human motivation were far more comprehensive and nuanced than that. In the aforementioned quote, he was specifically avoiding the pretence that good consequences from such economic activity arose as a result of the 'benevolence' of the artisans. He recognised it was far more robust than that. The artisans' own interest was to provide a viable and ongoing living for themselves and their dependents. To do that, as butchers, brewers and bakers, they would need to develop lasting relationships of trust with their customers who would be people with whom they came into regular contact. Such relationships would depend on the reliable provision of an acceptable product at a reasonable price, needing to last over their whole lifetime, rather than an individual transaction. That moral philosopher and enquirer is the true Adam Smith, not the advocate of short-term self-interest maximising economic man exploiting free markets.

Milton Friedman developed the neoclassical theory further in several directions, emphasising the microeconomic argument for the privatisation of state assets and provision, with the assertion that it costs the state twice as much to do anything as it costs private enterprise. He explained it to the Institute of Economic Affairs in London, as a 'sort of empirical generalization … and it is amazing how accurate it is.'[33] He provided no supporting evidence and there is much to the contrary as noted in the next chapter.

Friedman also made the argument for low flat rate taxation. He proposed a single rate income tax of 23.5 per cent as appropriate for the UK. The precision of the rate appeared to suggest detailed calculation had been completed though none was ever produced. Flat rate taxation results in money passed to the wealthy being increased, justified by the 'trickle down' argument, that the rich would invest their additional money, and that investment would in due course result in more jobs and income for the poor. That was different from what Smith had suggested: the rich paying rather more than in proportion to their income.

There is little evidence of such trickle down ever having been very effective, and since the 1980s computerisation and deregulation of capital markets, the trickle down argument lost whatever shreds of veracity it may have had before automated finance took over the world. The bulk of money passed to the rich is invested in high risk, high return speculative financial markets rather than in such mundane operations as manufacture or long-term research and development.

Friedman also argued that low rates of tax would anyway gain from the rich being less motivated to seek tax avoidance and evasion.[34] He later expressed his disappointment that when US tax rates were substantially reduced, a significant part of the benefit was invested in the pursuit of ever more elaborate avoidance and evasion schemes via offshore tax arrangements.[35]

The Friedmanite version of neoclassical economic theory is often nominated as neoliberal. However, neoliberal is a term which has been loosely used and its meaning is ambiguous and variable. It has therefore been avoided in this text, preferring to stick with the 21st century neoclassical nomination: neoclassical microeconomics with Friedman's variations, the most significant of which is the primacy of shareholder interests.

The institutional truth of shareholder primacy

There has been a long history of disputation over the legal status of shareholders, going as far back as the early royal chartered trading companies. Their owners, like the owners of any private property, had to accept full responsibility for the activities and liabilities of their property, whether or not they had any involvement in the relevant actions or decision-making processes.

The incorporated company was established as a legal entity in its own right, with its directors legally empowered to act on the company's behalf and when doing so legally required, as its agents, to act in the company's best interests at all times.

The critical distinction between the company and its shareholders was made right from the beginning. And right from the beginning, it was a bone of some contention, with suspicions in America of the 'unbridled power, as possessed by large landholders and dynastic wealth, as well as by government.'[36] A UK Act of Parliament in 1766 referred to the necessary protection of 'the permanent welfare of companies' from being 'sacrificed to the partial and interested views of the few.'[37] People of that era might well have imagined that 250 years later that problem would have been solved.

Markets in shares and bonds and insurance, expanded massively with developing industrialisation. The basic need was to invest in the development of the real economy. That included agriculture, the transportation infrastructure, the extraction industries – notably coal and iron ore – as well as textiles, manufacturing, distribution and associated services. The flow of funds was from the many dispersed shareholders, to be invested in the real industrial projects on which economic development depended.

With the coming of the railways, the 1844 Joint Stock Companies Act made company formation easier and cheaper, dispensing with the need for a royal charter or an Act of Parliament. Limited liability was added in 1855, freeing shareholders from direct responsibility for the activities of the company in which they invested, thus emphasising its independent status. Since then various Companies Acts have developed the concept of the company further, but the basic idea was settled.[38] Shareholder liability was limited to the money paid for the initial purchase of their shares; shareholders were owners of shares, not of the company itself. They therefore bore no responsibility for the company's activities. That is still the legal case.

However, there is a deep flaw in that concept of the company as a legal entity. It is established with all the rights of a legal person such as the right to sue and be sued. It is not a piece of private property which its shareholders own. They cannot simply come and take the company's assets as though they were their own simply because they own shares in the company. However, the protection and independence of the corporate legal entity changes when a shareholder has a majority of the equity – 50 per cent + one share. Then the law may not change, but the practicalities do. At that stage a shareholder becomes the controller and de facto owner, and the company becomes, in effect, an item of private property subject to control and disposal by the majority shareholder, who nevertheless retains the benefit of limited liability. The legal position changes when 50 per cent + a share is owned, but the threat of that change in ownership clearly exists with much smaller shareholdings.

The possibility of such majority shareholding being achieved is a potential threat for all publicly quoted companies, unless they have specifically organised protections from such abuse, as is customary in the capital markets of both Japan (with the keiretsu system of cross shareholdings, which are nevertheless open to their own form of abuse) and Germany (with the two-tier board system, which achieves a more reasonable form of balance of interests). Without such protections, the flaw in the corporate concept is undermining the independent legal status of incorporation which has led to the expression of what became known as shareholder primacy.

Friedman gave its first expression with the assertion that

> few trends could so thoroughly undermine the very foundations of our free society than the acceptance by corporate officials of a social responsibility other than to make as much money for their stockholders as possible.[39]

This variation from the neoclassical commitment to maximising profit, which appears to have been generally accepted, though never legally tested, has had profound impacts on the global economy.

Profit maximisation had not laid down how those maximised profits should be allocated. They could be invested in innovations of product or process, retained within the company as the security against a proverbial rainy day, spent on the further training and education of employees, invested in R&D, or returned as dividends to shareholders. Such allocation decisions were the responsibility of 'corporate officials' and were crucial to the survival, development and long-term prosperity of the company and, cumulatively, to the economy as a whole.

The duty to make as much money as possible for stockholders removes that executive discretion, replacing it with the simple unambiguous responsibility for maximising shareholder money. It is a fundamental change, which frustrates positive investment in the long-term development of the business, replacing strategic opportunities with the duty for short-term extraction of value for the sole benefit of shareholders. It emphasises not just the amount of returns to shareholders but also the speed of their delivery. The sooner returns are made the quicker they can be deployed in earning more returns, thus ensuring maximisation results in a short-term emphasis having priority.

That has clearly been detrimental for real business, for economies, for society and for the world as a whole, present and future. By 2012, there had been a 'multi-trillion dollar transfer of cash from US corporations to their shareholders' over the previous decade, and the City of London had achieved similar degree of disinvestment.[40] Over the same period the number of public companies in the UK had almost halved and declined by 38 per cent in the US. Similarly, the number of Initial Public Offerings (IPOs) declined by over two thirds, and by more than 80 per cent in the case of small and medium sized enterprises (SMEs), on which the hopes for a continuously improving innovative future rest.

When Friedman made his assertion regarding the primacy of shareholder interests, it was without legal or theoretical foundation. It was just another 'institutional truth'. It took ten years for economic theoreticians to come up with a justification referred to as agency theory. They did so by claiming that company directors were the agents of shareholders rather than their employing company, as was legally the case. Shareholders were thus claimed to be the principals in the relationship.

As agents, directors were bound to act, in accord with the long-established legal relationship, in the interests of their principals at all times. But the principal in that relationship was the employing company, with which directors invariably had a legal employment contract. The argument that shareholders were the principals with which directors were contracted to act as agents, could only be sustained by pretending the public company did not exist as a separate entity. Only then could directors be said to have a legal relationship with the shareholders. Various neoclassical economists got to work in this area and, in due course, came up with the assertion that the firm was 'a centralised contractual agent'[41] and a 'legal fiction'.[42] These much-cited contributions were the foundation of the theoretical justification for Friedman's assertion of shareholder primacy.

It was given substantial support by think tanks and lobbyists as well as by relevant members of the academy. In due course it became the established dominant belief across Anglo-America, accepted as such by bodies such as the American Business Roundtable, which came to assert that 'the paramount duty of management and of boards of directors is to the corporation's stockholders'.[43]

However, the simple truth is that the company is a legal fact, not just a contractual agent or a legal fiction. That is its whole point. Friedman's 'corporate officials' are actually appointed as agents of the company which is the principal in that relationship. Their contracts of employment and service agreements are with the company, not shareholders. Those contracts and agreements, in accordance with guidance originally given by the UK Institute of Directors, are specific about the requirement to act in the best interests of the company at all times.

A review of the legal position was conducted by Lan and Heracleous who found that nowhere in the world is there a legal statute which confirms company directors as the agents of shareholders. They quoted one item of American case law, *Dodge v Ford Motor Co.* in the Supreme Court of Michigan in 1919. Ford had retained a cash dividend within the company for its future expansion and the consequent benefit of its employees. However, the judge held that the firm was not a quasi-charity, but a business, and must be managed for the benefit of shareholders, rather than any other interested parties. Lan and Heracleous pointed out that

> the courts have only cited this case once ... which indicates the weakness of both its precedent value and its influence on legal doctrine. Corporate law in most Anglo-American countries still confers ultimate power to directors, not shareholders ... Shareholders' rights over directors are remarkably limited in both theory and practice.[44]

Shareholder primacy is therefore lacking in legal support and has only much falsified theoretical support. Yet it is still the widely taught and accepted belief which has wreaked destructions across the globe as outlined in Chapter 3. It is clearly rooted in the flaw in the incorporation process which provides no protection against the company becoming, in effect, an item of private property, when a majority shareholding is credibly threatened. That is what has enabled the institutional truth of shareholder primacy to overcome the law.

Ghoshal pointed out that, despite its obvious falsity, few managers could publicly question the shareholder primacy assertion. That remains largely true in 2020 though there are at last signs of the beginnings of change. Ghoshal asked where that enormous certainty had come from. His own explanation was that 'this assumption helps in structuring and solving nice mathematical models'.[45] That maybe a convenience for neoclassical economists, but its lasting potency has really depended on it maximising shareholder take (MST) from the real economy.

MST is the extraction of value for the benefit of shareholders including the already wealthy who, in reality, gain very little from increases in such inequality. Studies of wellbeing suggest that 'once an individual, a household (and indeed a country) is out of poverty, more income is not particularly effective in raising wellbeing or quality of life'.[46]

A 2019 discussion paper investigated the connections between employee wellbeing, productivity and firm performance. The focus was entirely on the internal workings of the firm rather than its external stakeholders. It was based on 339 independent research studies of more than 82,000 business units and almost 1.9 million individuals.[47,48] The conclusion was drawn that there was not only a strong positive correlation between employee satisfaction, productivity, customer loyalty and firm profitability, but that it was a causal relationship between employee wellbeing, and firm performance.

Friedman's fellow Nobel Memorial laureate, Paul Krugman, raised the question whether Friedman was profound theorist, or simplistic ideologue, populariser and propagandist of monetarism and the free market doctrine, whose ideas proved unworkable in practice and whose intellectual honesty was at least questionable.[49] Krugman concluded Friedman was all of these.

21st century neoclassical belief

The 21st century version of neoclassical microeconomics includes the Mont Pelerin/Friedman variations referred to previously, including most importantly of all, the assertion of shareholder primacy and the objective of MST.

Unlike in science, given sufficient support, a falsified economic theory can survive, but it does so as a matter of belief. As such it continues to influence behaviour. For the purposes of this text, the main components of neoclassical belief are assumed as follows:

- The core concept is the 19th century idea of economic man, motivated solely to maximise its own self-interest, which, for the maths to be calculable, can only be expressed in monetary terms, and depends on many unrealistic assumptions such as being fully informed of all possible choices, being wholly rational and values free in decision making, and so on.
- Business organisations exist to 'make as much money as possible for stockholders' (MST) and have no other social responsibilities.
- Shareholders are the principals in the principal:agent relationship with company directors/executives their agents.
- Free markets – markets completely free from government involvement as participant, taxer, subsidiser or regulator – are perfectly competitive.
- A progressive economy depends on minimised flat rate taxation and minimised involvement of the state, which is inherently bureaucratic and inefficient.
- Issues which are not expressed in monetary terms, such as moral or ethical values, ecological and social impacts and the evolution of economic systems, are incalculable and therefore excluded from consideration.
- The only precise way of taking account of money over time is by discounting. Thus the value today of £100 in 20 years' time is discounted down to not very much. Today's value of Mother Earth in 100 years is discounted to very little and is therefore not a significant consideration in mathematical modelling calculation.

Each and every one of these points of neoclassical belief is absolutely false. Nevertheless, it is clear that those theoretical inputs are having major impacts on how people contribute to the real economy. Moreover, those impacts are almost entirely negative, as outlined in Chapter 3.

Conclusions

Political-economics resolved into a left-right, socialism-capitalism disputation, a line of argument where both extremes are based on false microeconomic notions and both sides engage in sterile argument to achieve their own ends, irrespective of other considerations. Socialism as implemented mutated into totalitarian communism, which was incompatible with democracy. The neoclassical version of capitalism is also inconsistent with democracy given its exclusive support for a specific elite and for ever increasing inequalities. In first past the post democracies, much time, money and energy is wasted reversing the directional swings of the opposing party.

Nevertheless, the false and dangerously inadequate ideas of neoclassical belief still guide much political decision making in 2020. They ignore the messy realities of the real world from which knowledge and understanding of how things actually work might be gained. They take no account of the social and environmental contexts on which they impact, nor of time and the evolution of economic systems, nor of any human values. And they defy the logic of common sense.

The pretence that the free market decides the most efficient and effective allocation of resources is hugely damaging. First, there is no such thing as a free market; and markets free from government interference do not remain free and competitive for long. Without the benefit of extraneous regulation, competitive markets inevitably mutate towards cartel and monopoly, where financial players are focused on the predatory extraction of value, rather than investing in the long-term future. Thus, free markets fall naturally and inevitably into the hands of financialised monopolists whose power is reinforced by the false assumption of shareholder primacy. That is damaging to business, to the overall economy, and to wider ecological and social systems. The result is that long-term investment in real and sustainable progression has been converted into short-term extraction of value, for the benefit of shareholders, from whom there is no 'trickle down'.

Despite having been shown invariably to be false, neoclassical economic ideas and hypotheses persist as belief, maintaining their stranglehold on the global economy, notably in the UK and US.

According to that ideology, human greed is essential for the working of a healthy economy. Being empathetic or, as Adam Smith put it, having moral sentiment, is treated as both irrational and damaging to the economy and the general good.

Piketty identified the basic problem as the return on capital being greater than the rate of growth of income and output. Consequently, wealth grows faster than wages, continuously increasing the degree of inequality and seducing real economy entrepreneurs to mutate into what economists refer to as rentiers, non-productive recipients of returns for past accumulated wealth. He indicated that 'the market economy based on private property, if left to itself, contains ... powerful forces of divergence, which are potentially threatening to democratic societies and to the values of social justice on which they are based'.[50]

Unless reversed, the only logical end for that self-reinforcing process is some form of catastrophic revolutionary disruption.

Ghoshal argued that we must stop teaching the neoclassical version of economics, but that would only be the beginning. We also need to escape the grip on government decision making, exerted by the various components of the organised money establishment outlined in the following chapter.

2

'Old enemies of peace': constituents of organised money

Introduction

We have almost been here before. The 1929 Wall Street Crash, followed by Hoover's ideologically inspired austerity driven Great Depression, ushered in Roosevelt's presidency and his New Deal economic stimulus, the second wave of which he introduced as follows:

> We had to struggle with the old enemies of peace – business and financial monopoly, speculation, reckless banking, class antagonism, sectionalism, war profiteering. They had begun to consider the Government of the United States as a mere appendage to their own affairs. We know now that Government by organised money is just as dangerous as Government by organised mob.[1]

It seemed that struggle was subsequently won with the 1944 Bretton Woods settlement creating the International Monetary Fund (IMF) and World Bank, which were largely founded on a basis of Rooseveltian social democracy and Keynesian economics, with the aim of post-war reconstruction. That continued to challenge the predatory activities of international finance which became so destructive of the real economy. The IMF assisted the resumption of economic growth and full employment by promoting international trade and exchange-rate stability, while the World Bank helped poorer member nations with low-cost finance to support major capital investment to assist their long-term development.

The victory over organised money was, however, only temporary. Within three years, economists and representatives of what Roosevelt had referred to as organised money, were conferring in Mont Pelerin over their response to Bretton Woods.

After WW2 and its undoubted 'war profiteering', Eisenhower added the 'military–industrial complex' to Roosevelt's list of 'old enemies of peace'. Today, despite the prolonged freedom from global conflict, the military–industrial complex remains a powerful business component, supplying the most primitive destructions for profit, notably through the Middle East.

Organised money has been further expanded to include 'the ... academic-bureaucratic complex',[2] which includes those strands of academia that Ghoshal warned about – those that develop and teach theories that serve the interests of organised money.[3] They are further reinforced by the media and especially including those elements of social media that energetically promote neoclassical belief at every opportunity, along with a political sector which now includes the think tanks and lobbyists richly funded by the various other components of organised money. The whole is lubricated by the legally permitted revolving doors enabling immediate migration between those various sectors and government itself.

Organised money seems an apt description of that self-perpetuating establishment which, with the help of laxer regulation and 21st century technology, has a far tighter stranglehold on power now than it ever did in Roosevelt's day. Moreover, the global context is also quite different, with the population having more than tripled since then, and with ecological destructions continuing to reach new depths even as the tipping point is approached.

This chapter provides a brief outline of those various components of organised money, enemies of peace and progression. The struggle between socialism and neoclassical capitalism appears to have resolved into a fight to the death between social democracy and organised money. Roosevelt's concern was that organised money, driven by its insatiable greed, would steal the economy and devour it. The simple truth is rather more concerning than that.

The emergence of predatory finance

The seeds of the financial sector germinated with the ownership of private property, thousands of years ago. Adam Smith's model of the evolution of society focused on the progression of private ownership from the commons of hunter-gatherer society to the age of the shepherd, which necessarily recognised private ownership of flocks and herds, and the further evolution to the agricultural age, which recognised the private ownership of land. More extensive private property ownerships are difficult to envisage as anything other than inheritance or the product of success on the battlefield (broadly defined) or a close and favoured relationship with that success or its inheritance. The private acquisition of ancient commons, and the charging of rent and interest by its acquirers and their bankers, ushered in Smith's age of commercial man that was emerging as he wrote.

The unprecedented funding requirements of industrialisation created a whole new financial industry. Without it, the industrial revolution could not have happened. Industrialisation went far beyond the financial capacities of the old private property owners, the aristocracy and landed gentry. The essential infrastructural projects, such as the canals, and later the railways, required huge and prolonged finance. It took seven or more years from commencement of a canal project to the generation of its first income. That scale of funding was needed to pay the wages of teams of navvies and engineers and to purchase their tools and equipment as well as negotiating the land through which the canal was cut. It was only enabled through the establishment of a working financial sector and public companies funded by the sale of shares and bonds to large numbers of dispersed investors.

Thus from the dawn of industrialisation there has been a division between the real economy, which produces goods and services needed and demanded by the different sectors of the general population, and the financialised economy, which was greatly expanded to enable the industrialisation process and to support the real economy, on top of its traditional lead role in financing war.

Initially, that division between real and financialised economies was largely benign, with a tightly controlled retail banking sector dedicated to serving the real economy and the common good. But merchant or investment banking enjoyed the additional possibility of making money from speculative betting on the future value of securities, causing the occasional boom and bust. Such speculative bubbles have always, and no doubt always will, punctuate economic history. Tulip mania, the South Sea Bubble, canal and railway manias, the 1929 Wall Street Crash, the 1990s dot.com bubble and the bust of 2007–08 all demonstrate the volatility that is endemic to markets which incorporate the possibility of speculation.[4]

The defining characteristic of a bubble is that it will at some stage burst; that defines all the famous speculations. They invite analysis of their fairly simple processes to identify what might be done to avoid such disruptions in future. The start, development and end of such speculative markets has been widely studied and explained.[5] There is little mystery about them. Making money from such bubbles does not require great intelligence or hard work. The basic requirement is access to the necessary funding, a willingness to take risks, preferably with other people's money, and a certain amount of luck regarding the timing of investment and its disposal.

The essence of the speculative market is that its investors are not so much concerned with the substance of the assets in which they are invested. Their focus is on the probability that the security representing those assets, whatever they happen to be, will be priced differently in the future, either more or less, and therefore enable a profit to be taken. Such speculative trading serves no useful purpose for the real economy, only for the speculators who guess correctly, and their investors who may include pension funds and insurers as well as private individuals.

At the end of each stock market trading period, accounts were settled. Merchant banks could then decide in whose name, either the bank's or a client's, the various trades had been made over that accounting period. In effect the banks were deciding how much profit to take during that period and how much to allocate to clients. The power was entirely in their hands.[6]

Capital markets have always provided easy access for fraud and deception. Some limitations on illicit dealings were set by the avowed 'my word is my bond' culture which ruled financial houses in the City of London. It was deemed vital to make that claim to honesty and trustworthiness entirely credible. Corruption was also traditionally constrained by the regulatory system of closed shop cartels of jobbers, brokers and merchant banks which depended on long-established relationships between City financial houses. That limited, but did not prevent, the exploitation of easy opportunities for abuse and fraud, including the energetic avoidance and evasion of taxation through the system of secretive tax havens in large part established and controlled by the City of London.[7]

While ever 'my word is my bond' and the City's closed shop system operated, trading more or less hung together, with only the occasional rogue appearing to corrupt the system, including the occasional knight of the realm and even a Lord Mayor of London.[8]

The 1986 'big bang' computerisation of capital markets, followed by the process of deregulation and breaking up of the former closed shops, opened up financial trading to a whole new shadow banking sector of financial intermediaries. They were quickly aware of the ease with which the system could be exploited and abused but were lacking in any of the traditional constraints.

Consequently, over the past few decades, financialised constituents have developed, in accord with neoclassical belief, to serve their own wealth maximising purposes by extracting value from the real economy, rather than assisting its development and growth.

Retail banks had previously been regulated separately from investment banks and had not been empowered to trade in capital markets on their own behalf. The retail banking role was to provide a safe haven for customer deposits, paying out a sufficiency of interest which was largely dependent on the central bank's set interest rate. Retail banks were enabled to lend out a proportion of the deposits they held, as loans to individuals and businesses, making a profit by charging a higher rate of interest on their loans than they paid out to depositors. The safety of those deposits was guaranteed in the UK by the Bank of England, which required the retail banks to retain a defined proportion of their deposits as liquid assets in case of need. Retail banking was thus a safe and boring business.

Post 'big bang', deregulation allowed retail banks to become involved in trading on capital markets, which was far more profitable than its traditional retail business, though obviously also riskier. The pursuit of MST encouraged retail banks to increase their engagement with investment banking, setting up and taking over trading intermediaries and becoming deeply embroiled in the risky business of speculative dealing. It was a whole new financial universe set up for the 2007–08 crash:

> a vast unregulated shadow banking system organised internationally with credit markets, alongside the regulated banking systems of nation states. In the US alone, the balance sheet of the shadow banking system stood at around $25trillion on the eve of the crash – more than twice the size of the traditional banking system.[9]

Shaxson provided examples of how that financial universe became content to deal with criminally sourced funds.[10] Whether it was drug money, illicit funds from third world tyrants, money arising from such as Madoff's Ponzi scheme or the illicit trading of companies such as Enron and Worldcom, appears to be of no importance – money is money.[11] Nor is the damage done to third world nations by the likes of London-based Bank of Credit and Commerce International (BCCI). Questions of morality and ethics appear not to be of consequence to the newly financialised sector.

The focus of any new traders' attention is on the simple matter of growing the fund for which they are responsible as fast as possible, in order to progress up the fund management league tables. Most of these investment decisions have become fully automated, removing the need for professional financial expertise. After the 2008 crash, Reuters reported that 'tumbling technology costs have opened potentially lucrative ultra-fast trading strategies to tiny start-up players

... coming straight out of MIT [Massachusetts Institute of Technology] and setting up desks'.[12]

MIT was not alone. That ease of formation and the associated earning power seduced many new science and technology graduates into finance and away from the real economy where their education might reap its intended rewards. Fully automated ultra-fast trading was by 2014 estimated to account for over 80 per cent of the Wall Street and London trades.[13]

These automated systems, using ever faster hardware and software to beat other investors to profitable trades, deal on the basis of news reports, or rumour circulating (fake news has been shown to be deliberately created and circulated in the financial underworld for that very purpose).

Speculative traders invest and manage a surprising amount of money, either on their own behalf or for their depositors. Lanchester referred to the international market for swaps and derivatives at the time of the 2008 crash as having been estimated at '$54 trillion, equivalent of many times the value of the world's stocks and shares'.[14] They had only limited connection with the provision of finance for real industrial investment. Their main objective was, and is, unrelated to that original purpose of the finance sector. Easy profits from speculation, even though potentially risky, make it difficult to withdraw from that activity to support the more mundane needs of the real economy.

Thus, the prime purpose of stock markets has been subverted: they no longer serve as vehicles for investment, but for extraction and speculation.[15] That role reversal resulted mainly from the ideologically justified, but uninformed and careless, deregulation of newly computerised capital markets and the reorientation of finance and business to MST rather than to developing new technologies to satisfy future needs, of which there are many.

Previously shareholders were invested in companies for up to seven years on average and their expectations of returns were most likely based on some assessment of the prospects for the business concerned. After 'big bang', shares were held only for short periods, more recently in many cases only for nanoseconds. The markets themselves became speculative with prices depending on expectations of short-term price movements rather than depending on actual performance or fundamental valuation of stocks. They were consequently, in defiance of any hypothesis about efficient markets, more liable than ever to bubbles and bursts.

In the absence of efficient markets, investors are offered protection from fraud and deception by the big three credit rating agencies

(Standard and Poor's, Moody's and Fitch) the purpose of which is to assess the credit worthiness of shares, bonds and other securities issued by businesses or nation states. They 'rate' these instruments based on the likelihood that their investment will be repaid. For much of the 20th century the privately owned agencies appeared mostly to fulfil their public role despite the conflict of interest arising from companies paying the agencies to rate their own securities. However, they appeared unable to keep up with 'big bang' computerisation and deregulation. Enron was infamously rated as a good credit risk four days before its bankruptcy. That was followed by several major multinational errors. The agencies' real limitations were exposed when they failed to appreciate the risks involved in securitising sub-prime mortgages. Those securities were created so that their actual content, and therefore the risk involved, was deliberately hidden by devices such as Repo 105, which was instrumental in the failure of Lehman Brothers.[16]

It remains unclear whether the credit rating agencies are genuinely concerned with assessing risk and providing due warnings, or whether they have simply formed a 'casually dishonest' cartel to provide an elaborate form of window dressing in order to maximise the returns to their own shareholders. Similar ambiguity attaches to all regulation of the financial sector. It is overtly 'light touch' in order to be 'business friendly'. It is insufficiently resourced and operated by individuals whose prime associations are with the bodies that are being regulated. Consequently, financial regulation is ineffective.

Computerisation and freedom from closed shops and restrictive regulation opened the doors to new entrants who were not limited by the sector's traditional constraints, being driven only by the desire to make quick profits. One easy route to those quick returns was by exercise of the new freedom to support the predatory activities of big business as outlined in the following section.

Financialised business

Business historian Chandler identified business as 'the most powerful institution in the American economy and its managers the most influential group of economic decision makers', noting that any 'theory of the firm that ... fails to take into account the role of administrative coordination, is far removed from reality'.[17] One such theory is the neoclassical set of beliefs previously outlined.

In its natural and continuing pursuit of economic progression, real business continues to generate new technology, activities and consumptions which contribute to driving the real economy forward.

However, changes following the computerisation and deregulation of capital markets have also resulted in increasing pressure on real businesses to financialise their operations, reversing their beneficial economic impacts.

At some stage all markets cease growing and move into a mature, low growth phase of evolution. For business management, facing reduced rates of growth or even shrinkage of their main markets, and being under pressure to maintain their financial performance, the most obvious way forward is to financialise their strategy. The aim may be either to achieve a controlling share of their main market so as to be better able to control prices, or to diversify into new fields by the acquisition of an existing successful player.

Either way, the nature of the business and the requisite expertise of its top management both change fundamentally. Instead of expertise in any particular technology, product or market, they are necessarily led to expertise in finance, merger and acquisitions (M&A) and towards capital market dealing. That expertise is specifically focused on MST, rather than the balancing of other stakeholder interests in pursuit of 'creating a customer'. Focus on MST requires freedom from moral constraint so that the boundaries of legality can be fully tested.

Such financialisation provides opportunities for continuing to grow the business as well as extracting immediate financial rewards for shareholders. Mutation to financialised format is a natural evolutionary process.

The financialised entity is actively supported by financial institutions which have no knowledge, expertise or interest in the real products and processes involved, only some external assessment of future prices. Their role is to support the M&A bidder, providing short-term finance that can then be loaded as debt onto the balance sheet of the acquired business. That provides the opportunity for large scale returns from small scale investment, some of which would be repaid to the financial sector and some retained by the successful acquirer for future repeat of similar operations. The process is almost always destructive of the acquired business, either by simple asset stripping, or by its absorption within the acquirer and closure and/or disposal of remaining operations for short-term gain (see Practitioner notes XXV and XXVI).

There have been repeated reviews of the overall effects of such M&A activity,[18] which have almost invariably concluded that the effects are not in the public interest. Increasing the monopolistic focus and power of the acquirer only assists the extraction of value for the sole gain of shareholders.

The accepted mainstream legal and cultural position up to the time of 'big bang' was that company directors' prime duty was to serve the best interests of the company. The 1985 Companies Act stated that directors, being agents of the company, owe a fiduciary duty to their company to act in its best interests at all times and thus the best long-term interests of all stakeholders. The Institute of Directors explained that as meaning 'they must show it the highest loyalty and act in good faith in its interest'.[19]

However, that legally settled position does not fit with the increasingly dominant neoclassical belief. So the 2006 Act amended directors' duties as 'to promote the success of the company' but added 'for the benefit of its members as a whole', the word 'members' referring to shareholders. The insertion of 'for the benefit of its members as a whole' was then argued as confirming directors' duty to focus on the interests of shareholders ahead of all the other interested parties and, in particular, the company itself. Thus, the primacy of shareholder interests, proclaimed by Friedman and later falsely justified by agency theorists as outlined in the previous chapter, was given the possibility that its legality was at least conceivable. That was sufficient for organised money to exercise its power over government.

The general population is still reliant on real business, making things and providing services and platforms, for its progression. But when real business mutates into the financialised format, it becomes an important component of the organised money establishment. In that role, as an M&A predator destroying other real businesses, it takes decisions on the simple basis of MST.

In the absence of preventive regulation, mature industries therefore tend to become dominated by a small number of firms which form an effective cartel of big predatory corporates. It is those financialised corporate entities which provide the public front for government by organised money.

That process of financialisation has traditionally been fairly slow in its implementation. The growth of traditional real economy businesses was constrained by the need to build assets, whether in manufacturing, distribution or even in service provision. Growth costs money to build the necessary facilities and accrue the essential working capital.

However, those same necessities are required much less by today's Big Tech titans. The speed of their development is only increased by the network effects of growth, increasing the value of the platform provision, whatever it is. Moreover, the ever increasing scale of provision, such as the product range provided by Amazon, or Google's search facility, only adds to their attractions, with more or less immediate effect. That is achieved at no apparent cost to the user, since the intangible assets, such as intellectual capital, do not involve ongoing costs of use.

Growth, with its increase in the 'big data' of detailed user information, begets more growth at zero incremental cost. That is very different from the traditional real economy business for which growth is dependent on building new facilities and providing ever increasing working capital.

Technology start-ups, given they hit the right tech buttons, can generate explosive growth and rapidly achieve monopolistic proportions far ahead of any restrictive regulation that might be devised to constrain their activities to conform to the common good. Moreover, neoclassically devout governments, in both the US and UK, have relaxed regulation, permitting such monopolies to be established. That is in line with the economic ideology: in the US, if prices are reduced that is taken as proof of competitive market forces.[20] In the UK, whereas the Monopolies & Mergers Commission (M&MC) and the Office of Fair Trading (OFT) were formerly concerned with restricting the establishment of controlling market shares, the emphasis was moved, as regulation was reduced, to focus on the abuse of such market shares, rather than their establishment. Monopolistic power is readily achieved by the tech sector and has been made allowable, despite the real costs to society and democracy.

In the 21st century all those trends have been accelerated and magnified by the extremely rapid emergence and dominance of Big Tech (Google, Apple, Amazon, Facebook and others) which have created a new form of currency based on the value of captured user data. A whole new form of organisational platforms, such as Uber and Airbnb, exert ever tighter control over employees while escaping employer responsibilities. Such established practices enable predatory pricing to eliminate traditional competition. The resulting growth, driven by the network effects which generate funding, rather than consuming it as the business grows, has led to Big Tech outgrowing the established banking sector and is now in the course of reducing retail banking.

Big Tech progression is largely at the expense of traditional ways of serving existing markets, rather than creating wholly new markets. Its progress is therefore at the cost of existing providers. At this point in time, the true viability of Big Tech operation is uncertain. For the time being they are enabled to defeat existing businesses, but the total costs involved have not been properly identified. For example, Amazon by undercutting High Street retailers may succeed in wiping them out of business. But the retailers contributed business rates pro rata to their position on the High Street, contributing massively to other provisions for the public good. The new technology can readily out-compete the old, but the overall effect remains unclear, especially as the new technology is operated by organisations committed to MST.

Faroohar convincingly argues that Big Tech must be stopped,[21] though the more likely outcome might be that it will, like all previous bubbles, burst and come down to earth where it will in future be constrained by appropriate regulation.

Supportive strands of academia

The relevant strands of academia include the research, development and teaching of the standard microeconomic curriculum – the neoclassical version already outlined, which is delivered, at least in part, at secondary school and undergraduate levels, as well as in post-graduate business school education. Consciously or not, it serves the interests of organised money, playing a crucial role in the wider promulgation of neoclassical belief.

It provides the apparently respectable, theoretical validation of the ideology's dominance, explaining free markets as good for the overall economy and an inevitability of economic progress. That theorised explanation provides the underlying academic credibility which underpins much business school teaching and plays a particularly influential role in the education and development of succeeding generations of the various segments of the organised money establishment.

Khurana reviewed early American business school attempts to establish business management as a profession, alongside medicine and the law.[22] They failed in that ideal but were accepting of the 'robber barons' support for their own advancement. The Ford and Carnegie foundations, for example, funded much business education, and encouraged the adoption of economics as the foundational theory of business.

Khurana also noted the loss of pluralism in economics teaching, leading to mainstream acceptance of the neoclassical orthodoxy in the 1980s. Alternative perspectives, related to the macroeconomic concerns regarding the nature and causes of the wealth of nations, and also including economic history, had been taught previously to succeeding generations of political, academic and business leaders. But that pluralism was largely replaced by the single ideology-based solution to every economic problem as provided by neoclassical modelling.

In the UK, business management education was initially delivered by people with experience as management practitioners but with more limited academic standing. Consequently, there was considerable pressure for business faculty to achieve academic status through research and publication rather than the provision of training and education to improve management practice.

For similar reasons they sought to establish management as a scientific subject in its own right, quantitative, rational and technique based, with business school education evolving to become more oriented to the 'science' of economics.

A July 2013 report on business education confirmed the microeconomic version as then taught by business school faculty. *Institut Européen d'Administration des Affaires* professor Craig Smith suggested 'Students come in with a more rounded view of what managers are supposed to do, but when they go out, they think it's all about maximising shareholder value.'[23]

The rating of academic institutions has become dependent on the publications record of their faculty, which is assessed in the UK every five years or so. That assessment is critical to the institution's funding. Each faculty member is assessed as to their research publications, their score depending on the apparent standing of the journals in which they have been published. To a considerable extent acceptance of publications is dependent on their conforming to the research position of the editorial board members of the journal concerned. Non-conformance would tend to be grounds for rejection. This system then works as a further means of reinforcing the existing orthodoxy, whatever it is.

The changed focus of business academia has coincided with, and is deeply influential on, the financialisation of big business. Management has been established with a general expertise, deemed to be applicable to any situation, industry or technology. Finance and accounting provide the common language for managing these diversified corporations. Maximising shareholder value, the commonly used euphemism for MST, is accepted as the single common objective. It justifies the priority given to short-term deal making ahead of long-term strategic management. It is taught along with the supporting topics of agency theory, transaction cost economics and the open market in corporate managements.

The business schools themselves are under pressure to act according to the logic of what they teach. They are in a marketplace, subject to all manner of league tables which determine their market position. Students are apparently attracted on the basis of various considerations including the financial return they might expect from achieving their MBA qualification.[24]

Ghoshal argued that many of the worst excesses of recent business practice resulted from universities and business schools producing a student with no sense of moral responsibility.[25] University research and teaching units as well as business schools deliver and promote what has been referred to as an econocracy – rule by experts talking a language that is incomprehensible to the normal intelligent human being and which is having devastating effect on the overall economy and the common good.[26]

That obscure language is translated, accurately or not, into comprehensible messages by the media component of organised money which promotes the essentials of neoclassical belief. Nevertheless, an increasing number of economists and business school faculty expressly dissociate themselves from the whole neoclassical ideology as formerly noted by Routh[27] and also by Khurana.[28]

There is also much evidence of academic research funded by and subservient to the constituents of organised money.[29]

The media

The financial sector clearly leads the way, exploiting to the full all new opportunities provided by post 'big bang' technologies and the generally permissive deregulated culture that has been established. The financialised corporates form the more visible front which is widely recognised for what it really is: predatory on the real economy and the common good. They consequently take the critique and generally cover for the organised money establishment. Academia is the component which teaches the economic theoretical justification for the whole destructive fiasco, and has maintained the unlikely credibility of such theorising over its past 40 years.

The media is the component that has traditionally presented the propagandist explanations for free market excess. The organised money media seeks to persuade the general population to accept their argument that the free market solves everything for the best, justifying supportive government actions and reductions of assumed bureaucracy. In those endeavours the media has been highly successful.

The media is no more a coherent singularity than is business itself. There have always been various courageously independent organs across the globe. But traditional newsprint and broadcast media are dominated by a small number of financialised corporates such as the Murdochs, Harmsworths and Barclays. Moreover, all media are staffed and coordinated by many individuals who have internalised neoclassical orthodoxies at school or university and are oriented to its perspective.

Like other areas of business, the media is perpetually undergoing fundamental challenge by technology as well as evolution by M&A deal making. Traditional press has served the organised money purpose, and is now well into its decline phase. In its desperation to retain readership, truth in reporting news has been widely disregarded. Broadcast media is now subject, like the High Street, to new technology challenges, which threaten the role of such as the BBC. The standard mature phase consolidation appears now certain, as exampled by Murdoch's proposed takeover of Sky News, previously banned following phone hacking abuses, finally defeated by Comcast.

Online social media, maybe approaching its mature phase, but appears still well ahead of its effective regulation. So untruth goes largely unchallenged and unpunished. As with all such new technologies, appropriate regulation will necessarily follow some way behind, but the absolute essentials of factual reporting will surely catch up in due course.[30] When the social media sector started out, hopes were high that it would empower freedom of speech and the democratic process. At this point in time, it is more known for its role in the generation of fake news and the potential it offers foreign powers for interference in national democratic processes such as the alleged role of Russia in US presidential elections.

The pursuit of fact appears not to be a major concern for the most successful online media. Technology leaders such as Facebook, Google, Amazon, Twitter, Netflix, Instagram, LinkedIn, YouTube, SnapChat and others are transforming media, broadcast and many other aspects of contemporary life, while rapidly establishing monopolistic sectoral powers.

As with other sectors, it is subject to hostile or invited M&A attack from financialised corporates. So not only is its technology subject to fundamental change but also is its ownership and control. The original hopes for its benign contributions to progression have been reduced by malign effects. The sector is still subject to rapid change and increasing complexity. For the time being, free market ideology is limiting regulation, but obvious abuses attract attention and the technicalities of effective regulation will in due course be progressively implemented.

The political sector

The political sector comprises active and would-be politicians and their researchers and staff, in part paid for by the multi-billion-dollar funded lobbyists which promote the organised money interests directly to politicians, addressing specifically political issues focused on the self-interest of their funding providers. The sector also includes the multi-billion-dollar funded think tanks, including such as the UK based Adam Smith Institute, Institute of Economic Affairs and Centre for Policy Studies, all of which promote an overtly politicised ideology including the infamous reinvention of moral philosopher Adam Smith as the founding father of free market neoclassical belief. Such think tanks and lobbyists deliver analysis on behalf of their funding patrons, rather than being focused on the search for objective truth.

Politicians have responsibility for inputting the values, such as truth, fairness and justice, which might moderate economic decision making. But they have been taught the free market orthodoxy, which is explicitly values free. Consequently, there is pressure for them to be most concerned with achieving and maintaining power, gaining profile in the media so as to manipulate public opinion to support their chosen ideology.

The American administration in 2018 appeared set on reducing the democratic element of government, so that more of its activities might be taken over by private sector operators. Lewis notes the US constitution's weaknesses with regards the checks and balances built into the public sector. Each new administration controls around 4,000 senior public service appointments, which can be made on the grounds of political ideology rather than professional qualification and competence. Consequently, the US public sector lacks continuity and management independence, ceasing to operate effective restraints.[31] There has been a similar decline in the UK's political-economic checks and balances with the progressive weakening of competitive market oversight and the planned reduction in regulation of fair trading and monopolies and mergers.

Many of today's active politicians also tend to lack direct contact with the world that most of their constituents experience. An often repeated story of those who aspire to a career in UK politics is that they leave university with degrees in PPE or economics, get jobs as researchers or advisors to government ministers, leading to positions where they contribute to important decisions on truly fundamental issues. Those contributions are necessarily made on the basis of ideology, rather than any experience-based understanding. They then progress to standing for election themselves and becoming an MP without the benefit of real contact with the bulk of the people they represent or the real economy within which they work.

Consequently, little account is taken of the long term and wider concerns such as the ecological and social macro-systems. This is the setting into which politicians are introduced and over which global institutions such as the IMF and World Bank hold sway.

While not all politicians have been victims of such grooming, it takes a particular heterodox spirit to retain a focus on the democratically expressed objectives to which as political leaders they are committed.

Conclusions

This chapter has very briefly outlined the various components of the self-perpetuating organised money establishment. Together they are powerful enough to change the law to fit their requirements and to dominate government in Anglo-America and increasingly across advanced economies, thereby, as Lewis observed, 'undoing democracy'.

In most advanced democracies there is a carefully developed system of institutions providing checks and balances, built into the constitution, which prevents the nation state being easily taken over by some dictatorship or short-term extreme political thrust. The independence of the law and a permanent publicly funded civil service can provide such checks and balances. However, as noted previously, they have been seriously weakened in both the US and UK.

Social democracy is under threat, with democratic government becoming 'a mere appendage' of organised money. The UK's Companies Acts have been amended to reduce conflict with the ideology, and the government spokesperson of the day was persuaded to defend the change by expanding on the unfathomable notion of 'enlightened shareholder value'. In the US organised money has gone further with their political leader of the day having, for example, responsibility for making politically motivated appointments to lead the social services, opening up all sorts of opportunities for subsequent abuse.[32]

Knowledge and understanding of how the world works, and with it the development of technological expertise and capability, continue to grow apace. The ecosystem and the imperatives for a sustainable future are understood as never before. Survival, the fundamental aim of all living systems, requires the non-depletion of finite resources and non-destruction of life in its many forms. That may be within the grasp of the current population but appears of limited interest to organised money.

Government is responsible for deciding the direction in which we are headed as nations, as a global economy and as a species, as well as deciding the fate of Earth itself. The key battle appears to be that between the real economy focused on creating value and the financialised economy focused on value extraction. In Anglo-America the financialised has taken over government, using neoclassical belief to justify its predatory actions.

At a political level that dichotomy is expressed as between social democracy and government by organised money. That has replaced the old battle between socialism and neoclassically defined capitalism. While social democracy is values based and works for the common good; government by organised money is values free, aimed at maximising shareholder wealth, from which, like their 19th century 'robber baron' forbears, they might exercise the option to act philanthropically and achieve a legacy of apparent worth.

That is 21st century government by organised money. Individuals who populate its various constituents are broadly assumed to be driven by self-interest and so behave as neoclassical belief requires and predicts. Such individuals could be more productive if alternative assumptions were operative. There is an alternative. But that is not their current focus, as outlined in the following chapter.

3

Resulting profound wrongs, destructions, inequalities and frauds

Introduction

In 2010, Tony Judt opened 'Ill Fares the Land', his valedictory 'treatise on our present discontents', suggesting that 'Something is profoundly wrong with the way we live today. For 30 years, we have made a virtue out of the pursuit of material self-interest.'[1]

Those profound wrongs, carried out largely to serve organised money's best short-term interests, take many forms that damage the real economy, society and planet Earth.

The growth of global population is a further complicating factor in the current context of political–economic decision making, and is generally ignored as too inconvenient a truth. Concerns regarding population are not new. Malthus[2] recognised that population depended on the means of its subsistence, that it would grow when those means permitted, and that it would grow geometrically. Food supplies would only grow arithmetically, and therefore population would ultimately be limited by hunger and starvation, unless previously constrained by war, plague or disease.[3] Until the first industrial revolution Malthus was more or less correct. Since then, innovations in industry, agriculture and healthcare have prevented that global catastrophe, but it remains unclear how much more population growth such developments can be made to support, without inflicting irreversible damage on the environment.

Global population is now forecast to reach 9.5 billion by 2050, which some hold to be peak population, though non-Malthusian reasons for subsequent decline are unclear. Despite the concomitant ageing of the population, Japan and some countries in Western Europe are already experiencing what is probably the start of a reduction in native populations, potentially compensated by migration, which poses a different set of soluble problems.

The Economist described the financial sector as mired in 'a culture of casual dishonesty'.[4] That culture denies the imperatives of sustainability and population growth as well as social harmony, which are commonly excluded from political-economic consideration. But the culture does accept fines for fraud and criminality, simply as the cost of doing 'business as usual'. In the aftermath of the infamous Forex trading scandal, which involved banks colluding for at least a decade to manipulate exchange rates for their own financial gain, a Barclays trader succinctly expressed the culture as 'if you ain't cheating, you ain't trying'.[5]

That is the culture that encourages new and ever increasing inequalities and infrastructural failings, which lead to rising social unrest, and ignores the environmental destructions so well documented by the Intergovernmental Panel on Climate Change in 2018.[6]

These various issues are not controversial; they are widely known and reported. Why they have become so widespread may be less well understood. The people involved may not have criminal intent but need to earn a living for themselves and their dependents, and are driven by the witchcraft and institutional truths of neoclassical belief, measuring their own worth as revealed by their own income and wealth. However, the results of that system are much the same as if those individuals were criminally intent on exploiting every opportunity to maximise their own short-term financial gain at the expense of all other considerations.

The following sections provide a brief outline of the main destructive effects, starting with the corruption of real business.

Financialising real economy organisations

One of the most significant 'profound wrongs' is the corruption of businesses which exist to contribute to the real economy. Turning them into financialised entities results in them being focused on the extraction of value, rather than its creation.[7]

Since Adam Smith's pin factory observations, real business has been recognised as the prime driver of economic progression, continually developing new and better ways of working to satisfy consumer needs and wants. However, over the past four decades, real business has become increasingly financialised.

Without external regulation, mature industries tend naturally to mutate from being genuinely competitive to being dominated by a small number of successful but monopolistically inclined firms. Notorious examples include pharmaceuticals, agri-business, aerospace, armaments, telecoms, health insurance, professional services and banking. The ideological commitment to MST then focuses their power on the extraction of short-term value, rather than long-term investment for the benefit of consumers, the overall economy and the common good.

New technology industries, such as social media, online retail, internet search and provision, and the platform organisations providing entry to existing industries or alternatives, have all emerged in that culture of extraction and develop fast so that monopolistic control can be achieved more rapidly than ever. A successful formula can achieve global dominance over competing versions almost from start-up, rather than on a genuinely competitive level playing field entered in more traditional industries.

Facebook started in 2004, and over the following decade acquired a number of potential competitors, including Instagram and WhatsApp. The aim was to acquire and merge their innovative systems. In so doing competition was stifled, user contact details were acquired – as well as their profit potential. Regulatory checks and balances on such activities have not yet been developed and current regulation is restrained by the dominance of neoclassical belief.

In professional services, the global provision of audit, accounting and management consultancy is dominated by KPMG, PwC, Deloitte and EY – previously a 'big five' till Arthur Anderson self-destructed by complicity in the Enron fraud. Joined-up professional services have been permitted despite the obvious conflict of interest. Auditors' independent status, which is fundamental to their role, is clearly compromised when they also provide other services such as accounting and management consultancy for their audit client companies, as they invariably do.[8] But such objections have long since been overridden and the 'big four' continue to dominate their three global industries.

Referring to them as professional services has also been compromised by the change to their formation as limited liability partnerships (LLPs), muddying the distinction between their professional service based on trust and integrity and their financial operation as a form of business focused, in accord with neoclassical rule, on MST.

A similar compromise of interests has allowed retail banks to engage in investment banking services, trading in their own right, as well as on behalf of clients. The 2008 crash made those problems obvious and drew commitments to 'ring-fence' retail from investment banking, even to 'electrify' the ring-fence, though the meaning of the ring-fence, whether or not electrified, has never been made completely clear and has never been implemented. Re-establishing retail banking as separate legal entities would be essential to maintaining their separateness for when the next crash comes. The commitment to ring-fencing seems intended as window dressing.

The pursuit of monopolistic control of the market is a natural response to the pressure on management to ensure their businesses continue to grow and prosper, despite serving markets which are no longer in their growth phase of evolution.

The alternative to monopolistic control is to diversify away from the existing market focus onto some faster growing activity. Some mature businesses opt to pursue both monopolistic control of existing markets as well as diversifying into new areas.

Though diversification spreads the risk beyond the original business, it also adds complexity, creating an alternative focus for future development and an ongoing demand for investment in other technologies and industries. This changes the nature of the company. It started as a single business focused on delivering customer value through innovative development of its specialised resources. As a diversified business there is no longer that single focus for technology and professional expertise, it being superseded by a more generalised expertise in financial control and returns.

The easiest way to diversify is by acquisition of a business that has already achieved a competitive position in the chosen sector. The key expertise of the acquiring company therefore is focused on the financial skills required for effective M&A activity, just as it is with the pursuit of monopolistic power, raising the importance of financial deal making as the source of business success.

This financialisation route, whether to cartel, monopoly or conglomeration, is simpler and quicker to produce results than the development and coordination of real business. Moreover, by its restriction of competitive forces, it enables the extraction of greater value for shareholders. However, the mutation of businesses from real to financialised has the effect of reducing investment in future technological development and expertise, effectively limiting the progression from which the economy as a whole benefits.[9]

It also undermines the beneficial effects of competition. The increased focus on hostile acquisitions, notably of successful high technology SMEs, reduces the potential economic gain from their development. Thus the overall effect of financialising real business is damaging for the long term, the common good and the global economy.

Financialisation damage forces the change of focus from investment in long-term development of the company to short-term value extraction for investors. In the long term, this is perhaps the most profound and significant wrong resulting from government by organised money. It applies not only to businesses but also to individual people who become involved in the financialising processes, accepting the basic 'greed is good' tenets of neoclassical belief as simple facts of life. These individuals include many who have occupied university studentships in science subjects who might otherwise have contributed to resolving the world's sustainability problems, rather than extracting value and reducing the overall capacity to resolve sustainability.

Financialised culture and extraction of value

The managers and leaders of a financialised business are no longer required to have expertise with regard to technologies, customers or the development and support of people in their organisations. All that is required of them is a preparedness to make risk decisions, a responsibility which requires little knowledge and understanding of real business, and is exercised without regard to the possible impacts on other interests.

The only constraint on their financial dealing and extractions of value is the test of legality. Non-compliance with the law appears also to be accepted, so long as the anticipated gain is sufficiently large and the probability of wrongdoing being identified is sufficiently small. Such calculations are freed from consideration of personal liability in relation to decisions taken on behalf of the corporate entity, the standard resolution being in the form of corporate fines.

Many borderline non-compliances involve what are referred to as externalities, the avoidance of costs relating to, for example, the correction of pollutions resulting from business operations. Some of those pollutions are rectified at public expense. Others are not rectified at all and join the huge accumulation of externalities which are contributing to environmental damages. These are serious offences against society rather than accounting technicalities.

Over the past few decades neoclassical belief in the power and efficiency of business has led to the UK government outsourcing much of social and infrastructural provision to private sector contractors such as the 'big four' of Serco, Capita, Atos and G4S, whose main expertise is in the process of bidding for contracts, as was also the case with the now infamously bankrupted Carillion group. There are too many famous examples of such contractors' errors to list here, but the UK Ministry of Justice took back control of HM Prison Birmingham from G4S in 2018 after yet another inspection had reported prisoners used drink, drugs and violence with impunity and corridors had been found to be littered with cockroaches, blood and vomit. That was G4S who had famously presided over the 2012 London Olympics security fiasco.[10]

Outsourcing and privatisation have also resulted in substantial neglect of the real economy's infrastructure, including such mundane things as the failure of hospital, prison and school buildings, and the maintenance and improvement of the UK's water and urban sewer systems, much of which dates back to the Victorian era. Even the filling in of potholes on the UK's public highways has been made to take an austerity hit. Such avoidance of maintenance and improvement are largely hidden till disaster strikes. Infrastructural neglect is also evident in the closure of public libraries, parks, museums and art galleries.

The prime beneficiaries of such short-term savings by outsourcing provision are the shareholders of the companies involved, who are likely in many cases to be wholly unaware of the wrongs from which they benefit.

Similarly the supply of UK energy was disposed of to the big six energy providers (British Gas, EDF Energy, E.ON UK, npower, ScottishPower and SSE), whose main form of competition was restricted to pricing structures. There have been many instances of such private for-profit providers exploiting their non-competitive positions for shareholder gain.

Economically oriented politicians appear to be driven by the simplistic neoclassical idea that a market free from government regulation, will, by definition, be competitive. Its participants are therefore efficient, and its results automatically allocated in the most beneficial way. They may, or may not, be unaware of the financialised predators and their monopolistic power for exploitation.

A further problem resulting from the financialisation of business is the damage being done to the people engaged in those businesses. They are perverted from their real competence to becoming managers of an essentially predatory financial operation, for which purpose they are likely to mutate into what Ghoshal described as the familiar 'ruthlessly hard-driving, strictly top-down, command-and-control focused, shareholder-value obsessed, win-at-any-cost business leader'.[11] In that role, they can continue to wreak destructions.

Those public sector organisations that are not privatised are assessed against various key performance indicators nominated by uninformed politicians. Consequently, essentially non-competitive provision is loaded with all manner of administrative on-costs without any compensating gain. That has increased the cost of public delivery, presided over by successive UK governments, apparently innocent of the disastrous systems effects of their possibly well intentioned but ill-informed and ideologically driven interferences. The destruction of system efficiency and effectiveness then leads governments to believe Friedman's assertion that it costs a state enterprise twice as much as it costs private for-profit business to do anything. That assertion fits the ideology and may be self-fulfilled by the trashing of public services as outlined previously.

As a consequence, operations are contracted out to private financialised businesses which operate as effective monopolies focused on MST. This then adds a further dimension of cost to, for example, health provision, as well as refocusing away from serving the best interests of patients/customers.

Similar system effects impact on all natural monopolies. For example, energy supply delivers a standard product with a set means of delivery but is assumed to be delivered more efficiently by private means rather than public. Competition is limited to the creativity of pricing systems, which has become an art form intended to give the impression of real competition, while the actual result is monopolistically exploitative of customers.

Genuinely competitive markets are different, but governments have been led to trashing their operation too. Customers undoubtedly benefit from having different market participants competing for their custom. The reality is, as already noted, markets free of regulation, tend naturally to become ever less competitive. A market is not a system, but a metaphorical meeting place between suppliers and consumers, where systems compete, collude or mutate into monopolistic predators.

Organisations, such as NHS (National Health Service) hospitals, are being destroyed because their interdependent components are being made to compete, rather than collaborate, with each other to achieve overall system aims. At the same time, competitive markets are being allowed to become cartelised and monopolistic because the ideology dictates against extraneous regulation. Those destructions are the direct result of the financialised culture which is based on the witchcraft and institutional truths of neoclassical theorising, rather than real observation based knowledge and understanding of how such systems work best.

The result is that the financialised businesses continue their predation on the real economy, taking advantage of the enfeebled public sector providers.

The destructive effects of the financialised culture are well documented elsewhere. Mazzucato recounts many stories illustrating the essential distinction between value creation and value extraction, creation being the product of the real economy and extraction by the financialised economy.[12] Shaxson provides insights as to the ways and means of the financialised sector and its ultimately negative contribution to the world.[13]

Fraud and criminality

The 'culture of casual dishonesty' might be bad enough, but fraud and criminality, which extends far beyond the financial sector, suggests a culture which is substantially more committed, than 'casual'.

Financial derivatives such as credit default swaps and collateralised debt obligations, comprise securities deliberately bundled together so that the many non-viable components in their content, remain hidden. Repo 105 deals were an even more obvious example of intended deception: temporary sale of debt for the period when audited accounts were prepared and reported. The sole purpose of such devices was to mislead. The system of audit, certifying accounts as 'true and fair', is thus further compromised. Unless and until its original intent is legally reinstated, audit certificates appear to be worth little more than Enron's seal of approval four days before its bankruptcy declaration.

The economy has no doubt always harboured companies and individuals that have acted corruptly and dishonestly. In that it is no different from other areas of human activity. However, the extent of that corruption and dishonesty has clearly increased over the past few decades as regulatory powers have been systematically demolished.

JPMorgan and clients were hosted for dinner and entertainments at Buckingham Palace in November 2013.[14] That was only days after Morgan's agreed settlement of their $13 billion fine for fraud and criminality. Morgan's CEO, Jamie Dimon, was then still nominally subject to criminal investigation regarding Morgan's misdemeanours for which fine settlements then totalled around $19 billion. The possibility of Dimon being found guilty was obviously not taken seriously and he was given the official seal of approval by the Duke of York at Buckingham Palace. Such fines for fraud were regarded merely as the fees that had to be paid for participation in the modern financial sector.

A year after JPMorgan's night out, the *Financial Times* reported that, 'between 2009 and 2013 the 12 global bankers paid out £105.4bn worth of fines to European and US regulators for crimes ranging from mis-selling of mortgages, to rigging the Libor index of interbank lending rates'.[15]

They had also been fined for rigging the Forex market, as well as rigging various commodity markets, also for money laundering on behalf of various terrorist organisations and for Mexican drug cartels, not to mention tax evasion and the most energetic avoidance. It was also reported that those 12 global banks had also made additional provisions in their accounts for a further £61.23 billion of anticipated fines for crimes which presumably they knew all about, but which had not yet been uncovered. So a total of £167 billion, which Tett described as 'eye popping', at the same time pointing out that £167 billion was 'unlikely to be the final hit'.[16]

Not only was that £167 billion fraud not the whole story for the 12 global banks, but most financial houses appeared to have been behaving in a similar fashion. Barclays investment bank had been found guilty of fixing the Libor market, on which around US$350 trillion of derivatives depended, affecting pretty much all mortgages and overdrafts. This was the context of 'If you ain't cheating, you ain't trying!'[17] Barclays were fined £290 million for their 'wrong doing' and the investment bank boss, Bob Diamond, rather than being asked to bear any personal responsibility, was promoted to CEO of the whole group. In 2018, Barclays was reported as agreeing to pay US$2 billion to settle a US mortgage mis-selling probe which claimed the bank had 'fraudulently sold residential mortgage backed securities'.[18]

Heffernan adopted the term 'wilful blindness' to describe one aspect of financialised business which has become similarly mired. It was a term originally suggested by the trial of Enron bosses, Skilling and Lay, to describe their behaviour, which, while perhaps not originating with criminal intent, nevertheless *wilfully* ignored the responsibility to ensure criminal behaviour was not permitted on their watch. That is, so long as it appeared that shareholder interests were being served.[19]

Heffernan's prime focus was on BP's approach over the Texas City Refinery explosion in which 15 people died and 170 others were injured. An independent review concluded that the prime cause was a 'lack of effective monitoring and modelling approaches that provide early warnings and help to prevent such events'.[20] That review did not recognise the lack as wilful, though Heffernan's argument gained weight with the subsequent BP Deepwater Horizon catastrophe, which killed a further 11 people and spilled millions of barrels of oil into the Gulf of Mexico, doing unprecedented levels of environmental damage. BP's focus was clearly on its performance in terms of shareholder value – its blindness to other issues certainly appeared to be wilful and systemic.

The 'big four' privatising conglomerates – G4S, Serco, Capita and Atos – are focused on serving the best short-term interests of their shareholders, irrespective of the quality of service provided. A 2014 House of Commons Public Accounts Committee described the outsourcing industry as an 'evolution of privately owned public monopolies, who largely, or in some cases, wholly, rely on taxpayers' money for their income'. The outsourcing companies abuse the contractual system and taxation regimes to take out more and pay back less into the public purse.[21] A further noteworthy side effect of the privatisation process is that the state is effectively stripped of the resources and expertise to competently reassess future outsourcing contract bids.

Such firms invest in developing sophisticated means of avoiding and evading taxation and share the financial sector's willingness to act fraudulently in order to benefit shareholder returns. The list of such cases is far too long for inclusion here.

Since industrialisation, business has provided the means for resourcing our civilised society. But it now appears focused on avoiding that responsibility in order to maximise shareholder take.[22] Its global extent has been suggested by the leak of the Mossack Fonseca database of Panamanian tax haven activity,[23] the so-called Panama Papers. They comprised 11.5 million confidential documents of financial and legal client information leaked in 2015 to German newspaper *Süddeutsche Zeitung*, shared with the International Consortium of Investigative Journalists (ICIJ), and on public release by April 2016. They revealed the offshore financial industry's secret links to organised crime and tax evasion schemes, and exposed thousands of public officials and corporate executives as exploiting the shadow financial system for their private gain.

The 13.4 million confidential documents leaked as the Paradise Papers, followed the same route, with details starting to be made public in November 2017. Many leading corporate and high profile personal identities have been reported as mired in tax evasion and corruption, presumably on the strenuous advice of their tax advisors. However, it is the principals to such practice, not their advisors, who carry the responsibility. The extent of wrongdoing by those with power and influence reveals an astonishing level of corrupt and criminal activity which presents a substantial contemporary problem for business education and training.

Inequalities of wealth and income

The excesses of organised money, whether finance or financialised business, are experienced by the whole of society, which comprises both winners and losers. The winners, like the losers, depend on the public provision of necessary and desirable goods that the market would not, or could not, provide. For instance, all humanity depends on fresh air and clean water. More than that, even the most egregious of winners also depend on a variety of other public provisions, not just the 'regalian' items such as defence and law and order policing, but a surprisingly long list of others, including public highways and high speed internet access.

Inequalities within advanced economies such as the UK and US include increasing numbers of people trapped in unemployment or underemployment and consequently homeless, sleeping rough and dependent on food banks. There are examples of modern slavery.[24]

Such inequalities are being further emphasised by governments continuing the 'plunder of the commons'.[25] The UK public owns around £300 billion worth of public assets, in the form of land and buildings, social housing, public parks, forests, museums, libraries and art galleries and so on, which are being sold off to raise finance in lieu of taxation, in accord with the ideologically nominated austerity approach to balancing the government's books. This fire sale of public assets, as with the sale of corporate assets, has only a temporary one-off return but a permanent loss of public benefit.

The top end of the wealth and income divide has been well documented. Financialised business leaders have taken their excesses to new heights of inequality. Prior to the 1980s, chief executives of leading public companies were paid around 20 times the average shop floor worker's pay. Drucker pointed out 'Few top executives can imagine the hatred, contempt and even fury that has been created − not primarily among blue-collar workers who never had an exalted opinion of the bosses − but among their middle management and professional people.' He argued it could be 'no more than twenty to one without injury to company morale'.[26]

By 2017 CEOs of FTSE100 companies were paying themselves 312 times the average employee's pay and taking an annual increase of 11 per cent compared to less than 2 per cent for their average paid employees.[27] That exploding pay inequality has been accompanied by reduced growth rates, investment levels and productivity. Moreover, it has become apparent that, for the high paid, investment in professional advice regarding tax avoidance and evasion has become personally lucrative, as was noted by Friedman.

But 'corporate officials' do not in truth have a responsibility to make as much money as possible for stockholders; and they do have moral responsibilities as Friedman himself subsequently admitted. Those moral responsibilities include concerns for issues such as justice, fairness and sustainability, all of which are threatened by the pursuit of MST. That single variation on the neoclassical belief, from maximising profit to MST, is still contributing to corporate social, infrastructural and ecological destructions.

Inequality has grown dramatically over the past four decades, justified by the ideology. By 2020, the world's richest 1 per cent had more than twice as much wealth as its poorest 6.9 billion people, and the world's 2,153 billionaires had more wealth than 4.6 billion people.[28]

Oxfam's assessment was that inequality in the UK is rapidly returning to levels not seen since the time of Charles Dickens.[29] The Oxfam conclusions were further confirmed by Credit Suisse's 2019 Global Wealth Report.[30]

Those excesses are accompanied by avoidable destructions within advanced economies, which was symbolised in the UK by the Grenfell Tower fire, which caused 72 deaths, with more than 70 others suffering injury and 223 people escaping. What made it even more remarkable was the local authority's initial uncomprehending response to such a disaster and the denial of the various private sector organisations involved in erecting the tower.

The inequalities between economies are, of course, even more extreme. But yet, so far, the mainstream ideology which actively supports these inequalities remains firmly in place.

People at the bottom of the global heap are justified in feeling they are being treated with contempt by those at the top. They are unable to achieve a satisfactory income or standard of living in their home countries and are vulnerable to being misled into emigrating to wealthier countries where their capabilities might be employed. Individuals who are treated with such disregard might also be susceptible to being recruited into extremist protest movements, with further damaging outcomes.[31]

Unequal opportunity is not limited to those who lack proven capability or qualification at the bottom of the pile. For example, the World Bank reported in 2014 that Tunisia had 130,000 unemployed graduates, almost a third of the total, in a population of 11.3 million.[32] They too might be tempted by the apparent alternative futures.

Records of the unsustainable injustices and destructions currently being perpetrated are available elsewhere. That is not the purpose of this text. However, it is important to note that the inequalities of income and wealth are unprecedented and locked into a cycle of ever increasing divergence, noted by Picketty as the 'central contradiction of capitalism'.[33] Also, the widespread knowledge and understanding of those inequalities, enabled by modern communications technologies, are also without precedent. That awareness is already the cause of social unrest, violence and destruction, with several areas of the globe subject to military constraint and war, from which the military–industrial complex achieves further exploitative gains.

Ecological destructions

The final form of destruction considered here is clearly the most important of all. Unsustainable pollutions, finite resource depletion, mass species extinctions, global warming with its catastrophic implications such as sea level rises, which are forecast in due course to submerge around a third of human habitations. That all leads to an uninhabitable planet Earth unless we change radically what we are doing, and do so fast.

This is clearly a topic area with an already massive literature, and it is not the purpose here to repeat those threatened destructions in any detail. The Nature Conservancy website describes Planet Earth as being 'at a crossroads' and outlines the necessary actions required now to make the natural world sustainable.[34]

The result of no change will clearly be catastrophic. The 2018 report by the Intergovernmental Panel on Climate Change (IPCC) outlines forecast outcomes if global mean surface temperature rose by 2°C above preindustrial levels.[35] They would include ever more extreme weather, sea level rise and ocean acidification devastating wildlife, crops, water availability and human health, almost certainly increasing the probability of human populations to migrate and being displaced leading to the likelihood of civil disturbance and war.

Similarly, catastrophic forecasts have been made by specialist scientists of species extinctions, agricultural wastage and so on. Yet, the ideology ignores such issues, encouraging denial of all their effects, and firms continue to be supported in externalising various ecological impacts to avoid paying for their rectification. That despite the evidence of Australia's 2019–20 catastrophic bushfires, with similar experiences in California and the deliberately started Amazonian rainforest burning.

Avoidance of all these destructions is clearly feasible but can only be temporary. Given the current state of scientific knowledge and understanding, sufficient change may still be within reach. The drive to achieve that change could be this generation's motivator for business and economic progression. The reason appropriate change is being prevented is the continuing dominance of the free market economic neoclassical belief, which is supported and promoted by the organised money establishment.

Finally, it is worth quoting Sir David Attenborough as he spoke to the 2018 Climate Change Conference at Katowice, Poland:

> Right now we are facing a man-made disaster of global scale, our greatest threat in thousands of years: climate change. If

we don't take action, the collapse of our civilisations and the extinction of much of the natural world is on the horizon.[36]

Conclusions

The current generation clearly has an unprecedented set of challenges to face up to if they are to fulfil the prime duty of passing down to successor generations a planet that is at least as sustainable as it was when inherited.

Change is not an option. Paul Rogers proposed that three challenges face us over the next two decades, to which we must find answers.[37] First, if the world is to be saved, then what he referred to as the neoliberal model of free market capitalism must be replaced. The second challenge was to solve the climate change issue. The third was the need to control the culture of militarism. War, such as the 'war on terror', is not a solution. The mission in Iraq was not accomplished, nor in Syria, Libya, Afghanistan, or most other places the West has become embroiled in, which has produced large scale gains for its global armaments industry.

The standard political approach to such problems is to keep the lid on things – an essentially short-term focus which will avoid a real solution but delay the explosion till the current generation of politicians have moved on. The common sense alternative is to observe and try to understand in depth what the real issues are about and respond to them directly.

The challenges are so apparent, it is remarkable that an intelligent species such as ours should continue its progression to destruction. But that progression continues.

As this chapter was being written, the UK's Ministry of Defence was negotiating major outsourcing contracts with Capita despite its high risk rating, a former CEO of Anglo Irish Bank was jailed for six years for a €7.2 billion fraud, and Disney raised its bid for the majority of Murdoch's 21st Century Fox in response to Comcast's counter bid, with Rupert Murdoch quoted as saying 'We are extremely proud of the businesses we have built at 21st Century Fox and firmly believe the combination with Disney will unlock even more value for shareholders'.[38]

We are destroying the world at an ever increasing velocity. The solutions are known and largely understood. Humanity could avoid destruction if it so chose. The fact it has not, so far, engaged with sufficient action is because the self-perpetuating organised money establishment chooses to be guided by the false ideology from which it achieves such extraordinary short-term gains.

But at some stage in the not too distant future, change will happen, either as a result of reasoned argument, or the inevitability of destruction.

That is where we are now. It is not where we want to be.

PART II

Where do we want to get to?

Democratic governments have repeatedly indicated their commitments to what has been described as civilised society. Politicians have not been slow in proclaiming heroic commitments to such as universal human rights, equal opportunities, fairness, justice and freedom for all.

Commitments have also been set regarding the now recognisably fragile ecosystems within which the world operates, reminding this generation that they also have responsibilities to all future generations.

Knowledge of that fragility requires the amendment of human activity and the refocusing of invention and innovation onto achieving a fully sustainable planet.

Economic progression has made it possible to fulfil all such societal and ecological commitments. But achievement has fallen far short, with the destruction of ecological systems continuing apace, while a few people gain extremes of wealth, and others are trapped in squalor, ignorance, want, idleness and disease.

The opportunity to achieve permanent sustainability is apparently still available. If this generation succeeds in achieving sustainability, then future generations will recognise our contribution to their safe abode. If we fail, those fewer generations who follow will blame us for our greedy destruction of life on Earth.

4

Democratic commitments to sustainable progression

Introduction

Sustainable progression is necessarily defined by the basic system of morality on which democracy itself is based. It is fundamental to political-economic decision making, but it is not simply a matter of GDP growth, however that is defined.

Economic progression almost invariably depends on political decisions and political decisions almost invariably have economic consequences for the fabric of civil society about which there have been many heroic expressions of human aspiration throughout history.

The 1776 American Declaration of Independence expressed it as being 'self-evident, that all men are created equal', and that they are endowed with 'certain unalienable rights' such as 'Life, Liberty and the pursuit of Happiness', to which Lincoln's Gettysburg address 100 years later added the democratic principle that 'government of the people, by the people, for the people, shall not perish from the earth'. At the time there were almost 4 million African Americans held in bondage as slaves – 'Willingly, with deliberate purpose, our fathers bartered honesty for gain, and became partners with tyrants, that they might share in the profits of their tyranny.'[1]

All men – interpreted as all humanity – may have been created equal, and in terms of innate potential, nominated by intelligence and capability, that certainly appears to be the case. However, relatively few people have been permitted lives where their equality has been allowed fulfilment. That is not unique to the US, but an aspect of the human condition in most societies. Moreover, it is a widespread if not universal experience that a single sub-group of a population is permitted to manipulate systems for their own benefit, no matter the harm that might be done to others. Such is today's organised money establishment.

The UK has governed without a written constitution and so relies on the more pragmatic pursuit of humane principles being incorporated in its laws and cultural processes. That might be argued as in the spirit of Magna Carta, though more than 500 years later the UK was a major operator and beneficiary of the slave trade.[2] Despite progress, the achievement of equal opportunities is far from complete, and in recent decades that process appears to have been reversed.

The French elegantly distilled the same commitment down to three words: '*liberté, egalité, fraternité*'. But their fulfilment may be little further advanced than in Anglo-America.

German experience encapsulates all humanity's fragility, initiating the essentials of the welfare state in the 19th century, falling victim to the grotesque excesses of 20th century Nazism, and recovering to be as free, equal and communally enlightened as anywhere.

The Gettysburg principles remain valid definitions of the proper role and responsibilities of democratic government in the 21st century, to which must now be added the clear responsibility for the protection of a sustainable planet. Gettysburg can then apply to all future generations. That last principle might not previously have been recognised as relevant to political economy, but the implications of that error are now understood.

Environmental abuse is forecast to produce outcomes that far outweigh other crimes against humanity. But those lessons are yet to be incorporated in our culture and legal systems. Their truth and validity are still denied by members of the establishment who act as if in their own short-term self-interest with little regard for future generations. If our species is to survive, environmental stewardship must be acknowledged as a prime responsibility of governments across the globe.

It is widely agreed that those commitments would best be accomplished by the rule of law made available to all citizens, by democratic processes, operated on a regular basis, by all the people so governed. They elect their representatives to government to take decisions on their behalf, through the operation of a free and fair electoral system. Government by such a system would also require independent checks and balances by a permanent professional civil service and legal system, to restrain abuses of power by individuals so elected.

Environmental stewardship

Environmental devastation by the pursuit of economic ends is now understood as never before. The science may be impenetrable to the non-scientist, but the broad messages are clear. Human activity is generating various forms of pollution and waste. The result is damaging the ecosystems, causing polar ice caps to melt, acidification of the oceans and rising sea levels, mass extinctions of biological species and human habitations, causing a continuing vicious cycle of adverse effects.[3] The climate change euphemism all but hides the ultimate destructions envisaged by the relevant science and the urgency of its need for corrective action.

The destructions have been generally perceived as impacting the existing population. But their more devastating impacts for future generations are now also acknowledged. There is no logic in distinguishing between the worth of individuals who share our fleeting time on Earth and those who follow. Democratic aspirations must include a commitment to bequeath an Earth to future generations which is as viable as the one we inherited. The rule must be not to reduce the sustainability of Earth by one iota. To borrow from Florence Nightingale, the aim must be, referring to future generations, 'let us do them no harm'. But that is the minimum requirement. Nightingale was not just aiming to avoid harm, but to do much good. At the very least we should be aiming to pass on a planet that is better in some ways than the one we inherited and not worse in any way. The aim should be for global improvement, improbable though that may seem.

It is known what must be done to cut the generation of so-called greenhouse gases, and eliminate the waste of natural resources, including air and water, and cut other pollutions and the dumping of wastes, including food waste. But sufficient action is not being taken because the immediate economic gains are not calculably sufficient to pay the bill. Long-term effects tend therefore to be given scant attention.

Many individuals do live in accord with such 'rules'. But the need is for governments across the globe to take action to ensure it is in the interests of all individuals to comply, not just the intelligent and virtuous few.

The longer decisive action is delayed, the greater the damage with the possibility of various effects becoming irreversible, and the less likely action is to be effective and the more traumatic it will therefore need to be. Corrective action needs to be taken and justly rewarded now by global institutions, national governments and organisations as well as individuals.[4]

The literature on sustainability is huge and the overall message is clear. As with all predictions, there may be differences of detail, in this case as to timing and extent. But the overall message is simple, as expressed in the United Nation's Sustainable Development Goals declared in 2015 to be fulfilled by 2030:

a call for action by all countries – poor, rich and middle-income – to promote prosperity while protecting the planet. They recognize that ending poverty must go hand-in-hand with strategies that build economic growth and address a range of social needs including education, health, social protection, and job opportunities, while tackling climate change and environmental protection.[5]

The importance of this is not just to protect Earth as our habitat, but as an assertion of the interdependence of all human beings, including in particular this generation's responsibilities for future generations.

But the future value of the world and its populations is excluded from economic review because it is regarded as incalculable. In more meticulous assessments by discounting future cash flows, the value of the world in, say, 100 years' time is discounted to a present value of not very much at all, thereby offering a spurious pseudo-scientific justification for its exclusion from economic calculation. But it is an issue of moral principal, not economic, calculation.

Though scientific forecasts regarding the need for environmental stewardship may lack absolute precision, the destructions are such that the slightest risk of the science being right must be acted on. Denial of the science must be consigned to history.

The following sections outline democratic commitments that have been widely expressed. Though environmental stewardship may not have been recognised as a prime responsibility when those commitments were originally made, they are all now identified within the context of that fundamental commitment.

Human rights

The 1942 UK Beveridge Report identified freedoms from what were referred to as the five giant evils in society: squalor, ignorance, want, idleness, and disease. Prior to industrialisation in the 18th century, life in England for the vast majority was fairly short and uncomfortable if not 'brutish'. England's population had been constrained to around 5.5 million by unreliable harvests resulting in famine, and by poor public hygiene resulting in disease, notably dysentery, smallpox and consumption, with infant mortality around 1 in 15.

Industrialisation created the wealth to improve living conditions, and substantial improvements were made as recorded in measures such as infant mortality and longevity. However, the five giants remained: squalor in the slum living conditions in the new industrial mill towns;[6] ignorance as shown by unacceptably low levels of literacy and numeracy as well as the tiny minority admitted to further and higher education; want as widespread malnutrition if not starvation; idleness persisted, notably through the 1930s' levels of unemployment; and disease continued resulting from the limited health support available to the general population. All five were active threats to a progressing society.

Post WW2 UK democracy addressed the five giant evils through the provision of public housing, improved free state education, basic welfare payments for the poor, disabled and elderly, the provision of unemployment benefits and acceptance of government responsibility to maintain full employment as far as possible, and the establishment of the NHS. In the aftermath of war, social progress was achieved, the homeless were housed, those previously forced to beg on the streets were largely secured a survival standard of living, children were not only better educated but their adequate nutrition was underwritten by free provision at school, a third of the population which had previously been chronically undernourished received its first adequate diet, and public health famously made substantial progress under the auspices of the NHS.

All citizens had equal access to these revolutionary innovations. Beveridge recognised the risk of creating a state bureaucracy out of tune with the needs and wants of the people and emphasised that social progress was an essentially cooperative endeavour between the state and the individual. The government responsibility was to establish the minimum level of provision, but not to inhibit any person exceeding that minimum through their own individual efforts. The aim was to assist the people to improve their lot so that a healthier, longer lived and better educated society would be achieved from which all might benefit.

Today the five giants still exist and are particularly virulent in underdeveloped nations. For example, at the time of writing, the UNESCO Institute for Statistics reported that 617 million children and adolescents worldwide are not achieving minimum proficiency levels in literacy and numeracy. The figure signals 'a learning crisis … which could threaten progress towards the Sustainable Development Goals (SDGs)'. The data suggests that the problems are due to three main shortcomings.

> First, the lack of access, with children who are out of school having little or no chance to reach a minimum level of proficiency. Second, a failure to retain every child in school

and keep them on track. And third, the issue of education quality and what is happening within the classroom itself.[7]

Today people across the globe are increasingly aware through technology of how the other half lives. Those living in poverty are increasingly prepared to risk their lives to escape to achieve a more affluent situation. The achievement of survival with dignity in their home nation is a basic human right, which will only be achieved with the assistance of the developed world.

The United Nations Charter of 1945 declared its members' determination 'to reaffirm faith in fundamental human rights, in the dignity and worth of the human person'. That declaration was subsequently adopted by the UN General Assembly and later incorporated in the European Convention on Human Rights, agreed by member states of the Council of Europe, with its acceptance being a condition of entry for any nations wishing to join, enacted also by the UK Human Rights Act 1998.

The fundamental message of this internationally agreed legislation is that all individuals should enjoy the same rights to life, freedom and the pursuit of happiness so long as it does not interfere with the same fundamental rights of others. And they should do so freed from Beveridge's five giants: squalor, ignorance, want, idleness and disease, all of which are being revived in Anglo-America where ideologically driven inequalities continue to increase.

Equal opportunities

Those basic human rights were intended by law to be granted to all, no matter what their origin, circumstances or allegiances, so long as they were legal.

However, fine words do not necessarily produce results. Human beings may have laudable motivations but can too easily be dissuaded from their fulfilment. American blues queen, Billie Holiday, lamented the racially motivated lynch mobs still operating in USA well into the 20th century, referring to the strange fruit of black bodies hanging from the trees. America's segregation laws and practices were challenged by the civil rights movement, activated by courageous victims such as Rosa Parks refusing to obey the regulations requiring her to give her bus seat up to a white passenger. The movement led by Martin Luther King Jr, whose dream of 'freedom and equality arising from a land of slavery and hatred' brought official segregation to its end, initiated by

John F. Kennedy, enacted after his assassination, under Lyndon Johnson's leadership, but never completely eradicated.

Not only had the British presided over the slave trade till 19th century, but racial prejudice was accepted in the UK until after the last vestiges of empire were extinguished. The colonial experience included taken-for-granted racially based divisions, such as rail systems in Africa operating three passenger classes: European, Asian and African, referring to three highly differentiated levels of passenger accommodation. These were just pale latter-day reflections of the full bloodied empire excesses of invasion and slavery of indigenous peoples across the globe.

The South African apartheid system was only defeated in the 1990s; that defeat was accomplished without mass bloodshed, by the magnanimity and wisdom of Nelson Mandela's leadership with the courageous support of South African President F.W. de Klerk.

Such racial segregation and discrimination could no doubt be exampled across the globe, backed by law and established as dominant culture, both within nation states and between them. But its eradication requires more than just fine words.

Experiences in two world wars were heavy reminders of the interdependence between all peoples, quite irrespective of their origins or any other categorisation. Mandatory service in the armed forces placed all men in intimate, life-threatened proximity, where their interdependence was all too obvious. Heroism and cowardice were clearly no more distributed on the basis of ethnicity, rank, class or money than was intelligence.

Moreover, the domestic non-militarised population was also reminded of their interdependence by their wartime experience. Women, who had previously been largely constrained to domestic circumstances and a short list of low-ranking occupations, were recruited to 'man' the farms, factories and other operations deserted by those called up to military service.

People really were 'all in it together'. Therefore, health, education, a basic living standard, some security both financial and physical, and some fair distribution of such quality of life standards without prejudice, came to be regarded as a civilised target.

By the 21st century, discriminating against anyone on the grounds of their ethnicity had become illegal in most countries. And most advanced nations also upheld laws which proscribe discrimination against any individual because of their gender, religion or belief, age, disability and sexual orientation. Discrimination against anyone on any of these grounds is now mostly illegal at work, and when applying for access to employment, education, public services, and for private goods and services. Nevertheless, the ambiguity of established political processes continues, with actual performance falling far short of formal commitments described by the fine words.

Concerns for the treatment of people in work are now expanded by the Ten Principles of the UN Global Compact to include commitment that businesses should uphold 'the freedom of association and the effective recognition of the right to collective bargaining; the elimination of all forms of forced and compulsory labour; the effective abolition of child labour; and the elimination of discrimination in respect of employment and occupation'.[8]

Human rights and equal opportunities for all are now largely settled as legal requirements. Their enforcement and achieving justice for all are, however, far from complete in most societies. Real justice costs money and while in some states legal aid is available for those on low incomes, it is limited. Full justice is, as yet, available only to those who can afford to pay for it.

Social balance

A sustainable civil society would protect the environment from human damage to ensure the best interests of future generations are protected. It would defend basic human rights for all its citizens. It would also ensure they enjoy equal opportunities without any discrimination. If those commitments were fully achieved, what more could there be to make civil society sustainable?

Galbraith feared for the fragility of economic growth, which he saw as increasingly reliant on the production and purchase of goods that were not needed but for which demand was created artificially through sophisticated corporate promotions. The 'goods' which were in genuine demand were the public goods, such things as healthcare, education, a clean and healthy environment, increasing leisure and the public facilities for its enjoyment. Today he would no doubt have added a livable and sustainable climate. He identified the problem as one of social balance between the various components of the real economy, analysis of which he began quoting R.H. Tawney:

> It is not till it is discovered that high individual incomes will not purchase the mass of mankind immunity from cholera, typhus and ignorance, still less secure them the positive advantages of educational opportunity and economic

66

security, that slowly and reluctantly, amid prophesies of moral degeneration and economic disaster, society begins to make collective provision for needs which no ordinary individual, even if he works overtime all his life, can provide himself.[9]

Classical economic theory had been born in, and applied to, a world of poverty. It appeared less relevant to a world of affluence. Galbraith contrasted the US affluence in the late 1950s in terms of privately produced and advertised goods, with its inadequate provision of public goods, most of which were fundamental needs.[10] That was still true in 2008 with child poverty persisting even in the most advanced economy, and has advanced even further in the post 2008 decade of ideologically driven austerity.

Galbraith accepted that the balance between different private goods, such as cars, steel, fuel and insurance, would be best maintained through the operation of market forces, so long as the markets were competitive. He was concerned with the balance over the whole area of products and services, both private and public. For example, increased production of privately produced cars would require more publicly funded roads and if they were not provided in appropriate proportion, the economy would suffer, for example, through congestion and the consequent waste of fuel, time and money.

The problem of social balance was exampled by the city of Los Angeles as it was in the late 1950s.[11] The citizenry was affluent and known for its conspicuous consumption, but there was no publicly provided system of waste collection. It was therefore necessary for people to use home incinerators, which rendered Los Angeles air almost unbreathable.

The following half century saw the problems of Los Angeles becoming more general and global. By 2008, for example, the Beijing smog had to be artificially held at bay for the duration of the Olympic Games.

There is a need for both public provision of the everyday needs of society and the privately provided satisfaction of further needs and wants. Galbraith suggested that a stable society depended on a balance between private and public provision.[12] He referred to that as social balance, a rather more insightful perspective than the simplistic neoclassical aim to minimise state involvement in the economy.

Public provision of goods such as waste collection and disposal was essential. If such items were privatised and made chargeable, some citizens could not afford the luxury of collection and disposal, or even home incineration, and so the environment would be damaged for all citizens. Getting the social balance right was recognised as essential, not just for waste collection and disposal, but also for the essentials of life such as fresh air, clean water, an adequate road system, sufficiency of food and shelter for all, and effective systems of justice, security and defence.

The lack of social balance was also seen by Galbraith in the inadequate provision of healthcare, education, public law enforcement and housing which were leading to social dysfunction, increased crime and drug and alcohol abuse. The excessive production of unrecyclable waste is a 21st century manifestation of similar lack.

After around 40 years of 'government by organised money', the disparity between 'private wealth' and 'public poverty' has only widened. The throw away shopping culture has developed apace while the richest nation on Earth still lacks a universal healthcare system and leaves its poorest citizens homeless or in slum dwellings and tenements unfit for human habitation.[13]

That was the negative case for social balance, but Galbraith also made a positive case. A community would have been better rewarded by having better schools, parks and recreation facilities than simply, as an example of private wealth, bigger cars. Galbraith argued that the private investment in marketing bigger cars influenced the choice of citizens away from unpromoted public goods such as better schooling or hospitals. In that politicised world, the engineer or scientist who focused on developing a new device to make cars go better was a hero, while a public servant who proposed a new or improved public service was regarded as a 'wastrel'. Public expenditure was by definition bad, private provision good.

Galbraith also raised the concern of social balance of investment between material and personal capital. The distinction was fundamental. Public investment in material capital such as a school or a hospital was an increase in capital formation and a national asset. Investment in schooling increased the supply of educated human beings, of scientists and technologists on who the nation's intellectual capital depended. That capital formation in human beings was 'off balance-sheet', excluded from any census of public capital formation. It was nevertheless of prime importance to a nation's future development and would be especially so in an era of high technology when solutions are sought to such as global warming and resource depletion. Then the most powerful resources are various forms of intellectual capital which are all dependent on the capabilities of the people generating them.

Galbraith also included in his calculation of social balance the valuable but difficult to account for 'commons'. In the age of the hunter-gatherer, all resources were common to all people. But over time, some individuals and organisations took over ownership of almost everything, though excluding natural resources such as fresh air, clean water, the oceans and wildlife in its many forms, all of which are under some degree of threat. Beyond these ancient commons, there are many new forms which enhance the quality of civilised society which are also under ideological attack and need protection. These include such things as libraries, museums, art galleries, parks, beaches, village greens, rivers, the internet, open source software, and so on.

Physical assets cost to maintain, and local authorities pay. However, when local authorities are under pressure because of their lack of income and rising costs of operation, as when driven by a policy of austerity, they may be persuaded to dispose of their commons responsibilities, closing down libraries and museums, and selling off parks for housing development. Such actions provide short-term one-off gains in return for permanent loss of social benefit. Protection of the commons should therefore be a further commitment of democratic government in the interests of preserving social balance.

State or local authority owned housing which is rented to those in need is another complex category of asset, now clearly in reduced supply in the UK since they were made available for tenants to purchase at advantageous prices. That was another transaction with a one-off short-term gain for government, but a long-term additional cost, which is having to be more than compensated in the 21st century UK.

That all requires continuing investment to maintain their availability to all, everywhere. Those necessities of everyday life are too important to risk with private business. Should a private business delivering such a necessity go bankrupt, as happens not infrequently, the state would have to take over and deliver that provision. It is therefore important that the state does not lose the capability for such delivery should it be needed. Furthermore, the fact it is an absolute necessity, rather than a matter of real competitive supply, places the private business in a position of considerable power, which is fairly easy to abuse when the avowed objective of the private business is simply to make as much money as possible for its stockholders.

In most advanced economies, the state has also provided connected utilities such as gas, electricity, water, sewerage, telecoms and broadband. Such extensive state involvement was ideologically challenged, and supplies through those connected utilities were privatised and pretend competition was introduced to justify that privatisation. The results were predictably disappointing with prices being raised to maximise shareholder take and maintenance of the relevant infrastructure being neglected.

Balance and the real economy

In order to exercise effective environmental stewardship, deliver basic human rights and equal opportunities for all, as well as ensuring a degree of social balance, we need to achieve a healthy real economy.

Financial components of the economy, invented to provide investment for the first industrial revolution, have long since reversed their role so their impact on the real economy appears wholly negative as has been widely noted.[14] There is no trickle down of benefits to non-financial sectors, and as the financial economy grows, so those negative impacts increase. A fundamental distinction is therefore to be made between the real economy, from which everyone stands to gain, and the financial, from which all but a mall minority suffer substantial loss. It is a distinction that has been made many times, but yet is resisted in orthodox measurements of economic activity such as GDP and its growth.

That fundamental distinction between the real and the financial economies is confused by some real economy organisations, which continue to produce real goods and services, becoming dominated by the focus on maximising shareholder interests at the expense of everything else.

The real economy comprises a huge variety of different organisational forms, providing basic human needs for survival, the satisfaction of further wants and desires in order to progress, and the invention and innovation of new technologies which will be essential to the achievement of long-term sustainability of life on Earth.

Raworth described the base layer of provision on which the rest of the economy rests, as the 'social foundation of human wellbeing'.[15] It includes clean air and water, which were natural resources freely available to all until human beings managed to foul them up. Since then they have been increasingly recognised as precious commodities, along with the defeat of Beveridge's five giants by provision of social housing, education, a basic income, employment, health and social care, plus a host of other provisions such as public transportation infrastructure, adequate defence, security, the rule of law and continued support of the commons. Those are the basic social and infrastructural components of everyday life which need to be achieved with social equity as well as including the availability of some political voice.

Froud et al similarly identified what they referred to as the foundational economy, which exists so that 'lives can be lived to their full potential'.[16] It comprises both public and private components, which have been wasted and degraded over the past four decades of outsourcing and privatisation for the gain of rentier shareholders. That waste and degradation includes the hidden neglect of infrastructure such as the maintenance and updating of Victorian sewerage systems and water supply reservoirs and connections. In 2019, a failing reservoir dam in Derbyshire threatened the local township, which had to be vacated while necessary maintenance and repair were completed.[17]

The infrastructure in all its forms, hospitals, schools, public transport, water and sanitation, as well as the commons, clearly needs continuous maintenance and investment. Passing responsibility to MST focused organisations minimises maintenance and investment. Examples of such waste are well documented.[18] Ideologically driven politicians are not motivated to investment in important but unglamorous projects such as, for example in the UK, the upgrading and maintenance of Victorian dams and sewers.

As climate changes, crumbling infrastructures will face different conditions to withstand and will therefore need even more care and attention.

That basic mandatory requirement of a modern state is here nominated as the *social–infrastructural layer* of the real economy. It is not a choice. Its provision and consumption are necessary and cannot be rejected simply on the grounds that the price is too high. The normal conditions of competitive markets simply do not apply, so genuine competition has no ongoing role to play. Much of it is necessarily supplied free of charge at the point of delivery, and where a charge is made, it is as a contribution to the cost of supply, rather than being set at a level which maximises shareholder take.

Moreover, delivery of that social–infrastructural economy remains the responsibility of the state whether or not provision is contracted out. The state needs therefore to retain the skills and competence to coordinate delivery. Privatising and outsourcing social–infrastructural provision to private for-profit organisations, has a predictably sorry history, as cited in the previous chapter. The role of private for-profit organisations in areas where competition is naturally limited or which provide mandatory products or services should be carefully restricted and regulated.

Beyond that base layer of the real economy is a layer which includes a wide variety of non-mandatory provision of products and services, which is best delivered by providers operating in genuinely competitive markets. They work according to the normal rules of supply and demand, where providers seek to offer a better value product or service than their competitors. This is nominated here as the *progressive-competitive layer* of the real economy, which depends for its vitality on being genuinely competitive between suppliers. Systems engaged in this progressive–competitive economy are generally not state owned and need to make a sufficient surplus from their operations in order to survive and to prosper long term. Given freedom from regulation, it is a natural process for the progressive–competitive layer to become increasingly monopolistic, so as to control prices and thus their profitability, as was noted by Adam Smith.

The critical issue in assessing real economy activities in the progressive–competitive economy is the existence and degree of competition which operates. Markets which are genuinely competitive are best served by private sector organisations; public involvement is only needed to protect and preserve competition through the provision of effective regulation.

Beyond that progressive–competitive layer of the real economy is a *technological–revolutionary layer* of activity where the fundamental aim is to develop new technologies, products and services which provide revolutionary gains in efficiency, effectiveness and sustainability so that permanent progression without destruction might be achieved. Privately owned, competitive for-profit operators contribute hugely to this part of the real economy. But so too does the public sector, which has the undoubted strength of being able to take long-term and apparently high risk investment decisions aimed at achieving fundamental change without depending on the requirement to earn a short-term surplus.

Mazzucato pointed out that:

> most radical new technologies in different sectors – from the internet to pharmaceuticals – trace their funding to a courageous risk taking state. ... Despite the perception of the US as the epitome of private sector led wealth creation, in reality it is the State that has been engaged on a massive scale in entrepreneurial risk taking to spur innovation.[19]

NASA, the Atomic Energy Commission, the US government's Defense Advanced Research Project Agency (DARPA), the National Nanotechnology Initiative and the Apple innovations of iPod, iPhone and iPad are all noted as based on state developed technologies.

Even more importantly the state was, and is, behind the development of green technologies such as graphene, green generation and storage of electricity, and providing the financial commitments and long-term support for emerging technologies which private companies have been able to pick up and develop further. Similarly, the UK's NHS develops new procedures and drugs working in collaboration with the university research sector.

Without the state investing in the research at its blue skies start, private for-profit companies would have had much less to develop. That R&D is providing the impetus to achieve democratic commitments to sustainability quicker and more efficiently than could otherwise be done.

The US employs around 2 million people in its public sector working on both the social–infrastructural and technological–revolutionary layers of the real economy. Even today, despite the continued dominance of neoclassical belief, they have massive achievements to their credit, itemised in some detail by Michael Lewis.[20]

Those three layers of the real economy – social–infrastructural, progressive–competitive and technological–revolutionary – each play important and distinctive roles in economic progression. Political-economic decision makers need to base their decisions on real knowledge and understanding of how each layer operates, and how they contribute to the overall economy and the social balance within it. The false neoclassical assumption of the economy as a coherent singularity is hugely damaging.

It is the real economy, all three very different but interconnected layers of it, on which progression without destruction truly depends. Achieving democratic commitments will require increasing coordination between international frameworks such as the United Nations, the IMF, World Bank, and regional organisations such as the EU. They and various international trading agreements all need to be aligned with internationally agreed commitments. Clearly such complexities are beyond the competence of this text, but a systems approach to resolving such global progression suggests coordination rather than fragmentation and hostile competition will be the key to a sustainable future.

A rising rebellion

Neoclassical belief still rules, but there is increasing pressure to reject its orthodoxies in their entirety. From within economics, there has been a closely argued theoretical critique. Chang, Krugman, Mazzucato,

Picketty, Quiggin, Raworth, Shaxson, Stiglitz, and a host of others, are critical of that neoclassical orthodoxy, suggesting such belief is approaching the decline phase of its life cycle. It is clearly not working.

A fundamental aspect of this rebellion is the notion of achieving sufficiency rather than maximising, whether it is profit or shareholder take. Coyle recognised that the economic system was based to a large degree on qualitative factors such as fairness and trust and that when one of those is lost the threat is 'to bring the whole system down like a house of cards'.[21] Rather than a perpetual pursuit of economic growth, a more fruitful aim would be to focus on creating an economic sufficiency with a careful allocation of further surpluses to achieve sustainability in their various contexts.

Trebeck and Williams used the term 'economics of arrival' to signify that society collectively has the means for resolving economic problems.[22] However, as currently organised, the vast majority of the population, national and global, have no share in that resolution. The fruits of arrival seem to be 'rotting', while the continuing demand for more is pursued by those who already have far more than their fair share. However, the pursuit of continuing economic growth, which has been referred to here as in the UN's SDGs and noted by Galbraith, is not a valid economic objective. The distinction is made here between growth and progression, which refers to progress in the democratic commitments to environmental stewardship, universal human rights and equal opportunities with some achievement of social balance. Economic growth is at best irrelevant to those aims, and in practice its pursuit only adds to further inequalities and destructions.

A just and fair system of political-economic progression would aim to understand how all humanity, present and future, might share in the world's finite abundance. That would be the aim of the rising rebellion against neoclassical belief.

Conclusions

The democratic commitments outlined previously are not going to be met while we are ruled by neoclassical belief. It is heading us in the opposite direction, towards global destruction, with unsustainable damages and inequalities as well as an apparently corrupted establishment dominated by organised money.

If those commitments are to be fulfilled across the globe, the advanced economies must take the lead, investing directly in the social–infrastructural economy, renewing genuine competition in the progressive–competitive layer and investing appropriately in the technological–revolutionary economy to achieve the long-term development of technologies and modes of operation. Those lessons can then be followed by less developed nations, which tend to be first affected by both the discontinuities of the climate crisis as well as unsustainable population growth.

While the challenge for the current generation is huge, given sufficient energetic support, continually advancing technology might still provide the chance of a sustainable solution and even global improvement.

The focus of democratic governments needs to be on the long term, ensuring that any damage to sustainability, whether social or ecological, is always more than compensated by the perpetrator or by publicly funded reparation.

While democracy does not focus on the interests of any minority subset of the people it governs, it necessarily takes account of such groups, so that it might defend their interests by insisting on the rule of law and the protection of universal human rights and equal opportunities for all, as well as the more general commitments to sustainability, fairness, justice and freedom.

The solution has to be with the people who, in advanced democracies, vote their representatives into power. But the necessary checks and balances need also to be in place so that the power those are voted into is not absolute. The need is for action to be taken to ensure commitments are fulfilled so that the world is better able than it is now to support succeeding generations.

PART III

How do we get there?

---

250 years into industrialisation, humanity has achieved considerable knowledge and understanding of how people, individual organisations and markets work. We don't need a theory when the reality is there before us. All we need is the simple truth about what works and how.

Nevertheless, economic theories continue to dominate, divorced from observation of reality, neoclassical belief has been used to explain and justify the predatory exploitation of the real-world economy and its people.

The world is hugely different from what it was in Adam Smith's day when he observed the workings of pin manufacture and the productivity gains from collaborative working. The 1000 per cent rise in per capita income in advanced economies has been achieved by massive progression in technology and its application to existing and new forms of productive activity.

But some things don't change so much. The driving force behind all such invention and innovation is, as it always has been, the individual human being. And their greatest outputs are achieved by working in collaboration with others, within some form of organisation which exists to fulfil some clearly defined purpose.

Only if we understand how people and organisations work, can we identify the necessary actions to achieve progression without destruction. The realities of people and work have been observed in minute detail and the understanding gained has been applied and taught with repeated success.

Remaking the real economy is based on that foundation: real people as the engines of progress and real organisations in which they operate and which are themselves continuously innovating new forms of production, product and service.

There is a huge variety of organisational formats referred to here which are all able to contribute to progression without destruction. They include public and private services and producers, for-profit businesses, artisans, SMEs, LLPs, co-operatives, charities, publicly quoted companies and globally dominant corporates plus the new

'Big Tech titans'. That variety clearly involves many distinctions. But they also include many basic commonalities related to what Deming identified as the essential characteristics of an organisational system:

> A system must have an aim. Without an aim there is no system. The aim must be clear to everyone in the system. The aim must include plans for the future.[1]

Those simply stated characteristics are common to the effective functioning of all the organisation formats noted previously, and which from hereon will be referred to as organisational systems.

The following chapters outline how people as engines of enterprise, might drive the various organisational systems which make up the real economy, ensuring they are both productive for themselves and supportive of the macro-systems within which they operate.

5

Real people: engines of enterprise

Introduction

That people are an organisation's most important asset is an obvious truism, despite having the ring of pseudo management speak about it. Both individually and in collaboration with others, people are the creative force, inventers and improvers of organisational systems, and innovators of new products and processes in their various forms. It is real interdependent human beings who are capable of achieving all the changes necessary to achieving progression without destruction.

Major contributions are also anticipated from artificial intelligence and robotisation which might pose massive threats as well as opportunities. The basic assumption here is that, in due course, their regulation will catch up to ensure they will be made ultimately benign to human purpose, and it is human beings that will develop the regulation.

For the present it is the simplistic 19th century assumption of 'greed is good' economic man which poses the threats. It bears no relation to the complex reality. It is sometimes nominated as *homo economicus*, as though to give it the gravitas it so obviously lacks. It is necessarily based on impossible assumptions simply to make the mathematical models work. It clearly ignores inconvenient realities, but more than that, it is a self-fulfilling prophecy of human behaviour.

Real people are, of course, perfectly capable of negative contributions. They are likely to respond to their treatment in an equal and opposite manner. Treated as greedy, they may respond as such, rejecting their interdependence, minimising their contribution, and being actively destructive of organisational achievement. That is how *homo economicus* is expected to behave.

There is a huge empirical literature on human behaviour and motivation, which economic theorising is simply incapable of taking into account. The following sections provide a brief outline of the main critical contributions, the aim being to identify how people might best contribute to getting us to where we want to be. It is based on observation of human behaviour, both individually and collaboratively, in a wide variety of organisational settings.

Hierarchies of human need

Human beings are naturally curious animals, always ready to pursue new and different ways of doing things if the promise is sufficiently inviting and the risks not too threatening. But that preparedness to innovate is exercised within the context of human needs.

Adam Smith commenced *The Theory of Moral Sentiments* with an assessment of those needs. His opening remark was that though man is assumed to be selfish, 'there are evidently some principles in his nature, which interest him in the fortune of others, … pity or compassion, the emotion which we feel for the misery of others'.[1] (If Adam Smith was with us today he would undoubtedly apologise profusely for his gender specifics.) Such a complex notion would be anathema to neoclassical theorists who treated such concepts as irrational and therefore to be disregarded.

Having noted motivations such as generosity and altruism, Smith added further complication by suggesting real people experienced a hierarchy of such intrinsic motivations, the most basic being physiological, to satisfy hunger and thirst as well as keeping warm and safe. He summarised these as being 'to keep out of harm's way'. Smith recognised that human beings, like all living systems, are instinctively driven by the need to survive.

If that is threatened, nothing else matters. But if survival seems assured, motivation moves to higher-level issues, such as 'procuring pleasure and avoiding pain', which also involved 'preserving and increasing what is called his external fortune'. That was in order to supply the 'necessities and conveniences of the body' – the 18th century equivalent of human needs and wants.

Smith also recognised that earning the credit and respect of fellow humans was the top of the hierarchy of human needs. That rank and credit among equals would depend entirely on 'our character and conduct, or upon the confidence, esteem and good-will which these naturally excite in the people we live with'.[2] Microeconomic models are incapable of taking account of such variable and nuanced motivations and variability. However, that is the reality: aiming for survival while also aspiring to higher-level motivations.

At the same time, Smith also noted humanity's essential vulnerability to being seduced by other extrinsic factors, notably money. He referred to people coming together to fix prices for their own benefit against the interests of their customers.[3]

That messy but realistic picture of human needs and motivations has been confirmed by many other studies since. Maslow finessed Smith's hierarchy[4] identifying five categories of human needs: physiological, safety, love, esteem and, at the top level, self-actualisation – the need for personal achievement. Lower level needs became dominant should they cease to be satisfied.

Others offered simpler, apparently more empirically based, approaches, listing many possible motivations. Alderfer identified three levels of motivation. At base were what he referred to as existence needs. If they were satisfied, motivation moved onto satisfying relatedness needs. If those were then satisfied, motivation moved up to satisfying growth needs – the desire to be creative and to achieve one's full potential.[5]

The broad consensus from these various contributions was that there were three relevant groups of intrinsic human needs that motivate behaviour, which can be approximated as:

- survival
- interdependent relatedness
- achievement

The hierarchical idea appears valid. Being hungry or cold can easily become dominant considerations. But as soon as they are satisfied, those needs cease to be potent, and higher-level needs become the motivators of behaviour. Those higher-level motivations drive people to further progression. They might be simply to gain the respect of fellow human beings with whom interdependence is recognised, by the pursuit of some distinctive intrinsic achievement for which the individual might appear peculiarly well fitted.

Such needs and motivations of individual humans appear also applicable to groups of individuals working together within organisational systems. In some advanced economies, whole societies might be near the top of their hierarchy, while in underdeveloped nations, the mass of the population may be struggling to satisfy the most basic physiological needs.

In that wider global context, the wealth and waste of advanced economies has been made known, via modern communications technologies, to those trapped in poverty and continuous hunger. It consequently adds a further dimension to the hierarchy of human needs and their motivational and demotivational effects. Freedoms from 'squalor, ignorance, want, idleness and disease' are clearly essential requirements for global progression up the hierarchy.

Construed as a global imperative, the hierarchy may be far from simple to satisfy. Survival of the human species is interdependent with other biological species as well as the ecological systems of Planet Earth. The five freedoms refer to their availability to all humans. When those freedoms have been achieved, then humans are enabled to aspire to some higher-level achievement and progression, which might drive the world to a sustainable fulfilling future.

Motivation and demotivation

Herzberg's famous motivation-hygiene model was based on a series of interviews with some 200 engineers and accountants to establish factors that had motivated them and also factors that had been demotivating.[6] Five factors stood out as strong motivators: achievement, recognition of achievement, work itself, responsibility and advancement. The demotivators were identified as: company policy and administration, supervision, salary, interpersonal relationships and working conditions. These items were not prime motivators but if they were unsatisfactory, they could be major demotivators.

Gruenfeld and Foltman carried out a survey on attitudes to work among industrial supervisors and produced a list of 18 job characteristics. The five most positive were all related to aspects of achievement.

1 Greater opportunity for advancement.
2 Better opportunity for education and self-development.
3 More opportunity to see the concrete results of one's work.
4 Higher degree of personal responsibility.
5 More opportunity for independent action.

Opportunities for development and advancement were clearly valued more highly than extrinsic motivators such as money.[7] Money is not identified as a motivator in any of these empirical studies, but as a hygiene factor, a potential source of demotivation and discontent, either because of its absolute inadequacy, or it being relatively inadequate compared to the money others are known to be paid.

Frey took that demotivation a stage further, noting the crowding out of intrinsic motivators, such as achievement, by extrinsic factors which tend to become the focus of attention.[8] Frey noted the crowding out effect could also result from 'regulations with their commands, controls and punishments'.

Motivation for those who cannot, or do not, achieve in orthodox ways, such as fulfilling the commitments outlined in Chapter 4, may seek extrinsic achievement, for example, with displays of conspicuous consumptions and waste. Veblen poured scorn and ridicule on those wealthy individuals who made such extrovert demonstrations of their wealth, which for them becomes a culture.[9] For those born into it, money might readily become a real motivation, diverting them from pursuit of any more generally worthwhile objective.

The motivators and demotivators outlined here have been identified as characteristics observed in individuals in many different situations. The understanding may be flexible and imprecise, but it goes some way to explaining how individuals so motivated and demotivated might best work in collaboration with others to achieve some overall system purpose.

The management science of human relations

The idea of scientific management was based on the work of Fred Taylor,[10] who has been as misrepresented in the history of management as has Adam Smith in economics. The application of 'science' (work study and measurement) to the operations of different organisational formats and in particular manufacturing, was intended to bring management and labour together in productive partnership, from which both should gain. That was Taylor's declared aim as a committed Quaker. His intervention came after a century or more of worker exploitation and abuse by mill owners. That had resulted in legalised trade unions which were enabled to fight back against employers.

In that context, Taylor's methods were readily politicised. 'To organised labour, he was the soulless slave driver, out to destroy the workingman's health and rob him of his manhood. To the bosses, he was an eccentric and a radical, raising the wages of common labourers by a third...'[11]

Taylorism, or scientific management, was concerned first and foremost with the efficiency of work within organisations, its focus being on how such organisations could survive, rather than with how to divide the spoils of industry. Taylor himself claimed that resolving the power struggle was the end to which efficiency was the means, not the other way round.

Barnard focused on the polar opposites of management and worker, suggesting that 'human relations are the essence of managerial, employee, public and political relations.'[12] The dehumanising work on the typical industrial shop floor, of necessity working to the diktats of machines which threatened jobs, became the field of study for developing the necessary understanding.

Elton Mayo and colleagues observed work at Western Electric's Hawthorne Works with the aim of identifying links between working conditions and worker productivity. Their observations were at the time surprising. The so-called 'Hawthorne effect' was observed when increases in productivity were achieved following experimental changes in working conditions, no matter what the changes were. Those gains were generally ascribed to the interest and attention being given to the workers by the researchers. The Hawthorne Studies flagged up the importance of social and psychological factors in the working environment and the recognition of informal organisation structures at work.

The experiments suggested that workers were motivated by a 'logic of sentiment' and 'spontaneous co-operation' in the workplace.[13] Money was not the sole measure of interest, with its maximisation being the only operative human motivation. On that point, microeconomics and observed fact had become irretrievably separated.

Mayo concluded that the Hawthorne programme had highlighted 'the fundamentals of large scale industry' as management's responsibility for 'developing and sustaining cooperation' among the workforce.[14] The Hawthorne Studies opened up a new area for research with the possibility of new understanding of how work in industrial settings should best be coordinated, so that all the individuals would work as collaborating organisational members working for the organisation to fulfil its basic purpose.

Two opposing sets of assumptions about human motivation and behaviour were referred to by McGregor as Theories X and Y, both of which were patently self-fulfilling. Theory X, which McGregor subtitled as the 'traditional view of direction and control', assumed the 'average human being has an inherent dislike of work and will avoid it if they can'. Therefore, 'most people must be coerced, controlled, directed, threatened with punishment to get them to put forth adequate effort toward the achievement of organisational objectives'. 'The average human being prefers to be directed, wishes to avoid responsibility, has relatively little ambition, wants security above all.'[15]

The alternative Theory Y, which McGregor subtitled the 'integration of individual and organisational goals', included the following:

> The expenditure of physical and mental effort in work is as natural as play or rest ... The average human being learns, under proper conditions, not only to accept but to seek responsibility. The capacity to exercise imagination, ingenuity, and creativity in the solution of organisational problems is widely, not narrowly, distributed in the population. Under the conditions of modern industrial life,

the intellectual potentialities of the average human being are only partially utilised.

Theory Y appears wholly consistent with the approaches to human motivation based on empirical studies of people at work previously noted.

Thus, there was a straightforward dichotomy of approaches to the understanding of human behaviour, motivation and relations. One was based on serious study of human individuals and their activity in a wide variety of settings, which is the foundation of the organisational systems approach. The other is a simplistic application of the witchcraft and institutional truths of neoclassical belief. One is approximately right; the other is profoundly wrong. However, for the time being, it is the latter which still rules.

The leadership question

Ideology, as opposed to simple truth, has produced a system of governance which makes management subservient to a single interested party: the shareholder. Ghoshal argued that that approach 'had some very significant and negative influences on the practice of management ... by propagating ideologically inspired amoral theories, business schools have actively freed their students from any sense of moral responsibility'.[16]

So management itself was turned into a monstrous caricature of leadership, which Ghoshal described as ruthless, hard-driving and shareholder-value obsessed.[17]

Leadership is a fashionable term among would-be leaders who often treat it as a matter of charisma. Drucker rejected that idea. 'What matters is not the leader's charisma. What matters is the leader's mission.' In the UK Clement Atlee has often been referred to as a most effective political leader but was absolutely lacking in charisma. Drucker referred similarly to Dwight Eisenhower, George Marshall and Harry Truman having no more charisma than 'a dead mackerel'.[18]

Ghoshal's 'business leader' might seem well suited to heading up today's financialised businesses. But they would be entirely counter-productive coordinating a real organisation operated by real people. By focusing too much on control and financial end goals, and not enough on their people, such leaders make it more difficult to achieve their own intended outcomes.[19]

The alternative idea of cooperation, rather than the top-down direction, has always worked. It is in our genes, as with most species.[20]

Humanity's success as a hunter-gatherer depended on the cooperation within groups, with members dividing their labour for the benefit of the group as a whole. The success of cooperation depended on two human characteristics: the capability to make rational calculations; and an instinct for reciprocity, to repay kindness with kindness and to punish deception.[21]

W.L. Gore and Associates, maker of Gore-Tex fabric plus advanced technology products for electronics, fabrics, industrial and medical markets, further elaborated the point about cooperation. It is a private company co-owned by the Gore family and employees/associates, employing more than 8,500 people in nearly 50 facilities worldwide. Gore has been repeatedly ranked as one of the world's most innovative companies as well as one of the best to work for in the US, with its overseas units earning similar recognition in Germany, France and Italy, while its British plants have repeatedly headed the *Sunday Times* 'Best Companies to Work For'.

> There are no titles or conventional lines of command at Gore, where the only way of becoming a leader is to attract followers – if a project can't attract people to work on it, then it doesn't get done.[22]

The effective coordination of organisational systems ensures the organisation fulfils its fundamental purpose. To do that requires all people understand that purpose and their role in its fulfilment. It also requires the necessary training and personal development for all people, so they can play their full part in the organisation's processes and progression.

The money problem

Chief executives of FTSE100 companies now commonly exceed 300 times the average hourly paid wage, thus earning what Drucker described as the 'hatred, contempt and even fury' of fellow employees.[23] The majority of such businesses are in effect financialised and focused on extraction of value rather than its creation. As such, the leaders of those organisations are less concerned with the performance and motivation of individuals within their organisation. Their perspective is what Seddon referred to as 'command and control' management, which almost invariably has a negative impact on organisational performance and development.[24] Moreover, employees recognise they are colluding in that extraction process for the benefit of stockholders, which in most cases of financialised organisations, include senior executive managers.

Non-financialised organisations remain focused on achieving the organisational system purpose rather than simply MST. They are nevertheless affected by the problem of money and the extent of inequality in its distribution within organisations. Their purpose might be the continuous improvement of the satisfaction of some customer need or want by developing technologies, products and/or processes, but members of such real organisations are still demotivated by such inequality. Drucker's warning remains potent.

Rewarding one human being with more than 20 times the average wage, let alone 300 times or more, when they are all serving the same organisational purpose causes extremes of dissatisfaction, not just among those on the shop floor. It also becomes a dominant factor in the lives of those so rewarded.

Over the past four decades, inequality within organisations has been further accentuated by the ability of the top paid to take professional guidance on how to avoid where possible the payment of taxes or even to evade them altogether.[25]

Across much of today's corporate world, money has become an extreme demotivator, with those regarded as overpaid – top management – the focus of real 'hatred' and 'contempt'. That is a hugely negative effect within organisational systems that depend for their effectiveness on the collaboration of all their people.

But the money problem is even more pervasive than that. The same year that Friedman asserted the social responsibility of corporate officials as being to make as much money as possible for stockholders, Wilfred Brown published *Piecework Abandoned*. It was one of a series of publications in the Glacier Project focused on observing and understanding how organisational systems worked and how their people were affected by different approaches to management. Payment by results schemes such as piecework (wages paid per piece produced and by clocking on and off from the workplace) were commonly held to be the means of control and motivation of shop floor workers. Brown's experience led him to believe the opposite.

He concluded his text with the following:

> When our Company started to move away from wage incentive schemes, the large majority of those people whom I met in other companies shook their heads and said: 'From an idealistic point of view, this idea is good, but you will

be in trouble; you will lose output and you can't expect your customers to pay for your idealism.' 'Men work for money and work harder for more money'; said one of my friends. ... Well, those forebodings were not borne out. ...

My plea is that we should reject cynicism about people as the basis of organization, but, equally, we must reject idealism. In fact we must reject generalizations which are not well founded on objective observation. ... growth in civilization has been growth in the capacity of the individual to co-operate with others in society in pursuit of objectives of common interest. Our great institutions are all founded on assumptions about the potential sense of responsibility of the individual towards others. We are at fault in industry because we so often build our social institutions on the opposite assumption. ...

If we construct our social institutions on the assumption that people are incapable of responsible behavior, then we shall get irresponsibility. It is ridiculous then to cite such irresponsibility as evidence in support of our own cynicism.

Wage incentive schemes, in my experience, stimulate envy and greed, whereas equilibrium between personal capacity, level of work, and pay, stimulates cooperative behavior. ...

On the basis of greater acquaintanceship with reality, we can advance to more satisfying living conditions.[26]

The lessons of the Glacier Project apply far wider than the factory shop floor. Within the NHS, for example, hospital cleaners are a classic example. They are not required to have sophisticated skill levels, but the work they do is absolutely vital to the work of the hospital and it is essential that they fulfil their role carefully and thoroughly. Otherwise the hospital could become a centre of infection. Their pay level is inevitably at the lower end of the range, which in the knowledge of what other workers may be getting could be a significant demotivator. But, being made fully aware of the importance of their role in fulfilling the local system purpose, and being treated with the respect due to all human beings working in organisational systems, most individuals would work to fulfil their responsibility towards others. Treated with lack of respect they may well behave otherwise.

Piecework Abandoned has long been forgotten, though its message relates to all human beings, not just shop floor workers. Top executives are even less likely to be motivated to additional efforts and work than are their low pay workers by any payment by results schemes. Such bonus schemes have no incentive effect on the work done. They are paid by top executives to themselves simply because they can and are justified by the microeconomic models that require the commitment to 'greed is good'[27] and value a person simply according to their price.

Conclusions

These brief notes have focused on how people are observed to behave at work, capable of heroic achievement, though at the same time vulnerable to their better endeavours being crowded out by money. The work settings in which most of the observation took place, such as shop floor manufacturing, are subject to continuous change and development, and are hugely varied now including the Big Tech titans, as well as the Ubers of the gig economy which are, to a considerable extent, self-managed systems.

However, humanity itself is not so subject to rapid behavioural evolution and change. Much of what Adam Smith observed has been repeatedly validated by empirical research two centuries later. Our innate nature and motivations have been extensively researched and seem fairly well understood. Lessons have been learned regarding our motivation and demotivation, and also about the nature of human relations in work situations. We remain full of potential and vulnerability.

The real economy depends on the common sense application of that understanding to encourage the collaborative working of individuals – all individuals not just shop floor workers – within productive organisational systems. Those organisations have continued to innovate and develop technologies, processes, products and services, with ever increasing potential for achieving more than a sustainable global future, but potentially one of global improvement.

To disregard that knowledge and understanding, and to rely instead on falsified mathematical theorising, would appear to be a form of insanity. Or, it might be a corrupted collusion between vested interests to abuse the system for illicit gains. Either way, it is clear that the real human motivations are being misconstrued. For most people, the means of satisfying those motivations could be provided by working within, and contributing to, one or more of the various organisational systems, as outlined in the following chapter.

6

Organisational systems and their coordination

Introduction

Adam Smith's observation of the pin factory was an early description of an organisational system at work. It comprised a number of individuals working in collaboration with each other to fulfil the system purpose – in that case the production of pins. The individuals all carried out different parts of the production process and developed their particular skill and expertise, learning how best to use, and to invent or develop, specialised tools needed to carry out their part of production with continually improving efficiency. The result from such collaborative effort was, Smith estimated, around a 240 times increase in productivity per head, over and above what one individual could produce alone.

Despite the obvious and radical changes in technology since those days, that broad analysis remains valid. Individuals still need to collaborate with each other, rather than compete, in order to fulfil their system's purpose. As Deming pointed out,[1] collaboration rather than adversarial competition is a fundamental of everyday life everywhere, most examples of which are so natural they are not recognised as cooperation. We all accept hours of the day based on Greenwich Mean Time. Similarly, calendar dates and the international dateline are accepted across the globe. Red and green traffic signals are understood as meaning the same everywhere. As is the metric system of measurement. The list of such agreements is endless and by such cooperation, everybody wins.

Collaboration of internal system components requires their effective coordination. That requires understanding of human behaviour, motivation and demotivation, as already outlined. Such considerations are far beyond the capability of neoclassical mathematical modelling. But even if it were not so, a theory of the firm is completely superfluous, when the reality is there to be observed and understood.

Though organisational systems fall into many different categories, neoclassical belief makes the simplistic division between state owned and controlled organisations and privately owned for-profit businesses.

The former are assumed to be inefficient and bureaucratic, while the latter are assumed efficient and innovative. That is the neoclassical orthodoxy based on theoretical models which take no account of reality.

State owned enterprises can, of course, be inefficient and bureaucratic but they can also be hugely effective and innovative in ways that lie beyond privately owned businesses. Moreover, for-profit business can also be inefficient and bureaucratic, and are far from a singularity, with many different classifications falling under that label.

The critical division made here is between real and financialised organisational systems, acknowledging that both categories are complex and comprise huge variety. Real organisational systems are engaged in producing and delivering some form of product or service, based on the long-term application and development of resources (such as people, technology, facilities and money) to satisfy and improve the satisfaction of customer needs and wants and in so doing provide employment and resources to various stakeholders as well as developing the organisation further. Those real organisational systems are responsible for the continuous improvement of their various processes and the ultimate product or service they deliver. They are what Faroohar identified as the 'makers'.[2]

The financial sector includes some organisations which still serve real economy organisations by raising the funds needed for investment in real economy projects. But the sector is predominantly driven by MST, as defined by Friedman – Faroohar's 'takers'. The issue of shares and bonds for real economy organisations is a small part of the financial sector's activities, and is still largely focused on MST.[3]

That distinction between real and financialised, the makers and takers, though fundamental to economic progression, is ignored by neoclassical economics. Their progression is measured in terms for inclusion in GDP calculation, which makes no distinction between the real and financialised.

Systems analysis provides an alternative perspective, rooted in the observation of practical realities, as was Smith's observation of pin manufacture. Understanding the purpose of organisational systems is fundamental to their effectiveness as was demonstrated by quality specialists Deming, Juran and others, to the resurrection of Japanese manufacturing after WW2. It was instrumental in Japan's subsequent economic progression.

The systems approach has been repeatedly insightful as outlined in the following sections.

Organisational system characteristics and processes

Deming's definition of the organisational system was 'a network of interdependent components that work together to try to accomplish the aim of the system'.[4] The system must have an aim, which should be known and understood by everyone operating within the system, and it must also include plans for the future, recognising its role in the progression of the macro-systems within which it operates.

Deming's approach to quality control and management is one dimension of the systems approach to organisation that has a profound effect on the operational effectiveness of organisational systems.

Deming suggested that

> the job of management is inseparable from the welfare of the company ... Management must understand the design of product and of service, procurement of materials, problems of production, process control, and barriers on the job that rob the hourly worker of ... the right to pride of workmanship. ... Unfriendly takeover and leveraged buyout are a cancer on the American system. Fear of takeover, along with emphasis on the quarterly dividend defeats constancy of purpose.[5]

Taking full account of the behavioural nature of people working as system components, as outlined in the previous chapter, is another dimension.

Organisational systems operate, as do all live systems, by interacting with their environments. They intake from their environment and output into their environment, typically benefitting from a feedback loop with some automatic measuring and correction mechanism that enables the system to maintain a steady state. The human body replicates those system characteristics on many different planes. For example, we get hungry, we eat, our hunger is satisfied, we stop eating. We get hot, we perspire, the evaporation cools us down.

In social systems, inputs, processing and outputs are measured, analyzed and regulated, so as to maintain system operation and, if possible, improve it. The inputs to productive units, whether it is a factory, a hospital or even a web-based virtual provider, include some raw materials, physical work, knowledge and expertise relating to the individual processes, plus whatever fixed capital, such as software, hardware, buildings, plant and equipment, is required. There will also be ongoing need for funding of working capital and consumable items. The processes for a commercial unit will typically include purchasing, production, marketing, selling, research and development, innovation and training, plus the essential support services for those functions.

For mandatory basic provisions there is limited need for marketing and selling, but otherwise, approximate equivalent needs are apparent. Outputs include finished products and services, new knowledge and technologies, and newly trained and skilled employees, plus sufficient monetary surpluses to survive and develop long term. In the case of a public provider such as a hospital, the finished products are cured and healthy individuals, plus gains in knowledge and understanding which would be accrued just as with commercial systems.

Clearly, there are many forms of productive organisational systems beyond factories and hospitals, with broadly comparable characteristics and processes to which systems analysis is applicable.

Systems life cycles

As well as those resources and processes, systems also have to take account of the time dimension, an essential to systems understanding. Systems such as a biological cell or a human being, or social systems such as an organisational system or an industry, evolve over time progressing through different phases of a life cycle. Koehler illustrated that live open system life cycle by reference to a lighted candle, which usefully highlights many of the overall system properties and characteristics which change critically at the different stages of evolution.[6]

The prime essential system characteristic is the purpose which the system fulfils. In the case of the candle, it exists to provide light. Most systems are, of course, more complex than that, aiming to contribute to the fulfilment of some specific existential purpose, while also ensuring compatibility with the purposes of the larger systems within which they operate. Whatever it is, a system's purpose is fundamental to its existence and key to understanding the necessary working of system components and processes.

The basic purpose of organisational systems is to provide a product or service which satisfies a consumer need or want. Drucker summarised that for the private for-profit business as 'to create a customer'. That definition could be applied more widely, recognising the importance of identifying unsatisfied consumer needs or ways of their delivery, and devising sustainable means of their satisfaction.

At first when a light is put to its wick, Koehler's candle may spit and sputter and possibly go out several times before the wick achieves the temperature for ignition and is successfully lighted. This birth, introduction or infancy stage is characterised in many systems by such volatility and high rates of infant mortality, whether we are considering candles, human beings, business start-ups or new products.[7] In the case of start-ups, around half of them cease to exist within the first five years of operation.[8]

If the candle successfully lights, then the flame quickly burns up to its full size. This adolescent or growth stage is again typical of many systems in the speed and continuity of its growth up to a certain ceiling level which marks the start of its mature phase. The current generation of Big Tech titans – Facebook, Google, Uber, Amazon and so on – may be currently coming towards the end of that growth phase, with some even approaching decline of their original activity. It is a process of rapid learning and development. Again, this applies generally to social systems and in the case of organisations signals rapid rates of invention and innovation.

The speed of growth for businesses was traditionally determined by the ability to raise the necessary finance required to build new production facilities and pay for the necessary additional people and working capital, all of which consume cash as sales volume rises. Those constraints are less operative in the case of the high tech titans, which are enabled for rapid achievement of maturity with less need for continually increasing capital investment.

As the candle flame reaches its mature steady state, it again exhibits a common characteristic of volatility before settling down. The candle's volatility is manifested in a short period of flickering. Adolescent human beings exhibit similar volatility as parents might confirm as common experience. As businesses and products move from growth to maturity, they also experience a period of volatility as they adjust to the new low growth situation.[9] Some organisations will have committed funds to continued growth. If that growth is not realised, there will need to be some revision to strategic plans. Some organisations may find they are no longer able to generate sufficient surplus to justify continuing and either pull out from the process or liquidate altogether. The high tech titans have experienced the growth phase but not yet had to face maturity, though Apple appears currently to be doing just that, with its revised 2019 'strategic plan' based less on technological innovation and more on the application of its prodigious financial resources.[10]

In its mature phase steady state, the candle exhibits the general systems characteristic of maximum strength and efficiency. In the case of the candle this is the phase when it burns the maximum wax and gives off the greatest light. It will maintain this maximum energy conversion steady state as determined by its inputs of wick, wax and oxygen, and its system characteristics of size and composition of wick, diameter and length of candle, and availability of oxygen.

Human beings exhibit similar characteristics, in their maturity being at their strongest and physically and mentally most efficient stage. Real organisations are also at their most efficient stage. They also no longer require the continuing financial inputs to support continued rapid growth. So mature businesses are therefore naturally generating their maximum cash surpluses in the mature phase. The question of how to allocate those surpluses presents some challenging questions, which neoclassical belief avoids by focusing on MST.

As noted in Chapter 2, this is the phase when businesses come under extreme pressure to financialise. The existing strategy no longer enables continued growth, but the standing of the business and its management assumes continued performance increases. Moreover, such businesses will most likely have accrued a substantial cash surplus. Financialising of real business to become a predatory M&A wheeler-dealer is a natural system process, facilitated by lack of regulatory restraint which was formerly made operative with the intention of protecting market competition.

The candle's mature steady state will only end when one of the determining factors changes. For example, the wax is used up to the extent that there is no longer a full quantity available for burning. Or if the candle was lit in an enclosed space and the resource of oxygen was used up. At this stage the system goes into decline, but again the change from the mature phase to decline is marked by further volatility as the candle flickers and putters and frequently goes out prematurely before it has used up all its wax.

Real businesses that have resisted the pressures to financialise typically come under similar pressures when their main products and markets move to the decline phase. During maturity and the accrual of surplus resources, real businesses will have developed an appropriate strategy for addressing the decline issue. The phase change period is marked by volatility, as remaining businesses exit and close, belatedly financialise or are taken over by other businesses and are frequently stripped of their assets.

One of the intriguing aspects of this general systems life cycle model is the apparent breadth of its applicability. All manner of systems appear to share those general characteristics and are subject to parallel pressures and influences at the different stages and phase change periods of volatility. Social systems such as public organisations as well as businesses, whole industries and communities (Easter Islanders, nation states, empires and even Earth itself) may follow that evolutionary cycle illustrated by Koehler's candle.

They also exhibit similar characteristics at each life cycle phase, with industries, for example, being highly inventive and innovative during the rapid growth phase, multiplying the change effect contributing to industrial revolutions as outlined later.

Coordination of system components

Systems coordination may be the natural result of an evolutionary process, as in the case of biological cells fulfilling their role in greater systems such as the human anatomy. Such natural processes appear to exist as tendencies for all systems, but with social systems, coordination also involves a carefully deliberate role which, to be effective, requires detailed understanding of the system's purpose, components, products, processes and life cycle progression.

System coordination involves three separate responsibilities. First, the internal coordination of system components needs to ensure their effective collaboration towards achieving the overall system purpose. Smith's pin factory was a crude example but illustrates the point of collaboration as opposed to competition. Setting up system components to compete with each other in order to increase efficiency as prompted by neoclassical belief, has invariably proved dysfunctional.[11]

Second, external coordination is needed to ensure the system is compatible with, and supportive of, the external systems in which it is embedded. These critically include the social and ecological systems with which organisational systems interact. Being supportive of those systems is here ensured by positive contribution to the democratically expressed commitments including environmental stewardship.

Internal and external coordination is also responsible for interactions with the various organisational stakeholders, internal being employees, and external including customers, suppliers, shareholders and local and wider communities.

The third responsibility of system coordination is to ensure that internal and external coordinations are compatible and mutually supportive. This can be a highly challenging responsibility made more so by the likely conflict between short-term considerations such as making a sufficient surplus to ensure survival and long-term consideration for macro system sustainability.

Internal coordination, otherwise labelled management, is responsible for achieving system aims as they evolve over the life cycle, from start-up to maturity and decline. That involves, first of all, responsibility for the survival of the organisation in the short term and its longer-term development and progression.

What really matters is what goes on inside organisational systems, as demonstrated by Smith beginning his inquiry into the wealth of nations with observations on pin manufacture and the productivity gains available from appropriately coordinated activities. First, the purpose of the system must be clearly defined and understood, based on knowledge and understanding of the technologies and consumers involved. That understanding must be shared with all organisation members contributing to the fulfilment of that defined purpose, including understanding their individual and group roles in that fulfilment. Second, the definition of system purpose must include knowledge and understanding of change and the pace of change relevant to purpose fulfilment, including the system's contributions, positive and negative, to the climate crisis and environmental stewardship. System coordination also includes responsibility for the development of system resources including the training and development of its people.

Coordination responsibility clearly requires a basic understanding of the technology and processes of the organisation and how they interact with the social and ecological systems with which the organisation interacts. It also requires competence in financial control. The aim is to both fulfil its own purpose and be compatible and supportive of those greater systems.

Coordination is responsible for the long-term efficiency and effectiveness of system operations. That involves coordinating, operating and developing all the resources that the organisation uses to achieve its purpose. Those resources include people, fixed assets and the knowledge and expertise which creates, and is created by, research and development, innovation, and the application of money, which has the great virtue of flexibility as to its application and storage.

The fundamental motivations of the real people, who are the organisational system components, may not naturally coincide with those of the organisational system within which they operate. Nevertheless, they are unlikely to be the greed-driven robots assumed by neoclassical economics. People are not motivated, but can easily be demotivated, by payment systems as outlined in the previous chapter. That knowledge and understanding is essential to the effective coordination of organisational systems.

Coordination also involves responsibility for the continuous improvement and development of system operations, the innovation of new processes, products and services, the ever increasing understanding of consumer/customer needs and wants, and the development of new and better ways of delivery, all being supportive of the relevant macro-systems.

The effectiveness of coordination of all such activities makes the difference between a successful organisation and one which falls short of its potential and might even fail to survive. Most of these coordination responsibilities are only deliverable by people, so it is their coordination and development which matter above all else.

Organisational system ownership and control

As it is external to the system, ownership has no automatic impact on the system's internal operation. It does not directly affect the collaboration of system components, their achievement of system purpose, nor the system's compatibility with the macro-systems in which they operate. However, as outlined in Chapter 3, organised money guided by neoclassical belief has achieved dominant ownership over many real economy organisations.

For organisations operating in the public sector, this dominance is evidenced by direct political involvement in organisational purpose and their funding. State owned systems are vulnerable, even though they may be controlled by specialist sub-units, organised either nationally or through more localised authorities. The checks and balances originally built into such public sector operations are themselves subject to political interference.

Politicians, though most probably lacking the knowledge and understanding to contribute positively to system operation, nevertheless exert temporary power over system operations and might well be motivated to activate ideologically based initiatives.

The operation of such publicly owned and controlled organisational systems is therefore subject to variation according to the political decisions of voters. An unfortunate inevitability from such democratic control is that when the political orientation changes much waste is incurred reversing initiatives implemented under the previous regime. That compromise of public system operation according to the political dictates of the day works against establishing a consistent effective form of operation.

Several examples have been quoted in this text, including the politically driven focus on metrics which are ideologically convenient and easy to manipulate. The outsourcing and privatisation of public provisions, along with claimed responsibility for their operation, are further evidence of that political dominance over public sector ownership. Outsourcing and privatisations have had destructive effects as has been widely reported regarding the 'big four' outsourcing contractors and many others.[12]

If organisational systems in the public sector are to be coordinated effectively, they need protection against such ineffective external interference. Effective checks and balances need to be in place to ensure publicly owned organisational systems pursue the long-term sustainable democratic commitments and are not at the mercy of political domination with a short-term time horizon.

The potentially adverse influence of ownership on organisational systems can be even more damaging in the private sector. That ownership dominance is mostly focused on enforcing MST, with little regard for other issues.

However, company ownership is by no means a straightforward legal concept. Company formation specifically separates ownership from the corporate legal entity, by establishing ownership through the issue of shares, which process confirms the company as a separate legal entity and enables the grant of limited liability to share owners.

Share ownership rights and responsibilities are restricted as outlined in the opening chapter. Shareholders owe no debt to the company, fiduciary or otherwise, and have no responsibility for the survival and future success of the company and do not own the company as an item of private property. However, majority shareholding may become a credible threat by shareholders with around 25 per cent or more of the equity.

That compromised position has been further exacerbated by the general acceptance of the primacy of stockholder interests which empowers financialised corporates to become predatory on the real economy.[13] Internal operation of private sector organisations is commonly dictated by the commitment to MST. If the shareholders would gain more from the stripping of the company's assets and the closure of its operations, despite a continuing viability of its production, then, according to neoclassical belief, it is the duty of the relevant decision makers to asset strip and close, passing the resulting funds to shareholders. Moreover, according to the neoclassical belief it is perfectly legitimate for company directors to receive substantial bonus rewards for acting in such fashion.

The progression of financialised systems is largely dependent on exploiting ownership controls, such as through hostile M&A deals, which may damage and destroy the operation of the acquired real economy organisation. Such deals also reduce effective competition, increasing monopolistic power which operates only to achieve MST.

Protection from such ownership abuse is consequently a fundamental consideration for those with legal responsibility for real organisational systems.

Real competition and its protection

Competition is fundamental to the viability of organisational systems, whether in public or private ownership. It is a concept which the neoclassical belief simplifies down to free markets – markets free from state regulation. As already noted, the natural process of such free markets is to progress from being competitive in the early growth stages of evolution, to naturally becoming ever less competitive as markets mature with the natural unregulated result being monopoly or some form of cartel, as noted by Adam Smith.[14]

Competition is not a singularity, and its outcomes can be both positive and negative. If construed as the inevitable result of lack of government interference in the form of regulation, it can be dysfunctional, allowing some organisations to become dominant and, in pursuit of MST to be destructive by M&A and associated asset stripping. Deming gives many examples of what he refers to as adversarial competition and its negative impacts, compared to the results achieved from collaboration.[15]

That same ideological belief in freedom from regulation can also become dysfunctional if allowed or encouraged between individuals. It leads inevitably to the 1 per cent of the population who are led to believe they must be worth what they receive always seeking to achieve more, inevitably at the expense of the 99 per cent.[16] That dichotomy between individuals was summarised nicely in McGregor's Theories X and Y.[17]

The neoclassical claimed belief in competition reveals a convenient lack of understanding of what competition really is. All across the globe, there are towns and villages at the centre of which are so-called marketplaces, where in preindustrial days local agricultural/horticultural producers would bring their product for sale to the local population. In that highly localised situation, the producer and their customer would live in fairly close proximity to each other and might be in fairly regular contact. Any attempt by the producer to exploit the customer would be quickly recognised and punished accordingly, with potentially devastating effect.

The generally accepted market price of any produce would emerge naturally from the process of barter and competition. For a producer to achieve a premium price would require the product to be better or different in some way that was not available from neighbouring producers. That was how competition worked. The key to its validity was that there were many producers and the product or service on offer could be differentiated in some way from competing products or services, either in the product or service itself, or its mode of delivery and/or price.

Such competitive markets prevented exploitation by any single producer that might seek market dominance. As such, competitive markets still work for the benefit of the customer and the common good by ensuring that producers operate efficiently if they are to survive. It is therefore a vital contextual condition to which relevant organisational system coordination has to respond.

In their rapid growth phase of development, competitive markets motivate all sorts of innovations and improvements to differentiate a product from those available from other sources, making them faster, more intelligent, longer lasting, and lower cost. In so doing, new products, technologies, processes and ways of doing things are generated, which all ultimately benefit the customer and the common good.

Competition is thus a driving force behind efficiency and effectiveness of organisational systems. But it is a fragile commodity which requires protection.

Adam Smith explained the cartel problem: 'People of the same trade seldom meet together ... but the conversation ends in a conspiracy against the public, or in some contrivance to raise prices.'[18] It took a century before the law rescued the situation. Legislation was enacted in the US with the 1890 Sherman anti-trust law and its successors, which resulted in the breakup of some of the cartels and supposed monopolies such as Standard Oil.

Competition in the UK prior to the 1986 computerisation of capital markets was protected by the M&MC and the OFT, which could prevent and even reverse M&As which resulted in market shares being established of 25 per cent or more. Over the past 40 years, guided by neoclassical belief in free markets and deregulation, those protective regulatory bodies have been progressively reduced and discontinued.

Today, only the most extreme cases of anti-competitive M&As most obviously threatening the public interest are likely to be referred to the weakened regulatory bodies for consideration.

Thus, real competition has been progressively destroyed by cartelised and monopolistic tendencies, enabled by freedom from regulatory constraint. Hence: the big three or four dominating most mature industries for the predatory benefit of their shareholders.

The fragility of competition is rarely acknowledged – freedom from government interference being the primary concern for von Mises and

Mont Pelerin colleagues. However, if competition is compromised, the whole system collapses into one of monopolistic abuse, which is what has been not just allowed to happen but has been encouraged by neoclassical ideology.

Pretend competition and its failure

Guided by simplistic belief in markets free from government controls, and with apparently limited understanding of how such systems and markets actually work, successive UK governments have sought first of all to privatise and outsource state owned provision. Failing that, they have sought to introduce competition into the operation of their ongoing direct responsibilities for which collaboration, rather than competition, was the real key to productive operation. Such initiatives have been repeated many times and have invariably failed to achieve the intended result.

Experience with UK NHS hospitals is a typical example. Most politicians are likely to be more or less innocent of any real understanding as to how the NHS works. Instead they rely on ideology for guidance and that tells them that the NHS, being publicly owned, is inefficient and wasteful. A typical first intervention is to start trying to make such operations focus on some pseudo-competitive 'metric'.

Deming makes the point that measurement does not of itself improve performance.[19] Accident statistics do not reduce accidents. However, their measurement analysis and reporting does incur cost. So, of itself, measurement actually reduces performance. Typically, political intervention will establish certain statistics as key performance indicators and set target levels to be achieved. That is done as a proxy for real competition. The chosen metric tends to be one which is fairly simple to measure and adjust. Outcomes are then measured against those targets and reported on a continuing basis with results fed into published league tables of performance, which are presented as the competitive element. That 'unnecessary paperwork' substantially increases the administrative costs of running a hospital.[20]

The focus on selected NHS targets also has the effect of reducing attention on non-targeted areas of equally important work, thereby reducing their contribution to overall system performance.

It also tempts system components to game performance indicators by various dysfunctional means. For example, the calculation of patient waiting times starts when the patient enters hospital. Consequently, when waiting time targets risk not being met, patients have been queued up in ambulances outside hospital Accident & Emergency

Departments and will not be counted till they enter Accident and Emergency. During that delay, the ambulances thus queued up are not available to fulfil their intended role and purpose. Components within the hospital system are thus encouraged to compete with other components, rather than collaborate.

Moreover, the performance indicator makes no distinction between a patient queueing up with a sprained ankle and one with a more urgent need such as sepsis, a heart attack or stroke. They all affect the waiting times metric performance equally, though the urgency and seriousness of their needs may be completely different, and overall system performance would be more effectively met by giving priority to the urgent cases and accepting excess waiting times for the non-urgent.

The increase in costs without commensurate increases in budgets leads to cuts in essential NHS staffing, which may then need to be temporarily compensated by emergency hiring of agency staff at many times the cost of permanent staff, but with less familiarity and expertise in the particular specialised tasks involved.

Application of such performance measures and reporting directly interfere with the collaboration between the different components of the hospital's organisational systems on which real overall performance depends.

Collaboration within such systems in order to achieve the system purpose avoids those ideologically imposed on-costs, wastes and damages to the overall hospital purpose. Real competition is irrelevant to such situations. Political interference to impose pseudo-competitive measures of performance has done substantial damage to such non-competitive provision.[21]

That NHS example is just one of a huge number which have been implemented these past four decades. It has been noted at some length to illustrate the ill effects of such application of simplistic ideology rather than basing decisions on real knowledge and understanding of the systems involved.

Conclusions

The success or failure of organisational systems depends on the effective internal working of their human components and their collaboration to fulfil their existential system purpose. Organisation ownership, whether public or private, is external to system operation and has no automatic impact on the internal system operation. The orthodox neoclassical assumption that state ownership is by definition bureaucratic and inefficient while private for-profit organisations are necessarily efficient and effective simply lacks truth.

A real and more important distinction is between organisations that serve the real economy and those that serve the financialised economy. Real economy requires compatibility with – and support for – the macro-systems within which they work, including both ecological and social systems, in order to achieve full sustainability. The financialised economy ignores such considerations, focusing simply on the extraction of value from the real economy, setting aside all considerations other than MST and its growth.

However, a controlling ownership, whether public or private, can deliberately manipulate system purpose and the means of its achievement. That is what happens when an organisational system becomes financialised, or when representatives of its state owners enforce politically motivated interventions such as the imposition of false competitive metrics. The example quoted of the UK NHS indicates the potential for profound damage which can be done by ill-informed interventions. Protections against such controlling ownership have been available by various means such as two-tier boards, interlocking shareholdings, and various forms of co-operative organisation. Similar protections of public organisations are also needed against short-term political interventions.

Real organisational systems focus on continually improving their achievement of existential purpose, whether it is a direct contribution to the fulfilment of social and ecological sustainability, or the satisfaction of customer needs and wants in ways which are compatible with sustainability, as outlined in the following chapter.

7

Organisational systems interactions with the real economy

Introduction

The previous two chapters outlined how we get to where we want to be. They considered the internal components of organisational systems, the real people who are the engines of enterprise, and their coordination through life cycle progressions, noting the vital importance of protecting real competition in supposedly competitive markets and rejecting pretend competition in markets where real competition is not relevant or available.

This chapter now focuses on external interactions of organisational systems as they serve the different layers of the real economy, fulfilling their defined existential purposes and contributing to the fulfilment of the democratic commitments outlined in Chapter 4.

Constituents of organised money could also serve the real economy. They have the power and capability to make massive contributions, perhaps even decisive ones, to fulfilling sustainable democratic commitments. But, for the time being at least, they remain focused on MST, claiming neoclassical belief to cloak their actions with assumed academic respectability.

In that pursuit, constituents of organised money are limited only by the question of legality, which is sufficiently opaque as to permit much tax evasion and energetic tax avoidance as well as financial frauds, criminality and destructions already noted. Though fines are paid for such illegalities when identified, individuals are not generally held personally responsible, despite their contractual duties. Consequently, the financialised economy, driven by organised money, remains focused on destructive pursuits, rather than the fulfilment of the democratic commitments outlined in Chapter 4.

Galbraith flagged up the interdependence of public and private enterprise as key to real economic progression. That social balance is even more important now, when so much more is understood about ecological

107

destructions that will impact everyone. Technological innovation focused on ending and reversing those destructions will depend on contributions from organisational systems in both the public sector and the private, both of which are vulnerable to abuse by their designated owners.

To be effective innovators, public and private organisations depend on an appropriately focused strategy and a progressive culture. That way their capacity for invention and innovation will enable the development of new ways of progression without destruction, as has been demonstrated by successive technological revolutions. The potential for good and ill is unprecedented.

The need now is for a new green technological revolution to be given global support and access, if survival is to be assured. That can only be provided by the various organisational systems that serve the social–infrastructural, progressive–competitive and technological-revolutionary layers of the real economy. The following sections consider how those many and various organisational systems might best serve those very different layers of the real economy.

The social–infrastructural economy

The social–infrastructural layer provides products and services which people use or consume as part of 'the infrastructure of everyday life'.[1] That includes health and social care, education, water, energy, housing, a transportation infrastructure, the internet, the commons, defence, security and systems of justice. All those provisions must also include commitments to the environmental sustainability of their operations. Ensuring such sustainable provision is a basic responsibility of government.

Competition between providers is neither feasible nor valid. Water, gas and electricity, for example, are standard legally defined products which are supplied, as is waste drainage/sewerage, by permanent connections with end consumers. Such provisions are geographically defined, further frustrating any attempt to create genuine competition.

Organisational systems delivering these social–infrastructural products and services are effectively coordinated by commitment to the existential purpose, with all system components knowing and understanding that purpose and their own contributions to its fulfilment. System coordination also carries responsibility for the development of all resources involved, including its people, as well as its interactions with the macro-systems in which it operates.

Despite the US's reputed focus on private enterprise, the US civil service employs around 2 million people, ensuring people in need get food, including children getting proper nutrition at school, among many other fundamental achievements.[2] Political engagement with the US social–infrastructural economy, guided by neoclassical belief, has proved invariably destructive. The need is to establish effective checks and balances which will insulate the day-to-day operations of public enterprise from political manipulation for short-term gains.

The UK's social–infrastructural economy was firmly established post WW2 to fulfil the needs identified by Beveridge. Providing the infrastructure of everyday living must surely be the most basic of government responsibilities. Prior to the 1980s, public sector system components were more focused on their organisational purpose. In the case of a university, for example, that would be to achieve academic excellence in its teaching and research. In the case of a hospital the purpose would be to return its patients to good health as soon as possible.

During the past four decades of commitment to neoclassical belief, many such services and products have been outsourced and privatised, so that they are provided by organisations driven by MST. Consequently, their users and consumers are vulnerable to exploitation; an example was provided by hedge fund trader Martin Shkreli. Having bought Turing Pharmaceuticals after it acquired the rights to a life-saving treatment for AIDS/HIV and those with weakened immune systems, Shkreli raised the price by 5000 per cent from $13.50 per pill to $750.[3]

Such abuse, though mostly less extreme, has been repeated many times in the financialised pharmaceutical industry, contributing the opioid crisis among others. The social–infrastructural layer of the real economy is clearly vulnerable to such abuse by MST focused providers, some of which disguise their exploitative approach by creating pretend competition with elaborate pricing schemes and structures which are themselves exploitative.

Today's neoclassically deregulated, MST focused culture can also shape public sector systems. The result is that universities, for example, are under pressure to focus more on the short-term bottom line, achieving increased student numbers and a publications profile, rather than the pursuit of academic excellence however defined. Similarly, the role of hospitals has been focused on cost reduction and the positioning on league tables of conveniently measured metrics.

The social–infrastructural layer in the modern advanced state is a mandatory state provision that is only damaged by being forced to conform to the rules which should govern the progressive–competitive economy. That mandatory aspect of social–infrastructural provision has been emphasised by the necessary responses to the COVID-19 pandemic. It has posed a threat to human survival, and when survival is threatened, nothing else matters, not even neoclassical beliefs.

The progressive–competitive economy

The progressive–competitive layer of the real economy comprises a wide variety of non-mandatory provision of products and services. Organisational systems serving this part of the economy are many and various. They include those which are motivated to fulfil their system purpose by the need to be innovative and competitive in order to make a sufficient profit to survive in the short term and to develop and prosper long term.

As already noted, given freedom from regulation, it is natural progression for such competitors to seek to increase their market share and thus security and profitability, and becoming increasingly monopolistic, so as to control prices. The public sector involvement with the progressive–competitive economy is therefore not as producers, but as regulators to protect and reinvigorate genuine market competition. That regulation should not be easily removed by politicians driven solely by ideology.

Competitive organisational systems include a huge variety of different formats, from start-ups, sole trader artisan operations, SMEs, a wide variety of co-operatives, as well as large publicly quoted corporates that have retained their focus on the real economy as opposed to following the financialising route. The nature and aims of each organisational form evolves as they proceed through their life cycle.

Private organisational systems are usually referred to as 'for-profit' but that should not be interpreted as suggesting they exist solely for the purpose of maximising profit or shareholder take. They are funded mainly by private means and have to make sufficient profit to provide an adequate return to their investors as well as to invest in long-term future development.

Provision for the progressive–competitive layer is largely dependent on the competence of system coordination and its security from financialised control and abuse. The context is currently shaped by the dominance of neoclassical ideology. So a major determinant of the organisational form is the need to achieve effective protection against ownership abuse.

Artisan operations, like Smith's butcher, brewer and baker and other crafts people, provide their services in return for a sufficient surplus to support them and their dependents over their lifetimes. That means providing a reliable and trusted service on which a relationship with long-term customers might be based. Competition clearly plays a role in that reliability and continuity as it always has. A similar relationship of trust with the small number of employees involved is also beneficial. Artisans are not vulnerable to predatory attack, though they may be subject to competition from larger scale operations.

Start-up founding entrepreneurs typically need to attract investment from external sources, in order to invest in the systems development and expansion. That external finance can take many different forms of debt or equity or both, and is the source of existential problems. Shares might be sold to permanent or long-term holders, but they might also attract support from other sources and rapidly change hands becoming part of the fund management trade where the sole purpose of transfer is to make a quick return. Or they might fall victim to private equity which is enabled to invest without risking their own vulnerability to stock market raids or hostile takeover. Whichever route is taken, the external finance provided, can readily become subject to speculative dealing.

The need is therefore, for the founding entrepreneur to retain a controlling share, or as near to control as possible, so they would be able to mount an effective defence against hostile, predatory attack.

The transition from SME to large scale company is a critical change, needing to be undertaken with great care to defend the newly grown organisation from hostile M&A attack. Such M&A activity has always stoked the fear that 'the few' would take over the world at the expense of the many, as has actually happened across a broad front.

> It is the functioning of internal and external corporate governance that determines whether a company, or even a country, displays more of the negative or the positive aspects of the capitalist system.[4]

Though other orientations are legally available, both the US and UK are outsider shareholder oriented. Japan's *kieretsu* and Germany's two-tier board with employee representation on the supervisory board are both insider oriented, focused on protecting the organisational system from external predatory attack.

Real economy organisations can also be protected from predatory attack by establishing a co-operative format without public quotation.[5] In addition to normal membership shares, co-operatives may issue other forms of financial security such as 'privileged member shares', 'non-user member shares' and 'tradeable co-operative shares'.[6] In general, these are intended to provide a sufficient return to induce investment, but carry no right to any residual surpluses and may also have no voting rights.

Employee co-operatives can take various formats with shares held, in a trust on behalf of current employees, who may be treated to an annual dividend. Alternatively, shares can be held by a registered charity, on behalf of the operating company's members, the employees, who elect directors of the charity as well as the operating company. Scott Bader is a leading example, its shares held in trust by the Scott Bader Commonwealth Limited, a company limited by guarantee and a registered charity. The Scott Bader website makes the point that, with 'no external shareholders, we cannot be acquired so we are more stable and can plan ahead'.[7]

A further route to employee ownership is the US Employee Stock Ownership Plan system under which company shares are acquired through payroll deductions and sold back to the company at 'fair market value' when the employee leaves the company.

The vast majority of co-operatives are employee owned, though co-operative history goes back to the 1844 customer co-operative Rochdale Pioneers and before that to Robert Owen's New Lanark cotton mills, which introduced some semblance of social justice, ending the exploitation of trapped workers being forced to spend their wages at the company store.[8]

A key advantage of co-operative formation is its defence against financialised attack which stock market listed corporates are vulnerable to, as was the fate of chocolate company Cadbury in 2010.[9] Nor are co-operatives vulnerable to crude share raids with the aim of stripping assets, 'releasing' people and saddling what remains with massive debt, as was the fate for Debenhams[10] and Boots the Chemist. (Boots was taken over by a private equity operation, burdened with most of the debt raised for its acquisition and registered in the tax avoiding Swiss canton of Zug.) Protection from such predatory abuse is a considerable advantage for co-operatives. But the benefits go much deeper than that.

The internal benefit is in terms of the interpersonal culture of fairness and integrity, which engenders a spirit of commitment among all stakeholders:

> the commitment of people as human beings to their
> company and to future generations. They want to keep the
> company strong for their own sakes and they want to pass
> it on strong to the next generation ... They have human
> aspirations which include elements of conscience and of

generosity: they are much more than the money grubbing automata of economist's models.[11]

Internal commitment and protection from external predators enables firms to invest for the long term and take the necessary risks to innovate with new products and processes as well as ways of managing for the benefit of all. Work should not merely be a means to survival, but a source of satisfaction and personal development over a working life. That much should be achievable in the affluent society.

The technological–revolutionary economy

The technological–revolutionary layer of the real economy is best served by a combination of both public and private organisational systems working in collaboration with each other.

Involvement by the 'entrepreneurial state' operating in the context of rapid rates of innovation and change is outlined by Mazzucato:

> Despite the perception of the US as the epitome of private sector led wealth creation, in reality it is the State that has been engaged on a massive scale in entrepreneurial risk taking to spur innovation.[12]

Examples given include the US government's DARPA, SBIR (Small Business Innovation Research), the Orphan Drug Act and the National Nanotechnology Initiative. Publicly funded risk investment was not restricted just to defence and aerospace but also solid-state chemistry and silicon based semi-conductors, including such products as Apple's iPhone, iPod and iPad as well as protecting the intellectual property of firms such as Apple.

The technology on which the current generation of tech titans are based, largely originated from the work of people in state systems in the US and UK.

The entrepreneurial state has not in the past been at risk from organised money's predation and was therefore enabled to take a long-term perspective in financing fundamental research. However, the growing power of the financial sector, guided by neoclassical theorising, has led government to restrict entrepreneurial involvement of the state. Politically motivated affiliates of organised money who, for the time being, are in government are enabled to take short-term gains by restricting the state's investment in long-term research and innovation.

Lewis notes the substantial state contributions to the social-infrastructural economy as well as to the technological–revolutionary layer, but expresses concerns over ideologically motivated 'politicising the science',[13] which will probably result in further outsourcing and privatisation.

The various forms of public and private organisational systems, as outlined in the previous two sections, collaborate to serve the technological–revolutionary layer of the real economy. They bring their own particular inputs to the entrepreneurial mix.

An emerging SME high tech specialist company might be focused on developing technology further. It may have appropriate expertise in the right area but lack the resources to allocate them to the long-term project. However, if it is in an area that contributes to fulfilling democratic commitments, such as resolving ecological sustainability issues, the state, having the duty to achieve sustainability, could make the necessary investment.

The various formats of organisational systems, addressing the three layers of the real economy sensitive to their very different needs, could provide both a properly resourced social infrastructure including ecological sustainability as well as performing competitively to achieve further economic progression.

Systems innovation, strategy and culture

The progression that organisational systems achieve in remaking all three layers of the real economy largely results from their effectiveness as inventers and innovators. Both invention and its practical application as innovation, have been the focus of much empirical research.

The process of innovation is not necessarily a linearly logical and straightforward process, but is often haphazard and irrational, though dependent on having access to relevant knowledge and understanding.

Orthodox financial appraisal methods are based on readily quantifiable short-term results and the discounting of less easily quantifiable, long-term outcomes. That inhibits and prevents what might well be vitally important innovation. During a technological revolution, innovators need to be flexible and creative rather than simply driven by cost efficiency and tight control.

Factors which facilitate and inhibit organisational system innovation are identified as including two sets of organisational characteristics.[14] They relate to the strategic orientation of the organisational system, and to the organisational culture with which it operates.

Strategic orientation is defined along a focused–dispersed dimension, with a clearly focused strategy essential to effective innovation. That depends on maintaining effective two-way communications with external stakeholders, so that relevant information and knowledge is continually renewed. That includes, most importantly of all, communications with the ultimate consumer, so that their needs and wants are fully understood.

A focused strategy is also dependent on a long-term orientation rather than being dominated by the current position or the next quarterly result set. It necessarily recognises which organisational competences are core to the organisation's success and a commitment to ensuring they are maintained at the cutting edge for their industry. It also requires a clear focus on identifying and satisfying present and future consumer needs and preferences.

Those various factors are taken fully into account in defining a clearly focused strategic direction, a practical version of Deming's existential systems purpose. It also includes having effective systems of internal communication, so that the strategic direction or purpose is known and understood by all internal members.

The cultural element is defined in relation to a progressive–traditional dimension, which has much in common with McGregor's distinction of Theory Y and Theory X. A progressive culture involves an orientation to the interests and development of the people working within the organisational system, empowering them to contribute to the organisation's development, involving them in its decision making and leadership, and motivating their commitment to the organisation's progression. That requires real knowledge and understanding of what motivates and demotivates human behaviours.

A progressive culture also requires the organisational system to be based on the highest degree of corporate integrity. That involves ensuring the organisation's products and processes are all of high integrity both in terms of their overall intent and effect, but also in the way they are delivered to consumers. A guide to ethical business behaviour would commend behaviour which, if it were apparent, would increase rather than diminish the level of trust felt by the stakeholder or other party to the transaction or relationship in question. Top management has particular responsibilities for corporate integrity, including ensuring their take from the organisation is appropriate.[15] Despite today's excesses, there is no reason why Drucker's suggestion that 20 times the average pay packet should not still be an appropriate limit on top management pay if trust is to be maintained.

For organisational systems to be effective innovators they would need to operate with a focused strategy and a progressive culture. The innovative dynamic created by focused-progressive organisational systems can create a coincidence of organisational innovations. They can appear to spark off each other, igniting further innovations in adjacent areas, thus creating waves of change and innovation, as the first industrial revolution did in the late 18th century and as we now need to achieve with a green sustainability revolution.

Technological revolutions

Economic history tends to associate the names of Kondratiev and Schumpeter with the analysis of industrial revolutions. Kondratiev identified waves of innovation resulting from clusters of 'basic innovations that launch technological revolutions that in turn create leading industrial or commercial sectors'.[16] Schumpeter argued that the natural economic state was a stationary economy and that the prime cause of economic growth was technological innovation, which, according to the theory connecting innovation and economic development, occurred in 50-year cycles.[17]

A more systemic analysis was provided by Piatier, who outlined three such industrial revolutions, the third of which appears now to be approaching its maturity phase.[18]

Piatier's summary identified textiles, coal, the steam engine, steel, railways and the other industrial revolution industries as growing up and growing old together. The 1930s depression was not just a short-term economic crisis, nor a crisis of capitalism, but resulted from the ending of that great wave of major innovations.

Studies of industrial revolutions prior to Piatier had focused on the start and growth phases, but, like all live systems, industrial revolutions also have mature and decline phases which, in terms of economic effect, are as significant as their growth.

The second revolution had its embryonic phase in the 1930s and was based on oil, motor vehicles, aircraft, sheet steel, organic chemistry and synthetic materials. The growth from that revolution was interrupted by WW2, but was realised in the period of post-war reconstruction in the 1950s and 1960s, slowing down in the 1970s, brought to an early maturity by the oil price crises of the mid-1970s, and in decline by the 1980s.

The economic stagnation and high inflation experienced in that period was not the result of the failure of Keynesian economics as the Mont Pelerin neoclassicals suggested. Nor was it just caused by over powerful trade unions acting irresponsibly. The prime cause, according to Piatier, was the loss of innovative momentum in the second industrial revolution industries, which coincided with the OPEC engineered oil price hikes.

The third revolution was based primarily on computer and web-based systems enabled by electronics and information technology in a newly globalised format enabling the network society.[19]

The ability to computerise calculation also enabled the development of math and science based theoretical models which were made calculable for the first time and applied in many different areas such as molecular engineering and genetic engineering, as well as economic theorising.

For the first time, it coordinated physical, digital and biological developments which produced exciting new products and processes, demands for which now appear to be maturing and therefore slowing their economic impact. The economic slough which has engulfed the world since the 2007–08 crash of financial excesses may in part be evidence of the slowdown from the third technological revolution, resulting in all sorts of repercussions as human aspirations continue to increase. The result, on this analysis, is that later generations, for the first time since industrialisation, are less well off than their parents. Not only does this divert real attention from the ecological macro-systems which are in dire need of attention, but it also provides an additional source of social conflict.

The fourth industrial revolution, 4IR, has emerged with untold potential for good and ill. It is based on developments in artificial intelligence, robotics, the internet of things, autonomous vehicles, 3D printing, as well as nanotechnology, biotechnology, materials science, and renewable energy and its storage. These seem likely to have an even more fundamental impact on the way people live, work and relate to each other, and to do so more quickly than previous revolutions.

The current technological situation is therefore a complex mix of the maturing phase of the third revolution and the emergence of the fourth, which is at tremendous risk of being corrupted by global financialisation in pursuit of MST. That context is shaped by the 'Big Tech' operations of Facebook, Apple, Amazon, Google and other platform entities. The very real risk is exampled by Apple Inc, which unveiled its 2019 strategic push with a revamped Apple TV app which includes both original TV plus the ability to subscribe to third-party services, a games subscription service, a digital news and magazine bundle and a credit card in partnership with Goldman Sachs. It appears to be a fairly typical mature phase plan for a company that has run out of growth potential from further innovation in its areas of expertise. Its new strategy is devoid of technological innovation, which was the source of its founding and growth phase energy. It has now clearly reoriented itself to financialisation by capitalising on its accrued wealth and continuing market power.

That is exactly as the systems analysis of technological revolutions would predict. Similar initiatives can be anticipated from the likes of Amazon, Facebook, Google and others plus the new platform organisations such as Uber and Airbnb. They present new and different problems for re-establishing competition, but the same basic rules apply with the need to re-establish and protect competition when the technology serves competitive markets.

We have become so used to rapid technological development that it is difficult to imagine the process ever coming to an end, although its economic potential is finite. Biotechnology and genetic engineering have impacted agriculture, enabling productivity gains, but if applied with crude industrial scale savings for short-term gain as the sole objective, the long-term impact will be disastrous for agricultural output.

Molecular engineering is also making its impact with, for example, new synthetic materials. Graphene far surpasses the performance characteristics of steel at an inherently lower cost.[20] The technology of melting metal should in due course be consigned to museums and small craft units. However, unless constrained by liberating legislation to protect competition, the organised money establishment will naturally seek to monopolise the benefits from such gains.

Products and services are becoming cheaper to produce, more reliable, more flexible, more sophisticated and 'intelligent'. Flexibility and variety are instantly available. One-offs can be as cheap to produce as standard products. Labour costs have become less critical. The implications are revolutionary for all firms, large or small, whether actively competing at the forefront of technology or languishing as dominant near monopolists in the maturest of cartelised industries. The power of the financialised producer, driven by MST, also leads to the exploitation of planned obsolescence.[21]

The nature of work is being changed. Jobs are being eliminated on a potentially massive scale. The remaining work will either be in high skilled manufacturing, high skilled professional services associated with production, distribution and personal services, or lower level work offering flexibility through the part-time or zero hours contract working, magnifying the economic class divide. The employment

118

problem is further aggravated by the coincidence of technology reducing human work while global population continues to grow.

These further developments of the economy are being achieved and accelerated by the Big Tech organisations, which depend on the income derived from their capture and application of Big Data at no apparent cost. Realisation of that source of funding is still currently emerging and it might be anticipated that it will be some time before appropriate regulation and compensation is effectively implemented.

The necessary sustainability revolution

Judged by the pattern of previous experience, at some stage we will come to the end of this 4IR technological revolution. It has created vast amounts of new data, knowledge and understanding, and powerful new technologies which are revolutionising the world. It is full of threats and opportunities from its inventions and innovations. Huge new problems have been discovered and created, such as worldwide interference with democratic processes, revealed by the continuing leak of the Cambridge Analytica papers.[22] But possible routes to their resolution have also been indicated and are understood.

A revolution to access exciting new opportunities for a wholly sustainable future is now urgent. The potential for continuous development of renewable energy supplies is yet to be fully tested and implemented. That is the responsibility of governments. New forms of high tech organisation have been created that rise so fast they are means of extraction of money even before they have generated any. While still in their growth phase, such systems are able to stay well ahead of appropriate regulation. But as they mature and slow down, regulators will catch up. The problem is that seems unlikely to happen fast enough.

In the meantime, the potential for extracting value from Earth's finite resources, such as the remaining fossil fuels and non-renewable supplies, is still being made more profitable by neoclassically oriented governments and their climate crisis sceptical supporters. At time of writing the US government has announced its intent to increase support for its oil and coal industries,[23] while on fire Australia's prime minister has voiced his support for a balanced strategy of support for both coal and green investments.

The necessary sustainability revolution is the technological revolution comprising all the components necessary for achieving a fully sustainable Planet Earth suitable for human habitation. That would be Deming's declaration of system purpose.

The US initiative labelled Green New Deal seeks to correct both climate change and economic inequalities, combining Roosevelt's New Deal economic approach, investing public funds into job creation schemes, with the technological innovations needed to achieve sustainable Earth. It is the alternative to the currently still dominant MST–austerity combination. It seems unlikely to achieve sufficient progress while the neoclassical belief continues to influence relevant decision making.

While the sustainability revolution is clearly part of the technological-revolutionary layer of the real economy requiring both public and private engagement, it must be also be treated as absolutely essential to achieving a sustainable future. As such, it is also a key part of the new social–infrastructural layer, a fundamental role of the modern state, which is needed to be implemented across the globe.

Successive industrial revolutions and continuous technological innovation might give the impression that such developments will go on forever. But that may not be the case. We may be approaching the end of technological innovations. This may be the last ever industrial/technological revolution.

That is the context in which 21st century organisational systems operate in order to contribute to the achievement of humanity's existential purpose, which first of all is simply to survive, and ultimately to achieve further progression in our knowledge and understanding of how the world works best.

Conclusions

There are an ever increasing number of economists who, though they may not be content to set the whole of microeconomic theory aside, have nevertheless rejected the latest versions of neoclassical economics more or less in its entirety. Cambridge economist Ha-Joon Chang identified 95 per cent of economics as common sense 'made to look difficult with the use of jargons and mathematics'.[24] Chang also advised, among other things, that there is no such thing as a free market.[25] The market doesn't produce anything: it is a physical, digital, theoretical mode of exchange, not a system with a purpose or an organisation with coordinated components, unless, that is, it has been allowed to become monopolistic.

We depend on organisational systems to fulfil the democratic commitments that have been made. Applying economic theory to guide their governance and control has produced the profound wrongs, destructions, inequalities, frauds and criminality outlined in Chapter 3.

At the next stage of our evolution the consequences would be even more disastrous.

The alternative makes government responsibility clear. It is to grasp all opportunities for a wholly sustainable future. Technology is creating new possibilities for progression with new forms of organisational system, creating products and processes which can contribute to making the world sustainable. But it has also developed the power to destroy. So far, the lead organisational systems have stayed well ahead of appropriate regulation, a gap that must be closed.

The institutional truths that Galbraith warned of may all be unintended natural traps that humanity has fallen into. People may truly believe in the reality and worth of 'economic man' as a keystone of economic logic. It might be entirely coincidental that pursuit of those beliefs happens to result in unprecedented inequalities, financially benefitting the constituents of organised money and depriving the poor.

On the other hand, it might also be that the world has been cynically and deliberately taken over by some members of the organised money establishment, prepared to maximise their theft of the world's limited resources and be quite indifferent to all other consequences. If such were the case then the world is run by financial criminals, which is, as Roosevelt warned, more dangerous than government by organised mob.

Or it may be a combination of the two: either way, the result is the same. Though political-economic decision making is still mostly at the level of the nation state, its impacts and the impacts of economic subsystems of production and consumption, all clearly have global significance and are devastating ecological systems. Unless we change the way we live, the forecast population of 10 to 11 billion by the end of this century will be unlikely to inhabit a viable planet.

The systems approach to coordination of businesses, nation states and the global economy necessarily takes account of the dynamic nature and mess of the real world. It learns from observation and experience and from history, and it projects into the future. It does not abstract from that reality and seek to apply some unrelated theoretical construct in order to predict outcomes.

Observation and understanding of the real world is the foundation of the systems approach. This approach is also able to take account of human values and behaviour, which emphasises the importance of trust between all stakeholders and therefore of their integrity.

So we have the right people and the right organisational systems for the job they seek to do. We know what needs to be done. But still the organised money establishment is preventing real progression. So what action do we need to take in order to survive and for our children and their successors also to prosper?

What action needs to be taken?

PART IV

Action

We know where we are right now and we know the direction in which we're headed, and we know it's not good. That is the result of the world being guided by neoclassical belief, funded and promoted by its prime beneficiaries, constituents of organised money. The result is all manner of profound wrongs, destructions, inequalities, frauds and criminality which are making life on Earth progressively less sustainable.

We have identified where we want to be. As a species, our most fundamental motivation is to survive, which requires each generation to pass on to their successors, a planet that is at least as sustainable as the one inherited, so that they too, and their successors, might survive.

As sentient human beings, we also want to relate to our fellow humans and to progress and achieve in whatever way we can. We have expressed commitments to making basic human rights universally available and providing equal opportunities for all, as well as some degree of social balance, making it possible for all people to survive, relate and achieve.

Those commitments have been repeatedly expressed, but not enough has been done for their fulfilment. That will depend on human enterprise, people working individually and collaboratively in a huge variety of organisational systems to remake the real economy so that it is socially and ecologically sustainable.

Phenomenal success has already been achieved, developing revolutionary new technologies, products and processes. As at 2020, technologies are still developing but their application and regulation have not yet ensured their most beneficial diffusion, to ensure life on planet Earth is both permanently sustainable and progressively fulfilling. The next technological revolution must be focused, primarily and urgently, on achieving those sustainable outcomes.

The actions that appear essential to enabling that revolutionary change and remaking the real economy are outlined in the following chapter. That dream may seem far off in 2020. Time and resources are being wasted and action is becoming ever more urgent. In the end, appropriate action will be taken, or there will be a terminal response from people who have nothing to lose.

8

Systemic action for progression without destruction

Introduction

The systems approach to the real economy is simply concerned with what works, rather than theoretical detail or political ideology. First past the post democracies swing to and fro between the two ideals of left and right, wasting time and resource, undoing the initiatives of the previous orientation, frustrating the achievement of continuing progression without destruction which has now become urgent.

The previous swing to the capitalist right ended in the 1929 crash and subsequent austerity driven Great Depression – a notable failure of neoclassical belief. That was ended by the Roosevelt/ Keynesian move to the middle ground social democracy. At the same time, the socialist experiment was also failing, having mutated into totalitarian communism.

The 1970s 'stagflation' was a coincidence of stagnation arising from the slowing of the second industrial revolution technologies[1] combined with inflation arising from abandoning the gold standard, printing money to ease debt burdens, and OPEC-inflicted oil price rises. Nominating it as the failure of Keynesian economics helped to justify the reverse swing back to the currently still ruling version of neoclassical capitalism, further reinforced by the collapse of communism.

The 2008 repeat of the 1929 learning experience was followed again by an ideologically driven decade of austerity applied to the real economy in accord with neoclassical ideology. At the same time, funds were pumped into the financial sector following the crash, variously estimated at, around US$4.5 trillion in the US[2] and £435 billion in the UK and US$14 trillion worldwide.[3]

That crude approximation of the political-economic swings to and fro indicates the systemic movements that have taken place. We appear now to be approaching the end of the current neoclassical swing right, with its reducing levels of taxation and reduced public investment in the social–infrastructural economy disguised by outsourcing and privatisations and the euphemistically named light touch regulation, all aided by the new opportunities for both good and ill provided by the new 4IR technologies.

The result has predictably been ever more destructions, inequalities, frauds and criminality in what Shaxson referred to as a race to the bottom.[4] It remains to be seen whether the bottom will be hit and if so, how hard. Or whether the bottom might be avoided by the sort of actions outlined in this chapter which necessarily take account of the increasingly understood developing climate crisis.

Rather than seeking to embark on a swing back to some form of leftist alternative, the aim here is simply to enable the effective operation of all forms of organisational systems which contribute to the real economy and to limit those which extract from it. That will require their alignment with both the democratically declared commitments and the macro-systems within which they operate. Remaking the real economy will depend on organisations fulfilling their social and ecological roles efficiently and effectively as well as fulfilling the purposes for which they exist.

Actions to encourage the effective operation of real organisational systems are likely to be opposed by constituents of organised money which retain a controlling influence over government. It will therefore be essential to restrain those elements of organised money if real progression is to be achieved. That is simple to specify but will be rather more difficult to implement and may well depend on constituents of organised money exercising rather more than self-restraint.

Economists have long identified the flaws and misconceptions of neoclassical economics,[5] but since Keynes' era, a coherent alternative approach on which to base political-economic decision making has not been agreed.

The suggestion here is that microeconomic theorising is superfluous to requirements. The reality of economic activity can be observed, participated in and understood. The empirically based systems analysis of organisations provides that understanding which is the necessary foundation for effective macroeconomic decision making.

Organised money is still, in 2020, guided by neoclassical belief rather than those realities. Its restraint will, in the end, critically depend on the displacement of that belief system. That is becoming ever more urgent as, according to the science, the climate crisis continues to gather momentum.

Environmental stewardship and the global imperative

Environmental sustainability is not a matter for democratic debate. For the current generation of humanity, which has responsibility for this vital period of human evolution, sustainability is dependent on the behaviour and performance of all peoples, with the global imperative of environmental stewardship having top priority.

Sustainability will only be achieved at short-term cost to today's economy. The need is for investment in the long term to develop and implement new and improved technologies, and to close yesterday's low cost but destructive and polluting extractions and productions. That cost will have to be paid for out of taxation, which as Adam Smith argued should be levied on a progressive basis with the rich paying more than proportionately to their wealth and income.[6] Given today's technologies and the lagging of their adequate regulation, progressive taxation can readily be avoided. However, given the real ecological crisis the world faces, non-payment of taxes is definitely not 'smart'. Regulation is needed to catch up and put an end to evasion and avoidance.

The environmental issue is global, and its funding will have to be paid for by those who can, which means advanced economies paying more than proportionate to their wealth and income. That progressive taxation of nations would also be some acknowledgement of the fact that advanced nations have been the beneficiaries, in their early emergent phases, of the simpler but polluting industrial processes that emerging economies must now be denied. Advanced economies must assist the sustainable development of emerging nations if global sustainability goals are to be achieved.

We are all in it together and the need is for us all (all humanity) to agree the approach and implementation of appropriate measures, such as the funding of new environmentally positive technologies. That is a global imperative. However, vitally important though universal compliance will be, it must not inhibit advanced economies acting unilaterally to achieve the essential advances. If advanced economies lead the way and are successful in social and environmental terms, others will follow.

Global inequalities inevitably lead to unrest and rebellion in many different forms. The disadvantaged are motivated first of all to survive and to improve their lot and that of their children, and are prepared to risk their restricted lives to achieve those aims. The causes of their inequality, whether social or ecological, or even political (being dominated by some deviant tyrant), will only increase unless damages are reversed. Therefore, the rich nations, for their own self-interest, need to invest in improvement of the poor nations, so that domestic economies are livable, their populations educated, and all can be subject to minimum living standards.

That is the context in which the real economies of nation states operate. The following sections outline the actions needed to refocus all three layers of the real economy on achieving the sustainable democratic commitments of Chapter 4.

Rebuilding the social–infrastructural economy

This base layer of the real economy comprises products and services that people use or consume as part of the routine of daily life such as clean air and water, and that are recognised as precious commodities when their availability is threatened. It also includes social housing, education, a basic income, employment and health and social care, plus a public transportation infrastructure, adequate defence, security, the rule of law as well as justice available to all, plus continued support of the commons, such as libraries, museums, parks, rivers and beaches. Those many and various provisions are generally accepted as normal parts of everyday life in the modern advanced state,[7] which have to be provided in ways that are also fully sustainable.

Such necessities of life are required to conform to predefined standards, rather than providers competing with each other to achieve critical differences. In some cases, provision is only available by a single means of delivery or connection. So genuine competition between providers is neither possible nor appropriate and the normal rules of competitive markets simply cannot apply.

Nevertheless, the return to power of neoclassical belief in the 1980s ushered in the prolonged period of UK privatising and outsourcing of public provision that has led to the destruction of many public not-for-profit organisational systems. That includes the commons, which are being increasingly disowned and sold off by local authorities that bear responsibilities for their upkeep. In 2016 it was reported that around 100 public libraries a year are closing in UK as local authorities can no longer afford to maintain them following austerity driven cuts in central government support.[8] Similar devastation is being visited on other areas of the commons, such as public parks, rivers and beaches.

Much essential provision in the UK has been offloaded to the rapidly developed monopolistic 'big four': public service operators, Serco, Capita, Atos and G4S. Their primary expertise lies in the process of bidding for public service contracts, as was also the case with the now infamously bankrupted Carillion group. There are too many examples of such contractors' errors to list here. Some have already been referenced, such as G4S's uncontrolled abuse of Birmingham prison, which was as notorious as the UK government's £50 million waste on the Brexit necessitated cross-channel ferry contract with a company that had no ferries.[9] When the UK government announced increased investment in prisons,[10] it was only to increase their capacity to hold more prisoners, rather than spending on improved upkeep, counselling and training provided for inmates so as to reduce their reoffending and return to imprisonment.

The UK's reported spending on the social–infrastructural economy is also misleading because of the politically motivated headline catching investments such as the high speed rail link between London, the Midlands and northern England. The current estimated cost is £81–88 billion, some 40 per cent higher than originally budgeted, while delivery will take, as estimated in 2019, five years longer than planned.[11] Such projects hide the more prosaic, but vital infrastructure maintenance and improvement which is neglected in favour of the headline projects. The neglect has led to many emergencies and potential disasters, such as the threatened flooding of Whaley Bridge caused by failure of the ill-maintained 180-year-old dam.[12]

It is clearly not the case that private-for-profit is, by definition, more efficient and effective than the public sector operations could ever be. The only theoretical basis for that dogmatic assertion was that private sector operations were necessarily driven by the need to be competitive in order to survive and prosper. But social–infrastructural provision is not comprised of competitive activity.

Such necessities are and always will be the responsibility of the state whether nationally, or more locally, and are best provided by organisational systems that possess and develop the necessary expertise required in each case. Provision can be contracted out to private sector organisations, but the state retains full responsibility for effective delivery and so needs to retain expertise in each area of delivery.

That could be achieved by maintaining at least one state owned and controlled organisation operating in each area of social–infrastructural delivery, and to focus on the effectiveness and efficiency of all such operations, ensuring a progressively improving performance, either in terms of the product or service characteristics or the efficiency of their delivery. Continuing outsourcing or privatisations should only be permitted if the cost performance is superior to that achieved by the monitored state controlled operator.

That way, the not-for-profit state owned sector will be progressively rebuilt to serve those non-competitive needs. Such organisational systems would operate effectively and efficiently for the benefit of consumers, rather than exploitatively extracting money for the benefit of rentier shareholders.

The medium- to long-term effect of that revised systems approach would be the progressive withdrawal of private-for-profit operations from social–infrastructural provision, encouraging them to focus on the progressive–competitive layer of the real economy. That will certainly have a detrimental effect on shareholder gains and is likely therefore to be opposed by the constituents of organised money.

Action to rebuild the social–infrastructural economy should include consideration of the following:

- Public sector organisational systems retain full responsibility for some of the provision in all sectors and employ appropriate specialists with knowledge and understanding of all the real issues involved in their particular sector.
- Ensure the state retains the necessary skills and capability to operate and to be a benchmark against which private providers might be assessed. If falling below the state provided performance level, such privatised or outsourced contracts to be reversed.
- All natural monopolies should be at least part re-nationalised with the state owning a majority share.
- Establish an ongoing independent review of all UK infrastructure to ensure it continues to be fit for purpose.[13]

Re-establishing the progressive–competitive economy

Roosevelt identified 'business and financial monopoly' as the leading constituent of what he referred to as 'government by organised money' which he sought to address in the 1930s.[14] Monopoly was 'dangerous' then, but is far more powerful today as enabled by the current version of neoclassical belief and the new technologies now available. Free markets are a core concept of that belief: markets free from any extraneous interference from regulatory bodies or from state involvement in market provision.

Competition between providers in such free markets, according to neoclassical belief, will deliver the most efficient and effective ways of satisfying consumer needs and wants. Chandler's assertion that business was 'the most powerful institution in the American economy'[15] was made just as the 1970s stagflation prompted the rejection of the Keynesian approach and its replacement with neoclassical belief.

Competition is certainly a spur to efficient delivery, invention and progress. The most successful competitors will tend to increase market share and thus gain the ability to fund further invention and innovation, which assists further gains in market share. Thus, there is a natural process which sees competitive markets progress towards becoming monopolistic as the most successful participants advance. In due course it is natural for mature markets to be dominated by a small number of market leaders or even a single monopolist.

Since the 1986 'big bang' computerisation of capital markets, 'light touch' regulation has allowed most mature industries to be controlled by a small number of would-be monopolists, which fix and abuse markets for the benefit of their shareholders at the cost of all other stakeholders including the common good and the environment. In the new technology operations, that evolutionary process is extremely rapid so that the genuinely competitive growth phase of the market life cycle is almost non-existent.

Systems analysis recognises the need to regulate that decline in competition. Otherwise, the most powerful institution in the economy, being neoclassically compliant, will increasingly work to extract value for the benefit of shareholders rather than investing primarily to serve the interests of consumers and for a better long-term future.

The systems approach requires the re-establishment of genuine competition focused on creating rather than extracting value. That will be a fundamental change from the current acceptance of monopolistic extraction of value for shareholders. That extraction is from all other stakeholders, including employees, suppliers and customers, as well as ignoring environmental stewardship responsibilities. It is therefore important that competition is re-established and protected so it can again contribute to the efficient running of the progressive–competitive layer of the real economy.

The first step to re-establishing competition will be to break up existing monopolies and cartels. Companies considered as threatening monopolistic power were previously recognised in the UK as those with market shares in excess of 25 per cent. Monitoring and regulation was conducted by the M&MC and the OFT. Resourcing of both those bodies was subsequently much reduced and their roles have been merged into the Competition and Markets Authority (CMA).

The reduced resourcing of regulatory bodies results in the focus of their activities being on the pursuit and correction of very apparent market abuse. Regulation is needed to include a routine monitoring role in order to detect evidence of the building of monopolistic power ahead of its obvious abuse. Any such building of monopolistic positions should be the focus of close attention to ensure the protection of competition, with regulators empowered to initiate the breakup and prosecution of responsible entities.

The market power of such monopolistic operations is frequently achieved by mergers and acquisition as industries mature. Sometimes those deals are hostile and involve the subsequent destruction of the acquired entity. Such deals may quickly become irreversible. Other M&A deals may be by agreement of both parties. They can be even more destructive of the common good but are likely to be more amenable to reversal. An example was Glencore's merger with Xstrata, creating the world's biggest commodity trader, which had price fixing market shares of strategic minerals including nickel, zinc, platinum, chrome and copper, as well as being highly influential in grain markets following its acquisition of Viterra, and of thermal and coking coal. The merger was nevertheless allowed.

An effective regulatory authority will require adequate staffing and resourcing to monitor performances and initiate legal actions to prevent and break up monopoly and cartel operation, and to ensure relevant individuals be subject to investigation and prosecution as well as the corporate entity being similarly subject.

Some monopolistic situations also involve combinations that embody conflicts of interest which seriously compromise the roles and functions of the entities involved. Two such are audit and banking, as outlined in Chapter 3.

Audit is a professional role requiring specific qualifications to fulfil its legal requirements of signing off a set of accounts. As such, auditors are the private police force of capitalism and must be made truly accountable for their audit certification, For that role to be worthwhile, the auditor's certificate must be one that is trusted: that suitably qualified individuals have inspected the accounts in some detail and have established beyond reasonable doubt whether the accounts represent a true and fair account of the company's real financial position. For that certification to have credibility – which is its whole point – the auditor must be seen to be independent of the company being audited, rather than with some self-interest in the company's affairs. But auditors have been allowed to combine with accountants and management consultants, who may have lucrative contracts with the firm being audited. The independence of the audit is therefore compromised.

It is further compromised by being dominated by the 'big four' network organisations, which audit 98 per cent of companies in the

S&P500 and FTSE100 indices. Those four firms are now constituted as LLPs. Previously auditors were professional partnerships which stood or fell without liability being limited. The validity of their certificates rested on their professional competence and public trust in that validity. Moving to LLP meant that the partners would no longer be held to any personal responsibility for the validity of their certification.

Similar conflicts of interest apply to the retail and investment banking sectors which had previously been separated, with retail banks prevented from trading in capital markets. Retail banking was boring but safe as it was guaranteed in the UK by the Bank of England, so long as agreed levels of liquidity were maintained. Investment banking had no such formal protection. However, when the joined-up banking sector failed, it was bailed out as a totality, with shareholders being compensated for failure, as well as customers and other stakeholders, suggesting bank share ownership no longer involved risk.

New online technology provides whole new areas for market manipulation. Uber's entry to the London taxi market provides a relevant example. For decades, the black cab drivers' 'knowledge' meant when a black cab taxi was hired and some obscure address was requested, the driver would know how best to get there. Sat-nav systems and the Uber online platform can make existing people and resources quickly available to any location across London, without the need for 'the knowledge'. It was a clear advance of technology that increased the efficiency of delivery at much reduced cost to the customer, without detriment to the product delivered. The knowledgeable black cab drivers were the victims of that advance.

However, Uber's monopolistic position enabled the avoidance of employer responsibilities to provide any security of employment, minimum wage, holiday or sick pay. That is the nature of the new form of operation. Other operators entering the market might introduce an element of competition for driver services and may well offer those normal basics of employment. The present position is that the new technology is providing gains, but its regulation, either by competition or regulators, has not yet resolved. Similar considerations apply to other platform providers.

The speed of technological invention and its application remains well ahead of regulation. The 'network effects' are quickly accessible as the value of a new innovation is recognised. It can rapidly achieve scale without the frictions of traditional business building. The increasing scale of Amazon's product range makes it ever more efficient for customer use – currently estimated at around 40 per cent of US online shopping with more than 2 billion monthly users.

Similar network effects grant Google around 90 per cent of web searches in some economies and Facebook's increasing power over the media industry and, more importantly, the world's biggest pool of personal data, which is the currency that pays for these various 'free' activities.

Monopolistic power in these new technologies is achieved well ahead of regulators' ability to catch up, while the barriers to entry for new entrants continue to rise. Facebook's acquisition and integration of WhatsApp and Instagram, and Google's manipulative use of Android to prioritise its own apps show modes of limiting tech competition.[16]

The Big Tech titans have come to dominate not just the real economy but increasingly also the financialised. They need now to be 'tamed' and regulated adequately. One approach to be considered is the adoption worldwide of the single legal entity within any corporation, rather than the network of entities for which responsibility is readily avoided by closure.

Online technology also provides opportunities for market manipulation using personal information provided by online customers unaware of the misuse and value of the data they provide. For example, the UK's data protection regulator, the Information Commissioner's Office (ICO), found that sensitive personal data is being used illegally, without the owners' consent, by the US$200 billion online advertising industry, led by Google.

The European Union's General Data Protection Regulation (GDPR) was introduced in 2018 to protect the privacy of consumer personal information. When British Airways admitted a breach of its security systems had led to more than 500,000 customers having their personal data (including contact and credit/debit card details) leaked, it faced a £183 million GDPR fine for its 'poor security arrangements'.

This is a still rapidly evolving area of the economy. Online intellectual capital patents need special audit in order to maintain competition. Currently periods are excessive so that the innovative system grinds to a halt to await the initial benefits being fully exploited. That defeats the purpose of patents − to encourage and reward innovation − and now stifles innovation by making it possible for companies to constrain development in order to maximise shareholder value for up to 20 years.

In order to make private industry work again without being the predatory monopolistic monster it has evolved into, genuine competition will need to be re-established and protected. Making competitive markets competitive will require re-establishing effective checks and balances, as well as the restriction of the totalitarian powers of ownership over system membership.

Action to re-establish the progressive–competitive economy should include consideration of the following:

- Ensure statutory regulations define the boundaries of competitive, monopolistic and cartelised markets in sufficiently precise terms to enable effective regulation.
- Ensure staffing and resourcing of competition regulators is sufficient for purpose.
- Empower the regulatory authorities to monitor and investigate situations that might potentially compromise competition.
- Empower regulatory authorities to prevent M&A deals that would compromise competition.
- Empower regulatory authorities to reverse M&A deals that have resulted in competition being compromised.
- End professional conflicts of interest by separating the ownership of professional practices in audit from accounting and management consultancy.
- Make auditors truly accountable for their audit certification, with personnel held responsible for professional statements on audit certification.
- Review returning audit to professional partnerships without limited liability.
- Review the regulation and control of ownership of personal data, in order to return its value to its owners, the individuals to whom the data refers. One possibility is to make all such personal data, on an anonymised bulk basis, available to all competitors, on a fee-paying basis, similar to how patents work in relation to intellectual capital.
- Make social media and tech companies liable for any false information they publish online.
- Require disclosure and publication of source of all political text.
- Review the restriction of incorporated limited liability companies to a legal singularity, with the parent organisation having full legal responsibility for all the actions of all its subsidiaries including the prior activities of any acquired subsidiaries.
- Review patent protection law to ensure protection periods are appropriate to the relevant technology.
- Support United Nations initiatives to break up predatory corporate monopolists.

Refocusing the technological–revolutionary economy

While the social–infrastructural layer of the real economy is largely dependent on public sector not-for-profit organisations, and the progressive–competitive layer depends almost entirely on private for-profit organisations, the technological–revolutionary layer depends on a collaborative combination of inputs from both public and private sectors. State sector inputs provide vitally important long-term research which is foundational to subsequent commercial development by private for-profit organisations.[17] That collaboration between public and private will be essential to the green sustainability revolution needed to deliver critical results over the next decade. It is all about new technologies and their diffusion to make sustainability possible.

The technology on which the current generation of tech titans is based largely originated from the work of people in the US and UK state sectors. Mazzucato's analysis of the entrepreneurial state makes the connection with social democracy explicit: 'Companies like Uber and Airbnb ...would never have existed without publicly funded technology such as GPS and the Internet ... The digital revolution requires participatory democracy, keeping the citizen, not big business or big government, at the centre of technological change.'[18]

The current technological situation is a complex mix of decline from the third revolution and the emergence of the fourth, which is at risk of being corrupted from the start by global financialisation for the short-term benefit of organised money.

Technologies of the fourth industrial revolution are emerging with untold potential for good and ill. They are based on developments in artificial intelligence, robotics, the internet of things, autonomous vehicles, 3D printing, as well as nanotechnology, biotechnology, materials science and renewable energy and its storage. These 4IR applications seem likely to have an even more fundamental impact on the way people live, work, and relate to each other, than any previous technological changes. Moreover, they threaten to do so more quickly than any previous revolutions.

Clearly, they have the potential to make the essential revolutionary changes in how the ecological destructions, currently ongoing, might be reversed. The audit and correction of overall ecological destructions is a major concern for maintaining the technological-revolutionary economy.

Accelerating the technological–revolutionary economy should include consideration of the following:

- Provide public long-term financing of research and development of ecological sustainability.
- Establish an environmental audit authority and measure negative impacts and externalities.
- Ensure all environmentally unsustainable activities are fully compensated by ongoing taxation and fines for all damages.
- Introduce a state environmental subsidy for all green sustainable fuels and technologies.
- Introduce an environmental levy to be paid by producers of all goods which contribute to environmental damages.
- Introduce a progressively prohibitive levy on the extraction and use of all fossil fuels.
- Review the feasibility of a legal deadline on the extraction and use of all fossil fuels.

Restoring progressive taxation

Reference is repeatedly made to the evasion and avoidance of taxes, the distinction being between illegal evasion and legal avoidance. It is a distinction which invites professional expertise to identify the extremes of avoidance so that all opportunities for non-payment of taxes might be maximised without breaking the law. That clearly works against the intended purpose of taxation: to pay for the social–infrastructural layer of the real economy as well as investing in the revolutionary layer. Avoiding the payment of intended taxation by apparently legal means is just as damaging to the overall economy as evasion. Consequently, despite the additional difficulties involved, ending avoidance is required just as much as the illegalities.

In these days of high tech global communications, evasion and avoidance is simpler than it has ever previously been. It is made even easier by the City of London Corporation's web of quasi-criminal tax havens, which make the payment of tax by the wealthy largely a matter of choice. That system and culture is not sustainable. Their termination will certainly cost the financial sectors in the short term, but with a long-term gain for the overall economy and common good.

Taxation is clearly a global issue and global agreement would be advantageous, but national governments need also to act unilaterally to implement progressive taxation. Shaxson proposed 'country by country reporting' with governments sharing 'information about the local incomes and assets of each other's citizens'.[19] He also proposed prioritising the needs of developing countries for which 'tax is the most sustainable, the most important and the most beneficial form of finance for development'. Shaxson noted that international agreement is best; doing nothing is worst.

In sub-Saharan Africa, in 2015 the World Bank reported 413 million people living on less than US$1.90/day. 'Access to good schools, health care, electricity, safe water, and other critical services remains elusive for many people, often determined by socioeconomic status, gender, ethnicity, and geography.'[20] That is the result not just of growing population but also of illicit financial outflows of evaded tax having a net effect that far outweighs aid and investment.[21] Prevention of tax evasion is vital and requires individuals to be held personally responsible for corporate evasion. The taxation system should be revived to fund social–infrastructural investment as well as to assist technological–revolutionary progression.

Restoring progressive taxation will require consideration of the following items:

- Make avoidance of taxes illegal by default, its exceptions to be individually negotiated with the taxation authority.
- Establish a commission of enquiry to identify the UK web of tax havens and to propose the most advantageous action plan for their termination.
- Strengthen tax regulation to establish routine monitoring and correction of evasion and avoidance of intended taxation.
- Make taxation of wealth, inheritance and income progressive so as to redistribute those quantities and reduce extremes of inequality, which continue to rise with current regressive taxation.
- Sales/Value Added Tax to be made more progressive by lowering the standard rate but introducing higher rates for degrees of luxury items.
- Review onshore taxation, for example through land tax and minerals windfall taxation.

Restraining organised money

It is not possible to be certain how the various constituents of organised money are populated. Some members are intentionally criminal and entered the sector with the singular intent to extract value for their own gain by whatever means is available. But while the status quo enables such activity to go unpunished, it is not suggested here that organised money is itself a criminal conspiracy. Its constituents have been captured by the institutional truths of neoclassical belief and its impacts multiplied by the coincidence of new technologies. That is what lies behind and beneath so many of the damages, destructions, inequalities, frauds and criminality the world currently faces.

The overwhelming majority of organised money's constituents, being human, would be motivated to achieve and for their achievement to be seen and appreciated by their fellow human beings, rather than simply being focused on maximising their own self-interest. However, while they are led by neoclassical belief, they are taught that such altruistic contribution is simply irrational and damaging to efficient economy, when there are ready ways of avoiding such contribution. They might personally have laudable motivations, but in the hard neoclassical world of business, such generosity is not allowable.

The neoclassical fight is against the practicalities of rebuilding the social–infrastructural economy and re-establishing competitive markets. More than that, they will be likely to oppose the imposition of progressive taxation which will be essential to pay for those global social–infrastructural and ecological imperatives.

Remaking the real economy will clearly depend on the effective restraint and regulation of the various constituents of organised money. In terms of orthodox measures of economic performance, such as GDP growth, the restraint of organised money will produce some significant negative outcomes. That is partly because the financial sector has become too large a part of the overall economy, and will need to take a substantial reduction.

However, there are two qualifications to be made on that outcome. First, the orthodox measures are themselves inappropriate and inadequate, as noted in Chapter 9. Second, the financial sector may be large in numbers, but in terms of its impact on the broader population, the financial sector is mostly negative and relatively limited in its positive effects.

The key to restraining and refocusing organised money is necessarily financial, mainly through taxes, tariffs, subsidies and investment, aiming to focus sector outcomes on the real economy and the common good rather than MST. The following notes refer to the different subsectors of the organised money establishment.

The financial sector, among many and various roles, receives the value extracted by other organised money constituents and invests it for MST. The quickest and easiest way to do that is not by long-term investment in projects such as those aimed at resolving sustainability issues, but by speculative investment, using new technology, automated, algorithm-based trading systems. That process of dealing with the value extracted from the real economy is reported as increasing the quantity of money in circulation and therefore boosting the economy. The truth is it is mostly allocated to further speculative trading and so is not in circulation in the real economy and therefore has no positive effect, though its extraction invariably has a negative impact. Friedman, late in his life, expressed his disappointment at the failure of the quantity theory of money to deliver as anticipated.[22]

It has been proposed to implement a tax on all financial transactions, including those of automated algorithm-based systems, the aim being not simply to increase tax revenues, but to slow the transaction process and reduce the level of speculative dealing which serves no purpose for the real economy.

Financialised organisational systems: rather than entering the entrepreneurial struggle to create new value in the real economy, the quickest and simplest way to MST is by extracting value from already existing organisational systems by, for example, aggressive M&A dealing. That is the focus of financialised business, as opposed to real industry. The reduction of hostile M&A dealing could be achieved by reducing opportunistic deals by imposing legal requirements for periods of delay between announcing bids and their activation, as well as the delayed accrual of equity voting rights.

Academia makes multiple contributions to the development and promulgation of neoclassical belief. Despite the inputs of leading economists disowning neoclassical theorising, it continues to be taught and promoted by educational institutions to non-specialists in business schools and beyond, across the globe, providing an apparently respectable theoretical cover for organised money's activities. Its restraint must be largely a matter for professional economists, though excluding it from business school curricula, as proposed by Ghoshal,[23] would appear to be a first move.

The media supports and promotes the financial sector as key to economic wellbeing and in particular promotes the neoclassical culture, ideas and philosophy to the wider populations, so that its destructive activities are held to be economically efficient. Restraint of the media sector, notably including social media, would necessarily include the criminalisation of purveyors of fake news and making media directly responsible, both as corporate entities and the responsible decision takers, personally, for all information and communications published.

The political sector works, partly through its think tanks and lobbyists, to develop and promote further breadth and depth to the neoclassical volume. It is also partly achieved through the development of a political class, isolated from the real world, as ideologically driven trainees and advisors to practising politicians. Restraint would require limitations on the expenditures of lobbyists and political think tanks with punitive fines for any excess expenditures.

Government in a democracy depends on the people for its election, but depends on the constituents of organised money for its financial backing and support. It also depends on permanent constitutional structures to impose checks and balances on the powers of ideologically driven, essentially short-term, politicians. Restraint will require those checks and balances to be fully resourced and for further limits to be placed on the levels of financial support contributed for political purposes. Any excess contributions would be subject to fine and political disqualification.

The City of London is, in effect, the international headquarters of organised money with its established unregulated offshore markets. Funds from all over the world are attracted by London's permissive governance standards and apparent welcome to the money of criminals and oligarchs no matter how it was accrued.[24] Some analysts agonise over whether the City of London with its peculiar governance system – neither a local authority nor a direct responsibility of central government – is itself wilfully criminal, or just blind to fraud and criminality, in order to attract more business whatever its kind.[25]

Action to restrain all those constituents of organised money is likely to cause strong short-term responses. For example, those living in the UK with non-domiciled status do not pay taxes on capital gains or overseas earnings, unless they bring the money into the country. That has encouraged those with extreme wealth from whatever source to come to the UK, avoiding payments to the UK Treasury. Any threat to their 'non-dom' status will cause the super-rich to depart, leaving the UK financial sector in a weakened position.

Avoiding the restraint of organised money can only be temporary. Restraint will become an absolute essential to short-term survival. If delayed, restraint would need to be even tougher; the sooner action is taken, the less extreme it will have to be.

Actions to restrain organised money should include consideration of the following:

- Tax evasion and avoidance will be the special responsibility of an adequately resourced regulator with responsibility for review and termination of all avoidance as well as evasion.
- Banks will be fined and activities suspended for all fraudulent and criminal activities.

- Professionally qualified bank personnel will be held personally responsible for the decisions taken, including any fraud or criminality; any such decisions resulting in termination of professional careers.
- Return retail banks to separate ownership from other financial sector operations, with guaranteed central bank support for retail banks subject to maintaining agreed levels of liquidity.
- Support for investment banking will be restricted. Shareholders of a bank that fails are not to be compensated in any way by purchase of shares. No bank is too big to fail.
- Impose a financial transactions tax in order to reduce the automated speculative dealing, largely funded by extraction from the real economy. The tax would reduce transactions by making it less efficient and more expensive to operate.
- Limit the activities of lobbyists by restricting their expenditure on politically oriented activity, making the lobbyist firm subject to punitive fines for any transgression of those limits and, making the responsible individual subject to fines for any fake or factual transgressions published in any media.
- Regulate all political publication during election sensitive periods.
- Make trading in opaque securities illegal. All financial securities must make their contents absolutely clear, as is required with food products where the ingredients are required by law to be accurately listed.
- Bankrupted banks will not be bailed out by any compensation of shareholders, the bankrupted entity to be acquired by the state and its responsibilities to customers fulfilled.
- Review termination of LLPs, enforcing either professional partnerships or limited liability companies, with responsibility to relevant stakeholders.
- M&A activity will be limited by enforcing a minimum 9 months prior warning of any proposed deal.
- Equity voting rights will be accrued progressively after shares have been owned for a minimum of a year.
- Two-tier boards will be required of companies with over 100 employees, with employee representatives having 50 per cent of supervisory board membership.
- Pursue transparency so that companies and individuals are held to account on a country by country basis as to assets and profits, with automatic information exchange, prioritising the needs of developing nations to stop extracting ten times more than aid going in.

- Tackle the financial sector intermediaries, so that when a client is found guilty of fraud, the relevant auditor, accountant and lawyers are also held responsible.
- Change the financial sector culture with reform and rethink of corporate and personal responsibilities.
- Reduce waste reversing policies following government changes in first past the post elections, by establishing electoral systems of proportional representation.

Displacing neoclassical belief

Neoclassical belief serves the purposes of the organised money establishment, providing an apparently sufficient justification for its self-interested activities and decision making. Such decisions include the funding of lobbyists, think tanks and relevant strands of academia which promote and teach the models, concepts, hypotheses and assumptions of neoclassical belief. Organised money and neoclassical belief are thus interdependent and intimately entwined. The credibility of one without the other would surely not survive for long. While remaking the real economy requires organised money to be reduced, neoclassical belief should be displaced in its entirety.

Individuals are not simply motivated by greed alone. Organisations do not exist solely for MST. And markets, freed from government involvement or regulation, are not competitive for long. The mathematical models of neoclassical economics bear no relation to reality. The list of critical economists is endless. Even Friedman accepted that the economic models were unrealistic but argued that what mattered was whether they could predict outcomes.[26] Unlike in science, widely held economic theories tend to be self-fulfilling, so predictive capability is irrelevant. Hayek summed it up nicely in his Nobel Memorial lecture accepting that 'as a profession we have made a mess of things'.[27] He had seen nothing then, in 1989.

In terms of the resulting political-economic decisions, neoclassical belief has resulted in unsustainability at all levels of the economy. It commends short-term gains from one-off transactions which result in permanent losses to the public exchequer. In the UK these have been realised in various outsourcing and privatising of public provision and in the sale or closure of local council property including council owned housing. The result has been a one-off gain for the local economy, but with an ongoing permanent loss for subsequent years. Those losses are multiplied by the generalised belief in shareholder primacy, which justifies the exploitation of all such opportunities. Such ongoing losses are clearly not sustainable unless compensated by increases in taxation.

Instead of greed, real people, engines of enterprise, have a web of motivations to satisfy a hierarchy of needs, to survive, to socially interact and to achieve. Instead of MST, organisational systems exist to fulfil a wide variety of necessary purposes. Instead of free markets there is a wide variety of organisational settings that exist to provide 'the infrastructure of everyday life', its further progress and the revolutionary innovations required for total sustainability.

Shareholder primacy and freedom 'from any sense of moral responsibility' in its achievement are perhaps the most profound of all the errors of neoclassical belief. Exclusion of any consideration of values is an essential characteristic of its pretence of being a science, and persuades management to pursue the responsibility to MST without restraint.

Business school graduates have therefore actually applied neoclassical ideology at their place of work, enacting the form of management Ghoshal described, and the governance system which facilitates it. The result has been the financialisation of so many organisational systems, from which captivity they must escape if we are to achieve a sustainable future. Keynes was no doubt correct in his much-cited assertion that 'the ideas of economists and political philosophers, both when they are right and when they are wrong, are more powerful than is commonly understood'.[28]

Within economics there appears to be limited support for the simplistic neoclassical recipes. Nevertheless, it is still taught to non-specialists. Ghoshal was focused on the impact of neoclassical theorising within the business management context, but its influence is far wider than that. Non-specialists who are so influenced include those entering the subsectors of organised money: business, finance, the media and the various strands of politics. People entering any of those areas are likely to have been primed with the institutional truths of neoclassical belief and are likely to find themselves under pressure to act accordingly.

Neoclassical Becker held that 'the heart of the economic approach' amounted to nothing more than 'maximising behaviour, stable preferences and market equilibrium',[29] each of which is complete fantasy. Earle and colleagues referred to that as the 'econocracy' and quoted Keynes suggesting that the 'master-economist' needed to be a 'mathematician, historian, statesman, philosopher ... [and] must study the present in the light of the past for purposes of the future'. While the current text has no pretentions to qualifying as the work of a master economist, Keynes accurately describes the aim of this text, studying the present reality, in the light of past experience to guide future decisions.

Ghoshal argued that, to escape from the neoclassical belief system's grip, universities and business schools must, first of all, stop teaching it.[30] That first step is now urgent.

The breadth of subject area, suggested by Keynes, is needed for economics to be credible again, rather than simply a hook for soundbite politicians and their organised money associates. Raworth provides that breadth with the 'regenerative and distributive economy' meeting the minimum requirements of the 'social foundation', while existing within constraints of the 'ecological ceiling'.[31]

The Deming based systems approach also provides that breadth. Though focused on the variety of organisational systems and the collaboration of system components to fulfil the existential purpose, systems economics also takes account of the social and ecological macro-systems within which organisational systems operate, as well as their evolution over time.[32]

Replacing neoclassical economics in its entirety is the most important change that has to be made if we are to remake the real economy and achieve sustainable progression instead of the destructions, inequalities, frauds and criminality noted in this text. That will require a heroic academic faculty to deny neoclassical belief. That is the single action which might achieve this most important of all changes.

The displacement of neoclassical belief will require relevant strands of academia to define neoclassical microeconomics as economic history rather than a still relevant basis for economic decision making. That will require the espousal of a reality based alternative curriculum which takes account of democratic commitments to universal human rights, equal opportunities and the achievement of permanent sustainability.

Conclusions

Though the actions proposed in this chapter appear to be essential to establishing a sustainable future, they seem unlikely to gain much long-term support from the constituents of organised money who currently rule the world, despite the necessary pragmatic response to the COVID-19 pandemic attack on the real economy.

Governance must first of all seek to achieve mankind's long-term survival. The imperatives of sustainability must be observed, and transgressions punished beyond repeat. So the need for culture change is now urgent. Organised money's activities are highly damaging but that is not because the people intend it to be that way. Some may be criminally inclined, but most are no doubt perfectly well intended, persuaded by neoclassical belief. Whether innocent or corrupt is not of prime importance. What matters is the outcome, which is a crime against humanity which has to be stopped.

But rebuilding the social–infrastructural economy, re-establishing and protecting competition in the progressive–competitive economy, and reshaping the technological–revolutionary economy, are all essential to a sustainable future.

The first step that must be taken is to displace the neoclassical belief which justifies the actions of organised money. First, stop teaching it. Second, the academic researchers who have promoted its ideas, such as Milton Friedman, must be consigned to history.

The incompatibility of neoclassical economics with rebuilding social democracy needs to be addressed by coordinating international frameworks such as the United Nations, the IMF, World Bank, and regional organisations such as the EU and the various international trading agreements. These all need to be aligned with internationally agreed commitments. Clearly such complexities are beyond the competence of this text, but a systems approach to resolving such global progression suggests coordination rather than fragmentation.

This broad gestalten perspective suggests the main concern must be to challenge the two fundamental problems: neoclassical belief and the organised money establishment which grasps that belief and exploits it for its own narrow sighted gains.

The need then would be to accurately assess progression towards a positive solution. That is the focus of the final chapter.

PART V

How are we doing?

This text is written from the practitioner perspective, the focus being largely from within organisational systems. The primary concern is to understand what works and how such organisational systems might best contribute to the democratic commitments to ecological sustainability, universal human rights, equal opportunities and some measure of social balance.

An objective assessment of how we are doing requires a different, external orientation. The aim is to assess organisational system impacts in terms of progression without destruction, individually and collectively, nationally and globally.

The orthodox and continuously reported measures of economic progress are GDP and its growth. They have been the focus of much critique as immeasurable, inconsistent and illogical, as well as failing to take any account of the democratic commitments outlined in this text. GDP growth is not a satisfactory proxy for any real assessment of progress.

This final chapter provides an outline of existing objective external measures of progression which can take account of global, national and organisational level impacts.

The displacement of neoclassical belief and restraint of organised money remain the keys to a truly sustainable future, so assessment of that displacement and restraint will be crucial.

9

Measures of real progression

Introduction

Systems concepts are widely applicable. Life cycle analysis is recognised in relation to all living and social systems, including human beings and most of their creations: organisations, communities, products, technologies and nation states. It applies equally to planet Earth as the abode for biological species. Its fundamental resources are finite, so humanity and its subsystems have to live within their limitations.

Over the past 250 years, global economy and population have experienced the growth phase. They now appear to be experiencing the phase change volatilities as the global economy enters its mature phase. That requires the current population to learn how to live hopefully fulfilling lives, without further overall economic growth. Population is continuing to grow and will do so for some time yet, but it is also approaching its maturity when growth ceases and will subsequently decline, though the shape of that life cycle is unpredictable.[1]

The initiatives outlined in the previous chapter are intended to help address those phase change volatilities, mostly brought forward by continuing human abuse. If they do not succeed, then catastrophic outcomes threaten. The Easter Island parable is a reminder of what must be avoided. It suggests that measures of real progression must relate first and foremost to such global limitations.

That overall picture relates to individual nations differently, with the continuing growth of the industrialising states led by China, the maturing of the industrialised countries, such as the US, Japan and Germany, and the decline of the post-industrial states, led by the UK, which has taken the financialising route with its real economy being reduced by the ravages of organised money.

That simplification suggests how different nations might wish to measure their real progression differently, by focusing on measures of particular relevance to their individual situation.

The aim in this final chapter is to identify appropriate measures of progression without destruction. Environmental stewardship to achieve protection against the various ecological destructions is clearly a global imperative on which the whole of humanity depends. The pursuit and achievement of universal human rights, equal opportunities and some measure of social balance are also global considerations, with the most urgent emphases being given to those areas where they are least satisfied. The wealthier nations could choose to ease the plight of those victim states, or ignore them and face the inevitable rise in migration of those human beings seeking desperately to improve their lot or at least survive.

At the time of writing, such inequality is exampled by the plight of Yemen. Nearly 14 million Yemeni people are at risk of famine and an estimated 85,000 children under the age of five died from starvation in the three years to mid-2019.[2] That is a global calamity. Various charities are contributing to a solution, but it is being given inadequate acknowledgement and attention by governments and international organisations.

Measures of real progression need to be assessed on a global basis as well as on the various subsectors including international, regional and national performances. Ideally, the United Nations might measure all such progressions and report on a regular basis, so it is known and understood how much progress is being made and how much more needs to be achieved, with some agreed mechanisms for 'enforcing' compliance.

Politicians may be eloquent in their verbal commitments but are not so effective when it comes to action. For them to be effective will require, as outlined in Chapter 8, the displacement of neoclassical belief and restraint of organised money, so that progress can also be made rebuilding social–infrastructural provision on a not-for-profit basis, re-establishing competitive markets, and funding fundamental research to achieve the green sustainability revolution, notably including the generation and storage of clean energy and ending the burning of all fossil fuels.

Progress in strengthening the checks and balances of democracy is also required so that short-term politicians have some limits on the extent to which they might make destructive decisions.

None of these issues are as simple or straightforward as the standard orthodox measures of progression, such as GDP and its growth.

GDP growth metrics

Smith's enquiry into the nature and causes of the wealth of nations was conducted without the benefit of GDP measures, as were all subsequent economic progressions until the mid-20th century. Then, the standard measure of economic performance was Gross National Product which was roughly equal to the gross income of a country's citizens. The measure subsequently switched to GDP, the value of the goods and services produced within a country irrespective of who the producer was.[3] That change encouraged countries to be 'open for business' so that foreign entities might invest in and take over real economy activities, without the measured economy being reduced. The UK was a prime beneficiary of that change. In terms of GDP growth metrics, the UK also gained from the inclusion of fast growing foreign owned financial sector operators becoming UK based without being required to pay much in the way of UK taxes.

GDP has become the standard measure of the wealth of nations, and its growth rate the standard measure of economic progression.

Keynes set out the macroeconomic relationships between tools available to government and the size and state of the economy.[4] He also triggered the development of the first set of national accounts and GDP calculations in 1942.[5]

Coyle described its calculation as 'the product of a vast patchwork of statistics and a complicated set of processes carried out on the raw data to fit them to the conceptual framework'.[6] As a measure, it is full of ambiguities, inconsistencies and immeasurables, often exampled by the inclusion of prostitution and some criminal activity, but exclusion of unpaid housework, parenting and care for the elderly, which have been estimated to account for as much as 30 per cent of GDP.[7] Fioramonti also noted the neoclassical shortcomings such as the inability of GDP to take any account of moral values and sustainabilities.[8] Furthermore, endless economic growth in an essentially finite world is simply not possible.[9] Commitment to such continuous expansion is more a cancer than a virtue which sees rising health costs as a GDP good even though it destroys uninsured families.[10]

Any activity that can be exchanged for a price, or have a price attributed to it, can count as adding to GDP, irrespective of whether its contribution is positive or negative in terms of sustainability or wellbeing.

GDP measures also include the financial sector's predatory exploitation of the real economy as a positive contributor, taking no account of the vital distinction between the real economy and the financialised. Nor does it make any assessment of impacts on social or ecological macro-systems and their destructions. There are also ways that its calculation might quite easily be manipulated to better satisfy the current political ideology. For example, the privatisation and outsourcing of state operations involved bringing some operations which had previously not been included in GDP calculations within its orbit, thus boosting the apparent rate of GDP growth, for which associated politicians take credit, adding further weight to the neoclassical belief supporting those initiatives.

Other changes have made the GDP metric ever less appropriate as a measure of economic growth and general wellbeing. For example, new online technologies that achieve substantial increases in performance and reductions in prices might be shown as having negative impacts on GDP and growth.

Many critiques of GDP as a measure have been published.[11] Raworth replaced GDP growth with 'thriving in balance' between the ecological ceiling and social floor.[12] Mazzucato flagged up the vital distinction between creating value and its distribution, as well as noting the very real problems of measuring R&D, pollution, prostitution and rents.[13]

Despite those myriad problems, GDP growth remains the default measure of economic progress, its retention being consistent with neoclassical belief and supportive of the interests of organised money. The effect is to deflect attention away from what really matters.

Stiglitz addressed some of those problems by constructing 'Green GDP' accounts which would include calculation of the depletion of natural resources and degradation of the environment. Green GDP suggested that if 'correctly measured, the coal industry might have been making a negative contribution to the nation's output' which would have had 'significant policy implications'.[14] That argument was fiercely contested in the US by congressional representatives of coal states which benefitted from government initiatives supporting the burning of coal and oil. Clearly the burning of coal has one-off short-term positive contributions but permanent negative impacts of far greater consequence.

The problematic nature of GDP is well understood. Some adjustments might make GDP a more valid measure. For example, separate measures of real and financialised economic contributions to GDP might provide some useful insights. Similarly, measuring and reporting the separate positive and negative contributions to ecological sustainability might make GDP a partially useful measure.

However, in a world which needs to learn how to progress without economic growth, GDP has clearly become largely irrelevant and could be set aside.

Sustainable development

Sustainable development refers to the real progression in fulfilling commitments to environmental stewardship, the achievement of universal human rights and equal opportunities for all, as well as some measure of social balance in place of gross inequalities.

Many different suggestions have been made as to appropriate measures of that real progression. The urgent need for global partnership to achieve sustainability has been long understood. In 2000, the United Nations member states committed to eight Millennium Development Goals, which were to be achieved by 2015. They included addressing items such as poverty, health, education and some measure of environmental sustainability as well as the need for 'an open, rule-based, predictable, non-discriminatory trading and financial system' which included 'a commitment to good governance, development and poverty reduction—both nationally and internationally'.[15]

The UN's 2015 report of progress in pursuit of those goals confirmed that inequalities persisted including around 800 million people still living in extreme poverty with links to health disadvantages, child and maternal mortality, elevated school dropout rates, and inadequate sanitation. Each day, about 16,000 children die before celebrating their fifth birthday. Over the 15 years, conflicts had forced almost 60 million individuals to evacuate their homes; women continued to experience significant gender gaps in terms of poverty, labour market and wages, as well as participation in decision making; access to improved water and sanitation facilities remained limited for many people in rural areas; and measures of climate change confirmed totally inadequate progress was being achieved.[16]

Though it was agreed UN policy that the need was for those goals to be the focus of global, and national attention and also for individuals and organisational systems to be supportive, it was reported that by 2015, only 4 per cent of the UK public, for example, had ever heard of the MDGs (Millennium Development Goals).[17]

In 2015, the UN replaced the eight MDGs with 17 Sustainable Development Goals[18] as part of Resolution 70/1 of the United Nations General Assembly. The commitment was that they be met by 2030. Those SDGs covered much the same ground as the MDGs but spelled out the global imperatives in more detail including items supporting environmental sustainability, human rights and equal opportunities as well as challenging inequalities within and between states.

The United Nation's Development Programme explains the content of each SDG in some detail.[19] For example, SDG10 commits to reducing inequality. It indicates that income inequality is on the rise – the richest 10 per cent having up to 40 per cent of global income, whereas the poorest 10 per cent earn only 2–7 per cent. Income inequality has increased nearly everywhere in recent decades. In the

UK, that is nicely exampled by the BBC paying a football programme host an annual salary in excess of £1.75 million for work during the football season, at the same time withdrawing free TV licences for the over 75s.

Such widening disparities require sound policies to empower lower income earners, and to promote economic inclusion of all, regardless of sex, race or ethnicity. The UN also requires global solutions, by improving the regulation and monitoring of financial markets and institutions, encouraging development assistance and foreign direct investment to regions where the need is greatest.

The combination of increasing inequalities and increasing orientation of the wealthy to the financialised economy have hugely negative impacts on economic progress and have created a serious barrier to eradicating poverty. However, increasing inequalities are not inevitable.

The aim is for progression of those SDGs to be closely monitored and reported on a regular basis by suitably qualified individuals and organisations that cement global agreement on how all organisational systems can comply with the now urgent ecological and social imperatives. The UK government provided advice regarding its implementation, confirming the UK as committed to the delivery of the SDGs by ensuring they are 'fully embedded in planned activity of each Government department'.[20]

SDG17 commits to strengthening the means of implementation and revitalising the global partnership for sustainable development. But the progress report in 2019 included the following:

> significant challenges remain: ODA [Official Development Assistance] is declining, private investment flows are not well aligned with sustainable development, there continues to be a significant digital divide and there are ongoing trade tensions. Enhanced international cooperation is needed to ensure that sufficient means of implementation exist to provide countries the opportunity to achieve the Sustainable Development Goals.

In short, implementation progress is far from satisfactory.

Precise measures need to be developed and agreed to monitor progress towards the targets on local, national, international and global levels and across sectors. Also the connections between targets need to be properly understood, including synergies and trade-offs. For example, greater fertiliser use might increase food production and incomes locally but could exacerbate pollution and possibly long-term soil degradation. Such external effects are common experience in most sectors and must be taken fully into account.

Progress should be evaluated by relevant qualified bodies. Existing UN bodies, such as the IPCC and the Intergovernmental Platform on Biodiversity and Ecosystem Services plus other existing scientific-assessment bodies, should be instrumental in deciding how best to evaluate performance and achievement against relevant goals.

Establishing the means of evaluating performance and implementation of sustainable development projects and policies is still work in progress. But agreeing the targets and mechanisms for the effective focus and measurement of sustainability goals is a hugely important first step. The UN's SDGs are a close proxy for the Chapter 4 combination of environmental stewardship goals, the defeat of Beveridge's five giants, and the establishment of equal opportunities for all with the establishment of some measure of social balance. They could provide a satisfactory measure of how far those democratic commitments are being achieved, as well as the measures of ecological sustainability. They could also provide sufficient assessment of imminent or forthcoming destructions as measures of the need for further change of actions. They have the great advantage of being coordinated by leading international/global organisations, cooperating to encourage the integration of the SDGs in member states' national budgets.

They offer the best means of focusing on sustainability imperatives and the most likely way of achieving those goals. But the risk is ever present that they are just fine words and lack the necessary power and will to enforce compliance. The clear necessity is to make absolutely certain these are not just vain hopes or means of disguising malpractice but are implemented both urgently and ruthlessly.

It should also be noted that the two fundamental changes, identified as the key issues in the previous chapter – the displacement of neoclassical belief and the restraint of organised money, are not confronted by the SDGs. That is hardly surprising, but the reality is they are crucial and will remain as the key destroyers till displaced and restrained.

Real economy progression

The specific targets of remaking the real economy will vary according to the relevant national economy. Social–infrastructural provision is clearly best delivered by organisational systems which exist not for the benefit of shareholders, but to serve whatever the existential purpose happens to be. Returning outsourced and privatised provision back to not-for-profit organisational systems will therefore enable provision to be focused on that primary purpose.

Monitoring will require continuing measures of organisational system intakes and outputs plus some comparison with the public sector model operating in the relevant sector. A key measure will be the establishment of adequately resourced regulatory bodies which can conduct routine monitoring and enforce corrective actions on any deviations from approved progression.

Assessment of the critical measures of progressive–competitive provision will need to focus on the existence of effective competition. Key actions related to re-establishing competitive markets identified in the previous chapter included, most importantly, the separation of conflicts of interest in the areas of audit and banking, the achievement of which is fairly simple to measure.

These would be specific additions to SDG measures relevant and applicable to the UK situation and wherever those conditions apply.

Another key measure of re-establishing competitive markets would include the prevention and break up of monopolistic entities. That will be a fundamental change from the current orientation which encourages their creation by restricting the resources available to their monitoring, restriction and control.

The SDG measures include some of the technological–revolutionary provision for ecological and social sustainability based on measures of imminent and forthcoming destructions. They also note the need to change the nature and timing of required actions. Monitoring the level of resourcing of regulatory bodies will be a key measure of the success in remaking the real economy across the globe.

GDP metrics for all their inadequacies, inaccuracies and irrelevancies have the great virtue of apparent simplicity. An index based on a combination of SDGs with amendments according to national situations could also be created, and would provide an equally simple measure without the inaccuracy and irrelevance. Such an index would need to be created by the relevant international bodies with the SDG data to hand.

Democratic protection and renewal

The democratic principle, 'government of the people, by the people for the people', was the foundation of those commitments outlined in Chapter 4 aimed at, as previously, delivering the essential ecological protections to ensure the sustainability of life on Earth plus the necessaries for making that life worthwhile: universal human rights, equal opportunities for all together with some social balance. Roosevelt was fearful of the threat to democratic government posed by organised money. And he was right to be so.

Those threats have only increased since 1935, but democracy has been largely maintained in Anglo-America and most of the leading nation states, until now. Those threats include the out of control new technology social media, which is free to promote fake news and false rumours, both for short-term financial gain, and to rig elections.

Neoclassical belief challenges democracy with the alternative of government of the people, by organised money, for organised money. And a significant proportion of 21st century politicians profess that neoclassical belief which serves their own short-term self-interests. Their main skills appear to be in self-promotion and capturing sound bites in the media, especially social media, rather than the application of any knowledge and understanding to resolving the real problems the world faces.

Today's short-term politicians, largely paid for by lobbyists funded by financialised corporations, can do enormous damage. It is therefore important that democracy is subject to effective checks and balances to limit the disruptive waste that such politicians can wreak during their period of power.

Democracy is currently threatened as never before by that lack of effective checks and balances. When the US or UK agrees a course of action with foreign powers, it is no longer clear whether, in effect, it is a personal deal with that political leader, or whether it is one between nation states that will necessarily be respected by future governments.[21]

The state needs to rebuild its own expertise and competences into an effective permanent civil service with civil law that stands above party politics. That should be a permanent constitutional requirement, not a political option subject to destruction by the politicians of the moment. The civil service and the law should be required to provide a brief annual report to parliament providing an assessment of the effectiveness of such constitutional checks and balances.

Organised money restraint

The various constituents of organised money have the power to influence, if not control, governments. The only way that power has in the past been restrained is by mass violent revolt. In the short term at least, such restraint may therefore resolve into an option for organised money constituents themselves. If it is achieved in time, it will be by self-restraint.

The requirement is for the organised money constituents to recognise the realities of what they are doing and where they are heading the world and to make a Carnegie-like change of direction, from exploitation to philanthropy.

Membership of organised money has always been ambiguous, so the first step must be to identify the criminal and quasi-criminal activities and individuals, and remove them.

The original existential purpose of the financial sector was to assist and support the real economy. Today, that would include, most important of all, the support of ecological sustainability by investing in positive activities and closing activities which are having negative impacts.

Milton Friedman admitted to being disappointed with the results of lowered flat rate taxation which he had long advocated. He had anticipated the reduced levels of taxes would reduce the pursuit of tax avoidance, but the reverse had been experienced. An increasing amount of the tax saved was invested in the investigation of ever more cunning forms of tax avoidance provided by professional specialists.[22] Friedman had underestimated the power of neoclassical belief which taught that not seeking to avoid taxes would be irrational. A more philanthropic organised money would sympathise with Friedman's error and accept the necessity of progressive taxation of income, wealth and inheritance, as well as the need for properly resourced regulators to ensure the reduction and elimination of tax avoidance and evasion, and the detection and punishment of the latter.

Measures of organised money restraint would centre round the monitoring of progressive rates of taxation, subsidising the development and diffusion of green technology such as renewable energy, increasing tariffs on polluting technology and the sufficient resourcing of regulators.

Neoclassical belief displacement

This is the most important issue of all. Neoclassical belief is the cancer which is corrupting government by organised money and has to be removed. It is the prime cause of all the ills that government has contributed. Its permanent removal is an essential to human survival, not simply part of a political swing that might at some stage be reversed.

Neoclassical theorists and belief developers and promoters must become part of economic history. That can only be achieved by the academy itself. Measures of its displacement should include an ongoing assessment of relevant curricula content in business schools, university departments and advanced level school curricula.

A revised agenda: corporate purpose beyond profit?

We appear to have the capability to develop and establish permanent sustainability. But as corruptible human beings, we are by no means all committed to its achievement. Setting aside the criminally intent, we are divided between, on the one hand, the neoclassically inspired, 'ruthlessly hard-driving, ... shareholder-value obsessed, ... business leader'[23] and, on the other, the more enlightened organisational system coordinator, defined by Deming, Juran and colleagues, aimed at value creation and its preservation. Over the past four decades, neoclassical belief has been in the ascendancy, despite all the adverse evidence which observation of real systems has produced.

Now, at last, there appear to be some cracks in the neoclassical orthodoxy. Concern for the wellbeing of all was reconfirmed in 2019 with independent research studies confirming 'there is a strong business case for promoting the wellbeing of workers' and 'there are measurable objective benefits to wellbeing in terms of productivity and firm performance' which derive from 'improved ... customer loyalty, profitability and staff turnover'.[24]

Adam Smith, moral philosopher, had recognised that dichotomy between *wellbeing* and *ruthless hard-driving* with his observations of the pin factory and advocacy of compensating the 'mental mutilation' of workers with their free education. While ruthless hard-driving is simply counter-productive, the focus on wellbeing has been justified by both moral philosophy and real business. Those realities are again beginning to gain traction.

The Economist reviewed Appelbaum's book *The Economist's Hour*[25] under the heading 'When economists ruled the world',[26] referring to when 'charismatic intellectuals such as Milton Friedman ... spotted the chance to nudge history in their preferred direction'. For 50 years the Friedmanites held the ear of politicians, but their 'period of triumph ended in a fog of financial crisis, economic conflict and resurgent nationalism'. *The Economist* referred also to the neoclassically supportive legal scholar Richard Posner 'who promoted the notion that justice in the law meant no more and no less than economic efficiency', which contradicted anti-trust, 'allowing decades of corporate concentration and increasing market power'.

Appelbaum placed 'economists at the centre of the story, but they were often mere accomplices to a broader movement of conservatives determined to reverse the encroachment of the state'. He describes 'the easy ascent of a few ideas that appealed to the wealthy and powerful' and concludes that the 'end of the economist's hour has created room within the field for views that long struggled to get a hearing'.[27]

Further evidence of that shift in thinking was offered by the *Financial Times* which asserted it was time to 'reset' capitalism with 'A New Agenda'.[28] Tett raised the question whether capitalism was entering 'a new dawn', asserting that 'For decades shareholder interests have dominated the boardroom. Now bosses are busily promoting the idea of a purpose beyond profit.'[29]

US chief executives had issued a collective statement on the purpose of the corporation, abandoning their long adherence to shareholder primacy. Organised by former shareholder primacy advocates, the Business Roundtable,[30] under the leadership of Jamie Dimon, had pledged 'a fundamental commitment to all our stakeholders', with prime concerns for employees and communities. That is Dimon, CEO of JP Morgan, referred to in this text in the fraud and criminality section of Chapter 3. Dimon is now a leading light of Chief Executives for Corporate Purpose (CECP), 'a CEO-led coalition that believes that a company's social strategy—how it engages with key stakeholders including employees, communities, investors, and customers—determines company success'.[31]

The CECP website reports that

> it has grown to a movement of more than 200 of the world's largest companies that represent $6.6 trillion in revenues, $21.2 billion in social investment, 14 million employees, 23 million hours of employee engagement, and $15 trillion in assets under management. CECP helps companies transform their social strategy by providing customized connections and networking, counsel and support, benchmarking and trends, and awareness building and recognition.

That is the CECP website. But is it for real? Similar confusion is created by philanthropic acts, which may seem magnanimous to the population at large, but which may be trivial for the individual donor.

So, is CECP just window dressing by the robber barons to cover their own personal extraction of value? That fundamental question should be asked of all the extractors of value. The truth is difficult to establish at this phase of change. Do they continue to extract value unabated for themselves? Or do they accept some approximation to Drucker's suggestion that they should limit their pay to no more than 20 times the average pay in their organisation?

Would they support Adam Smith's progressive taxation of income and wealth? Or do they continue to support the total misrepresentation of Smith's position by the neoclassical didacts?

Do they condemn the evasion and avoidance provided by the offshore network of tax havens? Or do they continue to support those havens and avail themselves of their benefits?

The Economist, Financial Times, Business Roundtable, CECP and others appear enlightened in terms of, at least, acknowledging stakeholder and ecological responsibilities. But their true intentions remain unclear, while progression without destruction is becoming ever more urgent.

Conclusions

The grossest of inequalities by the conspicuous consumers and wasters for doing very little good, clearly breeds the 'hatred and contempt' Drucker referred to. But the inequalities are now many times more extreme than in Drucker's day and are continuing to increase. We are also very much more aware of the ecological destructions we are wreaking on planet Earth than we were only three decades ago when Drucker wrote of 'Post Capitalist Society'. Yet we continue to destroy.

Today's population confronts challenges never before confronted in the 195,000 years of human existence. The opportunities are there for constituents of organised money to act not just philanthropically but as the all-time heroic saviours of mankind and planet Earth. Or they can opt to continue their destructions.

The universe and all that is in it is a super-macro-system of some kind. As such, it must, according to Deming et al, have an existential purpose. That notion appears to have invaded the consciousness of man from very early times. According to human imagination, this world with all its wonders must have some deep explanation as to the reason for its existence. Various philosophical and faith-based explanations developed, which also asserted the necessary values that all people be required to live by. In general, those values were benign, except when in opposition to alternative value sets.

The systems explanation accepts that such purpose is beyond our calculation, but recognises the basic human motivations to survive, and to interact positively with fellow humans, and to achieve. That simple hierarchy of needs can take account of the developing knowledge and understanding of our world and its increasingly apparent frailties.

Achievement is available in many different forms. The creative application of all the sciences, arts and humanities are forms of achievement, as are generosity and kindness aimed at contributing to making the world a better place for all species including fellow humans. But the pursuit and application of knowledge and understanding in order to aid survival on planet Earth is perhaps the most fundamental and valuable focus for satisfying the need for achievement.

Without the overall guidance of philosophy or faith, it is perhaps not surprising that human individuals might become increasingly amoral or immoral, in pursuit of their own self-interest, a condition encouraged and justified by values-free neoclassical explanation and belief.

The constituents of organised money may be able to extract value for their own personal gain, and they may be enabled to evade and avoid their due contribution to the common good. But they cannot escape the fundamental need to make survival, for themselves and their progeny, the greatest achievement of all.

The IPCC makes it clear that to ensure survival we will need to keep temperature rises below the 1.5°C global warming threshold. That will require the halving of global emissions in the next 10 years and getting to net-zero carbon emissions by 2050.[32]

Klein argues that it is not impossible, but that we will have to achieve radical change if we are to succeed. Roosevelt's New Deal demonstrated the revolutionary change that could be achieved over a decade:

> More than 10 million people were directly employed by the government; most of rural America got electricity for the first time; hundreds of thousands of new buildings and structures were built; 2.3 billion trees were planted; 800 new state parks were developed; and hundreds of thousands of public works of art were created.[33]

Today, with our hugely faster and globalised technologies we could achieve far more. Headed in the right direction, the Green New Deal could achieve the necessary social and ecological changes. At last there is some mounting pressure for the displacement and despatch to history of the neoclassical economic belief which is obstructing satisfaction of the need to survive.

We know where we are. We know where we want to be. We also know how to get there. The people with the power to achieve change need to act. If they do, they will go down in history as the all-time heroes of the human species. If they continue to maximise their own extraction of value from the system, they will rightly be condemned by all other members of mankind, as the arch criminals of all time, for as long as our species survives.

Practitioner notes on real organisational systems

The following are notes of practitioner experience in real organisational systems as they create or extract value. It refers to a 40-year period from the mid-1960s. That may seem like ancient history, but human beings don't change much, and the understanding outlined is far more relevant to today's much changed world than the 19th century neoclassical theorising on which so much present-day decision making is still based. Specific references to issues especially relevant to remaking the real economy and escaping destruction by organised money are *italicised*. The notes outline the basis for economic understanding on which this text is based. It is the alternative to the maths-based theoretical models that even Friedman accepted were not realistic. The lessons drawn are all explanatory and supportive of the main text analysis.

   I Royal Air Force
  II Management trainee
 III Billposting
  IV Site getting, space selling and accounts
   V Management education
  VI Junior management practice
 VII Introduction to manufacturing
VIII Personnel matters
  IX Production control and buying
   X Work measurement and standard costing
  XI Payment systems
 XII Quality control
XIII Reflections on manufacturing
 XIV Retail and distribution
  XV Organising for growth
 XVI Standard product range
XVII Centralised warehouse and the travelling salesman
XVIII Corporate planning
 XIX Mergers and acquisitions
  XX Management sciences
 XXI A financialised business
XXII The asset stripping game
XXIII A further step to corruption

XXIV Joining a 'blue chip' corporate
  XXV Company planning specialist
  XXVI Boston box for real
  XXVII The view from corporate headquarters
XXVIII A company in context
  XXIX Personnel and industrial relations
   XXX The Bullock Report
  XXXI Preparing for M&A
 XXXII Inputs from the City of London
XXXIII Researching industrial innovation
XXXIV Joining academia
 XXXV The academic industry
XXXVI Practitioner conclusions

I Royal Air Force

Experience in the Royal Air Force (RAF), based mostly in Aden, supervising the loading and unloading of aircraft, demonstrated the interdependence of organisational roles of all people.

The real work was done by a local labour force. The RAF role was to make sure the freight loads were distributed on aircraft so they could both take off and land safely. It was a simple enough task. For most aircraft, around two thirds of the payload should be located in the front third of the load space with the rest distributed down the length of the plane, gradually reducing towards the tail. There were some technicalities in preparing an accurate trim sheet which carried the detailed calculations of weight distribution both taking off with full fuel tanks and landing at the end of flight, portraying them geometrically. The approximate weight distribution, outlined previously, appeared to work OK for most freighter aircraft.

The loaders were mostly of Yemeni origin with some from Somalia. Though poverty stricken by UK standards, they were intelligent people and fun to work with. One of their favourite tricks, which invariably shocked RAF personnel, was stamping out cigarette ends with their bare feet, an achievement only attainable by those who had never worn shoes or socks.

They understood perfectly well how to load aircraft. They would spread the load properly without supervision, but if treated without respect, they might misload the aircraft and cause their supervisor the greatest trouble, having to unload and reload the plane, possibly necessitating its flight to be rescheduled with potentially serious consequences, at least for the supervisor.

That experience demonstrated the very *real interdependence of all people, working together within organisational systems*, no matter how apparently unequal they might appear to be. That interdependence is fundamental to system operation and to human life.

II Management trainee

Mills & Rockleys Ltd (M&R), then the leading UK outdoor advertising contractor, operated a management trainee scheme which lasted a full year on an extremely modest salary gaining experience in most of the company's operations, culminating in three separate week-long courses at Ashridge Management College.[1]

Trainees were also encouraged and funded to take the necessary qualifications for membership of the Institute of Practitioners in Advertising.[2] IPA members were mostly advertising agency staff, rather than people working with media companies, but the latter gained from the additional understanding of their media's role in the broader context of advertising and commerce generally.

The traineeship offer, and its acceptance, were clearly a declaration of some commitment on both sides, with the presumed intention of longer-term employment with the company.

Billposting was a form of advertising that had been around for thousands of years but is still a powerful and cost effective medium. Typically placed around high traffic areas (both automotive and foot traffic), posters had many advantages over other media as to their cost, effectiveness and longevity. However, they had to be a quick read and were not good for providing detailed information. Their most important role was in increasing brand awareness as part of national campaigns, which is still true in the 21st century. Though the outdoor medium has developed new digital formats, panels still carry paper and paste posters.[3]

I reported to the manager of the Derby branch that first morning, and he explained the intention was that I would work with that branch for three months, getting to know all that was carried out by the branch office, and including the posting of bills. *If I didn't really understand all the work being done, how could I expect to manage it effectively!* I was reminded of that many times noting the damages caused by initiatives imposed by uncomprehending controllers and politicians.

III Billposting

The first task I was introduced to was mixing the paste under close supervision. Then after a couple of days, I was promoted to poster folding and quickly learned how crucial it was to fold bills in the appropriate order. A billposter, at the top of his ladder (a woman would be unlikely to be so rash as to take this job on), needs to retrieve the next folded sheet of paper from his bag, confident it is the right one to be posted next on the billboard.

After three days of poster folding, I was promoted to billposting itself.

A billposter's day starts by being issued with the day's duly folded posters. The job is to post these on the round of billboards for which the billposter is responsible. The skill of the job is to post the bills accurately, without gaps or undue overlaps, so that the various component sheets connect with precision to form the whole. The poster sheets are thoroughly wetted in the paste so that as they dry out on the billboard, they naturally shrink leaving no bubbles or voids. In their wetted condition, the poster sheets can be extremely fragile, requiring the utmost care in their handling. At the top of a ladder and in varying weather conditions, which usually include a certain amount of breeze, ensuring the poster is not damaged requires considerable skill. Ensuring a bill is so posted that it will survive intact for the full 13 weeks of the typical poster ad campaign is serious work requiring real skill.

To issue an appropriate number of bills to each billposter requires some assessment of the workload involved. That work includes travel between sites as well as posting, so the numbers of posters to fill the working day is clearly variable. Assessment of such workloads is not a clinically accurate process, so the way of accommodating the variable inaccuracy was for the billposters, once loaded with their day's work, to drive their vans to Joe's café for a morning cup of tea. Typically, this would last for around half an hour each morning. If it looked to any one billposter that their day was going to be over busy, they would slip out of Joe's early, or even not appear at all, so they could complete their allotted work. A similar process might occur at the end of the day, for those who finished their workload in time.

So the company was paying up to an hour's wage each day for people to spend in a café. Apart from that relaxation, I discovered that people actually worked hard to fulfil their workload through the rest of the day, and did so *completely without supervision*. The arrangement was apparently known about and accepted by the branch manager, though so far as I knew it was not the subject of any formal acknowledgement or agreement. It was *a system that seemed to work on the basis of some trust on both sides.*

The Derby area was divided into five routes, each being the responsibility of an experienced billposter, some with apprentice mates. The poster sites on each route were numbered and categorised by price. The allocation of poster campaigns to each site was a branch responsibility, very often in consultation with a representative of the advertising agency who booked the campaign. A large proportion of posters were silk screen printed by M&R's own subsidiary, which was one of the leading UK poster printers.

All sites would be inspected every few weeks by branch sales staff, occasionally accompanied by an ad agency rep. Following inspection, a report would be submitted providing an overview of the condition of posters on the round and giving details of any damages requiring rectification. That would be expensive, requiring a replacement poster as well as the cost of time and transportation. *The quality of a billposter's work*, minimising the need for rectification, therefore contributed much to the viability of the branch operation, as well as being *a matter of some personal satisfaction for the billposter.*

One of my billposting experiences was posting a 16-sheet poster at the top of a ladder some 10 metres up on the side of the old Hippodrome Theatre in Green Lane. The bottom of the ladder was on the edge of a very narrow pavement so that at the top of the ladder, it was more or less vertical. This gave me many nightmares, waking up in the middle of the night imagining I was falling backwards off the ladder.

Reflecting on the value of all that experience, I appreciated it provided a *detailed understanding of the work involved and the people doing it.* The various jobs were not technically sophisticated, but did require some physical dexterity and skill, as well as occasionally some personal courage. They did not lend themselves readily to automation.

The gains from that extremely primitive experience were worthwhile. *Understanding the work being done and the people doing it meant that managers were able to be flexible and collaborative with work and workers*, no matter what improbable circumstances occurred. All the individuals involved understood the purpose of the M&R branch and their role in it. That existential system purpose seemed fairly obvious and was never voiced. Billposters were *treated with respect* by the system coordinators as demonstrated by the Joe's café routine.

IV Site getting, space selling and accounts

My next move was to Norwich to spend a couple of months with one of the firm's leading 'site getters'. This role involved the identification of potential poster sites which would be economically viable. That meant that they would be clearly visible for a sufficient traffic and long lasting to make their erection worthwhile. They would also need to be negotiated for a rent at which a sufficient surplus might reasonably be expected.

Having identified the potential site, the site getter role also included identifying the relevant landlord and negotiating the erection of the advertising boards at an economic rent, and getting planning permission for their erection.

The Norwich branch was responsible for Norfolk, Suffolk and Cambridgeshire, which involved high mileage driving around that area, getting to know people in local government planning departments and understanding their basic disposition regarding the different areas covered. It also required a full understanding of the planning regulations and their processes, as well as being wholly aware of proposed building developments in the area and getting to know the relevant people in the developing companies. The site getter had to be a personable, intelligent individual but not necessarily possessed of any particular skill set.

Most outdoor advertising is for national brand promotional campaigns with only a relatively small proportion of space being sold locally. In most cases the best and therefore most expensive advertising sites were occupied by national advertisers and while these typically changed posters every three months, the sites were let on a TC (till countermanded) basis, which enabled only occasional access to top space for local customers.

Nevertheless, local sales were crucial to branch viability. If all available space was sold, then the branch office would be highly profitable. If only 70 per cent was sold then it might be only slightly above break-even. The difference was mostly down to local sales, achieved by developing relationships with leading local advertisers.

Understanding the roles of site getting and local sales, gaining some appreciation of how they could contribute to the viability of branch operations, and the required expertise were significant issues for company success.

My final in-company move as a management trainee was to Head Office where all the processes and different geographical areas were tied together as a coherent whole and the trainees were able to observe, if not participate in, the interactions between the various sub-units and the centre. The main learning was from participation in the Accounts Department where we saw the daily routine of handling incoming orders and their dissemination to the relevant branches, the processing of payments and receipts, the calculation of trading results in terms of profit and cash flow, and the monthly reporting of a set of draft management accounts which included reported profit and loss and cash flow statements. *This role was another essential support function, assessing how well the overall company was fulfilling its purpose of outdoor advertising provision on a sufficiently profitable basis.*

The traineeship year was rounded off with the three courses at Ashridge, dealing with managing people and finance for non-financial managers.

V Management education

The finance courses at Ashridge focused on reading and understanding balance sheets and profit and loss accounts, being made aware of the crucial difference between cash flow and profit and its critical importance as a business expanded, with profit growing but cash surpluses being consumed by the growth.

The programme on people management was focused on the *motivations of people at work* and introduced me to Maslow's hierarchy of human needs from survival to self-actualisation, the motive to achieve one's full potential. We also learned of Herzberg's motivation-hygiene theory, which introduced the persuasive concept of factors that might be demotivators.

These courses were interesting introductions to management theory which emphasised the importance of human relations between the various human components of an organisation. The most memorable item of the Ashridge experience was a keynote lecture by Dr Christopher Macrae, Principal of the College, arguing that *the continuous pursuit of ever increasing profit, risked corrupting people into behaviour which was unethical, if not illegal.* Such behaviour might have a short-term reward, but in the long term it would inevitably lead to corporate damage. Every *lasting business needs to be trusted by all the parties with which it interacts.* That was the message from the then Principal of Ashridge, who further argued that therefore *management must act at all times with complete integrity. Integrity was more powerful than money. Sufficient cash might ensure short-term survival, but absolute integrity was essential to long-term progression.*

VI Junior management practice

My next appointment within the company was to be assistant area manager of the Yorkshire region, centred on Hull, with sub-offices in Scarborough, Doncaster and Pontefract. That new role seemed really to be a continuation of the trainee experience, though the salary was now livable. It involved regular inspection and reporting on the different poster sites around the Yorkshire region, responsibility for the preparation of the monthly branch management accounts and their reporting. Plus, in any absence of the branch manager, the assistant manager agreed such pragmatic decisions as might be required from time to time.

I also had direct responsibility for the Pontefract and Doncaster sub-branches, some peripheral engagement in the site getting and sales functions as well as continuing to serve the wider Hull branch functions. They were all roles I understood thanks to the trainee experience.

I continued in this role gradually establishing some competence in the various tasks involved. Then, quite out of the blue, I received a telephone call from Head Office requesting me to make a temporary change in job and help sort out a mess that had been made with Mills & Rockleys (Electronics) Ltd. The business had outgrown its original base in Coventry and had moved to a brand new factory on the Gillibrands Industrial Estate at Skelmersdale. Would I therefore get myself over to Skelmersdale forthwith and liaise with Don Phillips the managing director and Jack Clyde, a parent board director who had special responsibilities for the electronics operation?

VII Introduction to manufacturing

The move into electronics – silk screen printed circuits – was a natural development for M&R from its silk screen printing of posters. A circuit of electrically conductive tracks, pads and other features was printed with acid resisting ink onto copper clad laminated insulation board. The unprinted copper is then etched away leaving the printed circuit which was then cleaned by removal of the acid resisting ink. Holes were then drilled through the centre of the pads so that electronic components could be mounted on the board and soldered in place.

For high volume production, a custom designed machine tool replaced the drilling. Then the circuit profile cutting and drilling was performed at a single stroke of a power press at the beginning of the production process. Similar mass production methods streamlined the various other processes including mounting and soldering of components. Mass demand for such circuitry was then exploding with obvious benefits in production costs.

M&R clearly had the potential for large scale production but designing the most efficient circuitry to achieve a given task was a severely complicating factor. M&R had fortuitously come together with Don Philips, who had the required genius for seeing a physical piece of electrical kit and being able, intuitively it seemed, to draw the relevant printed circuit diagram. His circuits invariably worked and were efficient in their use of copper clad laminate.

Mills & Rockleys (Electronics) Ltd (M&RE) had been set up as a separate subsidiary company in small premises with limited production facilities but had succeeded in gaining a number of prestigious production contracts, demonstrating the potential for major and rapid growth. The decision was taken to establish a new, purpose built and equipped factory. Skelmersdale had been chosen as the location because of the government support for investment then available in the form of Regional Development Grants.

The small scale Coventry plant was moved to Skelmersdale, with a dozen of its key employees. However, the entire shop floor staff had to be recruited locally. This was a problem since Skelmersdale New Town was opening a number of new factories on its industrial estates and while new town housing development was also progressing, synchronising the two developments was far from perfect.

There were also problems with the control of raw materials purchase and storage as well as their issue onto the shop floor and control of their production and delivery. This array of initial problems prompted the decision to seek some assistance from elsewhere in the company and hence the request for me, temporarily, to join Electronics. I quickly realised that *management experience in outdoor advertising was no foundation for management in Electronics.*

VIII Personnel matters

My first role was in the area of personnel and initially involved travelling to neighbouring populations, carrying out multiple interviews for shop floor operatives who were mainly female. The jobs on offer, for which training was provided, were to fill the various roles progressing circuits round the plant, from printing, to etching, drilling, eyeletting and soldering components, plus inspection and recording as batches of work progressed through production.

It took several weeks to recruit a full shop floor. During that initial phase, I was the de facto personnel manager. One of my earliest experiences was to take an interview with a group of women who were working in the etching section. That entailed loading and unloading racks of printed boards into a large temperature-controlled bath of bubbling trichloroethylene which etched off the unprinted copper. It was an evil liquid apparently, since replaced by less noxious stuff. The women's role was to lower the racks into the bath of trike, accurately time their period of submersion in accord with the thickness of the circuit copper, remove the racks of circuits from the bath, drain and clean off the circuit boards.

The trike bath did have powerful extraction above it, so fumes did not escape into the workstation atmosphere. But the work did inevitably involve close encounters with noxious emissions.

Jack Clyde, formerly a senior partner with management consultants Urwick Orr, parent board director with special responsibilities for M&RE, asked if he might observe the requested interview. To this end he sat at the back of the interview room when the women entered. Their issue was, it turned out, a claim for 'dirty money', since this group were the only people on the entire shop floor required to work so close to such conditions. Their claim seemed not to be unreasonable, but could clearly lead to a never-ending series of claims for the special conditions applying to any particular workstation. It would be important not to start those other hares running by agreeing compensation for those on the etching workstation. It was agreed the effectiveness of the extraction system would be checked at regular intervals, but that 'dirty money' would not be paid. Industrial relations at Electronics remained harmonious – *another example of the interdependence of people in organisational systems.*

IX Production control and buying

After the first few weeks at Skelmersdale, I was asked to remain on a longer-term basis with the Electronics operation, which I was keen to do. I was then assigned to work in buying and raw materials control.

When a customer order was received, its content in terms of base raw materials, copper clad laminate, components and other items, was identified and ordered from the manufacturers. The order was acknowledged, and a delivery date confirmed. When the items were received, an inefficient process was initiated, involving, for the larger orders, breaking it down into separate batches of work, each with a job sheet identifying the customer and order, plus the details of the work to be done to complete the order. Then all batches were issued onto the shop floor to join the queue of work at the first workstation. It was not a systems approach to that process.

The choice of jobs to be done at that first workstation was in effect down to the supervisor concerned, though they would work loosely according to date of order receipt. One of the roles on the shop floor was referred to as 'progress chaser', whose telephone number was quoted to all customers and who would be their first contact should they wish to chase up the progress of their order and its estimated delivery date. The progress chaser was frequently in discussion with section supervisors to persuade them to work on a particular batch of work, the delivery of which had been promised to anxious customers. The progress chaser's job was, in effect, to correct systems failures.

Over time, this process resulted in backlogs of work being established at most workstations. This had two unfortunate results. First, it produced an excessive amount of work in progress tied up on the shop floor, representing a lot of money doing nothing. Second, that weight of work in progress made it more difficult to maintain control of customers' orders and to be able to reliably schedule delivery dates. In turn, that made the progress chaser's role more important to customers and at the same time less effective on the shop floor.

It was corrected by implementing *a proper system of production control* achieved under Jack Clyde's guidance. I spent some months recording the progress of all work through the plant, producing rough estimates of the production capacity of each of the ten main workstations, and an equally rough estimate of the time taken at each station for the main categories of work.

These rough estimates were sufficient to suggest that an efficient use of resources could be achieved with just two weeks of work in progress on the shop floor, as opposed to the then actual shop floor load which was over three months of work. By focusing on that reduced load, it was relatively simple to make a huge improvement in the control of work completion and delivery. At the same time the money tied up in work in progress on the shop floor would be reduced by around 80 per cent.

So one weekend was spent marking all the job sheets of work batches actually on the shop floor, 20 per cent to be worked on, and 80 per cent to be set aside. We had briefed all section supervisors about the change and explained why it was happening.

I was surprised, that Monday morning, when supervisors no longer had a choice as to what they should work on, how smoothly the change went. They clearly appreciated the common sense of the change being implemented. Subsequently there were occasional blips when a workstation ran out of scheduled work, but they were normally simple to resolve. The reduction in shop floor workload took some time to work through the system, but in due course, work in progress was reduced to around 20 per cent of the former level and customers were clearly satisfied with the much greater accuracy of delivery promises and the apparent speeding up of order processing.

Another gain from the new system was that circuits could be combined so as to make the usage of copper clad laminate more efficient. Circuits came in a wide variety of shapes and sizes whereas laminate was a standard size, around 60 × 100 cm. By carefully fitting jobs together on a standard sheet, the off-cut waste could be minimised, an advantage that was rarely realised with the former disorganisation.

The main lessons from this experience were *the value of system analysis and its potential for achieving effective change. Also it was clear how costly external interventions could be if made by those without understanding of the systems involved.*

X Work measurement and standard costing

All those changes were based on rough estimates of workloads and the work content of different jobs. The next step was to make those rough estimates more reliably accurate. That required measurement of the work involved. I was therefore trained in a simple system of work measurement known as Primary Standard Data (PSD), a version of MTM (Methods–Time Measurement), developed by Fred Neale of Urwick Orr.

Neale spent a day at the factory and introduced a consultant who worked on site for several weeks, measuring, and teaching me how to measure the operations of the first four workstations. The system involved studying the work movements involved in the different jobs in a workstation. It was important to study an individual who was experienced in the particular role and from that experience had naturally developed the most efficient ways of doing the job. Across the whole of the shop floor, that experience-based expertise was crucial to the viability of the production process.

I completed the work measurement for the rest of the workstations, subject to occasional visits from Urwick Orr, plus a couple of visits from Neale himself. At that time, according to Clyde, management consultancy in the UK differed from custom and practice in the US. *In the UK, a management consultant would seek to train a client employee in the systems and methods involved in their consultancy assignment and would typically revisit the client unannounced and unpaid, on several subsequent occasions to ensure the assignment had maintained the intended impact, as*

Neale did with me. US practice was, as far as possible, to retain the relevant expertise gained on the assignment within the consultancy. Client personnel were not trained unless it could not be avoided, and consultants only revisited the client on a paid-for basis at the client's request. The American way is now common practice across the globe dominated by the big four consultancies driven by the need to MST.

The PSD based work measures were used as the basis of *a standard costing system, on which a measured day-work payment system was based.* It was also the means of estimating the cost of new jobs and therefore the quotations provided to potential customers. This had previously been a notoriously inaccurate process, resulting in some jobs being taken on which were quoted at prices which were too low to be sufficiently profitable. *The availability of more precise information was a clear system gain.*

XI Payment systems

Measured day-work was a payment system which, though based on work measurement, was not individualised and paid by the piece. Payment was at a regular guaranteed rate for achieving the agreed quantity and quality of work for each workstation, based on the work measurement and the capabilities of the relevant machinery and equipment. Output falling below the agreed standards was paid pro rata, while achievement standard was rewarded with a pro rata bonus. That gave it *the added benefit of being fair, which was a key ingredient in measured day-work, unfairness having been identified as a prime source of worker demotivation.*

Wilfred Brown outlined measured day-work systems in *Piecework Abandoned,*[4] which also provided an evidence-based analysis of the damaging effects of payment by results systems, as quoted in Chapter 5. *Today that knowledge and understanding has been set aside so that bonus payments are applied to top management and highly paid financial sector jobs, even though the results of their work are not accurately measured, or even, in most cases, measurable.*

XII Quality control

The final developments at M&RE with which I had any contact were in quality control. Production had previously depended on final inspection to ensure that appropriate quality was achieved, prior to delivery to customers. It was not unknown for whole batches of finished work to fail to meet the required standard and have to be scrapped. That meant they had to be produced all over again, which was hugely expensive and turned the relevant job into a substantial loss maker.

With external consulting assistance, a proper system of quality control was implemented, based on the work of Deming and Juran. *The essence of the difference in quality control was that instead of inspecting bad quality out at the end of the production process, good quality was built into the process from the beginning.*

At M&RE this was done by replacing final inspection with a system of roving inspection which would assess work at any and all workstations. Continuous quality measures were also set up such as concentricity of a machine tool pressed hole in a printed circuit pad. If it was becoming progressively less accurate, it would be picked up and corrected before going out of tolerance. The result of picking this up at an early stage of production meant that the necessary timely corrective action could be implemented rather than continuing to process already 'scrap' circuit boards. Thus, by building quality in, rather than inspecting it out at the end of the production process, huge savings might be made. As Crosby put it: *'Quality is Free'*.

XIII Reflections on manufacturing

M&RE provided a huge learning experience, gaining some real management practice. It was initially in various processes of manufacturing, but the principles had a much wider application. That *experience in manufacturing was of an organisational system at work which all the trained employees bought into. They understood the basic purpose of M&RE and their own roles in fulfilling that purpose. The organisation provided the essential training to people so as to better fulfil their roles. The idea that the organisational system existed, along with all their personal efforts, simply to earn more money for some far away unknown shareholders would have been wholly destructive and demotivational.* Robotisation of manufacture in many such situations does not change those fundamental considerations. So far, human beings have remained mostly in control.

My next management experience, which was in distribution assisting in the organisation of Mills & Mills Ltd (M&M), another M&R subsidiary, engaged in the retail of office furniture, equipment and stationery.

XIV Retail and distribution

M&M originated as stationery and office equipment retail shop based in Coventry. From there it had grown in the region with three other stationery outlets, but with its main activities in the distribution of office furniture and equipment for which it had a substantial warehouse and a large scale showroom of office and board room furniture and equipment.

The company had acquired two similar businesses, one based in East Anglia with outlets in Norwich and Ipswich and one based in Nottingham with shops, warehouses and showrooms in Leicester and Northampton as well as Nottingham. With these acquisitions, it had become the largest such business in the Midlands and East Anglia.

The main manufacturers of office furniture worked through exclusive distributorships for specific geographic areas. The M&M plan was to expand its geographical coverage, mainly by acquiring other regionally based companies with the same major supplier distributorships. That expansion would provide the opportunity to increase the profitability of the business by achieving scale economies. However, as currently organised, few real savings were being made. With each addition, the company had taken on more warehousing and showrooms as well as shops, with the result that, though it was growing, the business was actually becoming more complex and less efficient.

There was concern that the company's growth plans were not really viable. The obvious need was to streamline and integrate the operations, so that fewer showrooms and warehouses served larger geographic areas. *Such a profitable growth business would, along with M&RE, spread the parent company's range of activities, becoming less dependent on the fortunes of outdoor advertising which was a mature low growth industry.*

I moved to M&M, with *the primary aim of identifying a credible expansion plan which took full advantage of the potential synergies and economies of scale that might be achieved through effective system integration.*

XV Organising for growth

As at M&RE, *the first job was to obtain real information about the business, before thinking about making any definitive changes to its operation.* The focus was primarily on the office furniture and equipment distribution and how its organisation might be streamlined and better integrated with the stationery retail outlets, which were also intended to grow.

The initial idea had been to establish regional showrooms and warehouses and close down the more localised facilities. That would enable some growth to be achieved without the necessary on-cost of a new showroom/warehouse in every town served. It also seemed there might be benefit in promoting a reduced range of furniture that would be stocked and actively promoted. That might have a similar effect as the establishment of the effective production control system at Electronics. It would reduce the required stocks in warehouses and showrooms, just as Electronics work in progress had been reduced.

These ideas seemed plausible but needed to be based on factual information as to what was actually being sold and where. So my first job was to analyze the detail of past sales by checking through sales records, including the geographic point of delivery, approximated by reference to the nearest urban area. These records were intended to be useful when it came to deciding the most effective location for the regional warehouses.

The analysis of sales revealed some interesting data regarding the movement of furniture between depots resulting from customer enquiries. A customer in Nottingham might enquire about a particular item which was not stocked locally but was in stock in, say, Ipswich. If the potential sale was large enough, the item would then be transported to the Nottingham showroom for the customer to inspect. With over 2,000 different furniture items in stock, transportation between depots of customer enquiry items was surprisingly frequent, amounting to a considerable additional cost. Some items appeared to be extremely well travelled. Establishing a reduced range of products would eliminate much of that waste.

During the process of extracting sales data, a more radical plan emerged. Instead of regional warehouses and showrooms, the possibility was conceived of a single central warehouse and to move away from selling furniture and equipment through showrooms to sales by catalogue. The plan was formed also to focus on promoting a much reduced 'standard' range of products which would be featured in the catalogue and offered at significantly discounted prices. The stationery outlets were included in the planned expansion and were to feature a space in each stationery shop allocated to promote catalogued items of furniture and equipment.

The closure of many warehouses and all showrooms would release a considerable sum of money which could be invested in achieving further expansion. That expansion, without the concomitant addition of further warehousing and showrooms, would produce substantial scale improvements in efficiency and profitability.

It was *a plan of system sufficiency and controlled growth and expansion with the emphasis very much on the long term: a very different set of actions than would have resulted from a focus on MST.*

XVI Standard product range

The first thing that had to be done was to identify the product range that would be featured in the catalogue. Furniture was typically manufactured in a number of different wood finishes and colour shades, such as light, medium and dark oak and similar shades of mahogany. It had to be decided what range of finishes would be included in the discounted standard range and therefore kept in stock available for immediate delivery.

The standard product range would be based on estimated sales volumes based on an analysis of sales and trends over the previous three years, plus information about product range changes over that period.

Based on that analysis of these voluminous records, a standard product range was proposed, and after much discussion and negotiation, finally agreed. It was crucial to achieving system efficiency.

Advertising agents were then hired to photograph, design and produce the catalogue promoting the standard range as well as providing details of alternative, non-standard items which could be made available but without the discount and promise of immediate delivery.

XVII Centralised warehouse and the travelling salesman

Deciding the location of the proposed central warehouse was an interesting problem. All other things being equal, the most effective location would be that which minimised the mileage of delivery vehicles. That would depend on what products were delivered to where. Data as to the quantities of product, measured in terms of van loads and destinations, were available from the invoice analysis which had been undertaken.

Jack Clyde had a practical, if approximate, method for identifying the location of such centralised services, based on data regarding invoice values and delivery locations to indicate the most efficient warehouse location in terms of delivery mileage.

Then I heard about a thing called the travelling salesman algorithm, which was apparently used for solving that sort of problem, establishing the shortest route for a salesman to travel round customers in different locations. I was told it was a special case of linear programming.

The Clyde approximation suggested a location a few miles east of Newport Pagnell. It was a methodology that had sufficed for management consultants long before computer maths was available to solve linear programs. It reminded me of other practical approximations I'd experienced such as the loading of

RAF freight aircraft. This whole text is a form of approximation, made in order to provide the alternative systems perspective to provide distinctive insights regarding systems processes and outcomes, rather than being drawn into detailed analysis of individual factors.

Data was provided to a member of a university maths department, which in due course reported back that the travelling salesman algorithm suggested the best location would be a few miles east of Newport Pagnell!

The brush with the travelling salesman algorithm made me very aware of my own lack of theoretical knowledge and qualification. Warwick University was then reputed for its Mathematics Institute and Warwick's School of Industrial and Business Studies was proposing to offer a BSc in Management Sciences. I imagined such a course might be useful. I enquired if the course could be attended on a part-time basis, but that was not available.

XVIII Corporate planning

There had been discussions at M&R regarding the establishment of a corporate planning department which would oversee such issues as the strategic direction of the company's long-term development and its financial planning. Establishing such departments was becoming a fashionable idea among major corporates at that time. *The idea was mooted that I might complete a management sciences degree as a company employee on half salary, working for the company during the vacation periods, and agreeing to return to full-time employment on graduation. It was anticipated I would resume work becoming involved in the corporate planning role. The whole arrangement was offered by word of mouth with no formal agreement. I accepted on a similar basis.*

All that had to be done was to gain the necessary qualifications for university entry and to be accepted by Warwick University as suitable for their Management Sciences degree programme. This was done by gaining acceptable GCE A Level passes in Economics, Economic History and British Constitution plus a satisfactory score on the Princeton Test for graduate study in business. That was the forerunner of today's GMAT test, which its official website indicates as 'the test that's accepted by more than 6,500 graduate business programs worldwide'.[5]

XIX Mergers and acquisitions

While I was still working at M&R, it had been agreed to takeover fellow outdoor advertising contractor, David Allen & Sons Ltd and change its name to Mills & Allen Ltd. M&R was a public limited company, quoted on the London stock exchange. Though the Mills & Allen chief executive was a Mills family member, the Mills family did not have a controlling interest in the company's shares. David Allen & Sons Ltd, which was the second largest UK outdoor advertising contractor, was a family owned business with no public quotation.

M&R seemed a moderately ambitious organisation, motivated to develop by careful steps as with the subsidiaries I had worked with. My experience of the company was entirely positive. They had provided great experience as well as support for employee personal development.

Merging the two businesses could clearly achieve significant savings of overhead and admin costs, as well as simplifying outdoor advertising contract provision for client agencies. At that time there was increasing sensitivity by regulators to the risks of M&As resulting in the monopolistic control of markets.

Although it was M&R that acquired David Allen & Sons and the parent company's board of directors was dominated by those from M&R, the Allen family were the major shareholders with a holding which might readily be extended to over 50 per cent if the need arose. That could protect the company from hostile takeover by any opportunistic asset stripping predator, but it also handed that protection to the Allen family shareholders. It proved a catastrophic mistake for M&R.

XX Management sciences

I joined Warwick's first intake of students on its BSc Management Sciences degree, which listed its main components as macro and microeconomics, statistics, quantitative methods, operations research, behavioural science, organisation theory, accounting, financial analysis, marketing research and business as a system.

Behavioural science and organisation theory covered a lot of ground from its late 19th century classical or structural manifestation led by Henri Fayol, who was CEO of a French coal mining company. He saw the job of management as to forecast and plan, to organise, command, coordinate and control. Forecasting, planning, organising and coordinating, seemed to line up with my experience. The command and control element was presumably resulting from Fayol's era and industry which were fairly ancient history.

The subject area also included some analysis of Fred Taylor's *so-called scientific management, based on his work measurement and studies of work methods at Bethlehem Steel Corporation. My experience with Fred Neale's PSD at Electronics had provided a good introduction to Taylor's work. His stated aim was to organise work to produce the maximum prosperity for the employer and for each employee, which included their development as well as immediate income. The interdependence of all people working in an organisation was fundamental to Taylor's approach. The more recent representation of Taylor as a tool of human exploitation was not included on the programme.*

Behavioural science included Elton Mayo's five-year study of the human impacts of work at Western Electric's Hawthorne Works.[6] Initially this work was aimed at understanding the issues related to labour turnover and how this was related to working conditions, fatigue, accidents and the like. *Mayo's studies uncovered the importance of the informal organisation structure and the social systems affecting cooperation between management and workers. The 'human relations' approach suggested that management succeeds or fails in as much as it is accepted without reservation by the workgroup concerned. This gave the lie to Fayol's command and control approach.*

The human relations approach was further clarified by *Elliott Jacques researching industrial organisation at the Glacier Metal Co which demonstrated that piecework payment and clocking systems, far from optimising production and individual work satisfaction, actually hindered both. Together with the work of Eric Trist and the Tavistock Institute of Human Relations, the mechanistic, top-down, monetary approach to organisation was largely replaced.*

That more enlightened approach to organisation was supported by many empirical studies of human motivation in work situations. *Herzberg identified positively motivating factors, including personal growth in its many forms, and potentially demotivating factors, including pay and payment systems, flagging up two diametrically opposed views of human behaviour in organisations. On the one hand, the top-down, command and control mechanistic approach and, on the other, the work satisfaction, human relations approach, both nicely encapsulated by McGregor's self-fulfilling Theories X and Y, which themselves go some way to explaining the dichotomy between the neoclassical version of capitalism and the social democracy of Roosevelt and Keynes.*

Management sciences also included approaches to corporate strategy which were then emerging. Especially prominent was the approach advocated by the Boston Consulting Group (BCG) which focused on the effects of cumulative business experience on total costs. The two dimensions BCG used for analysing corporate strategy, which became known as the Boston Box. It was a model I was destined to become familiar with and learn to disparage as superficial and very open to abuse and fixing. In *Management: Tasks, Responsibilities and Practices* Peter Drucker wrote that *strategic planning 'is not a box of tricks, or a bundle of techniques' and it is 'not forecasting'. For Drucker it was a creative, systematic approach to entrepreneurial decisions.*

XXI A financialised business

Before the first year at Warwick was complete, Mills & Allen had been taken over. It had been made known to some City financiers that the Allen shareholding was available for purchase. That made the whole company vulnerable to takeover, rather than being protected by the substantial family holding. The possibility of such a deal was communicated to Jim Slater, the high profile CEO of the City takeover specialist, Slater Walker Securities Ltd. Slater Walker passed it on to one of their satellite companies, Barclay Securities, which demonstrated the predatory destructions of the real economy that can readily be inflicted by such financial operations.

Barclay & Sons Ltd had been a long-established wholesale chemist, which for financial purposes had the necessary asset of a stock market quotation. Slater Walker protégé John Bentley acquired Barclay, changed its name to Barclay Securities and financialised its reason for existence. That was the company that, with the Allen shareholding already spoken for, mounted a stock market raid and acquired Mills & Allen.

Bentley had served two years as a City stock analyst and had progressed, with backing from Slater Walker, by the very simple means of exploiting the difference between the market value of corporate assets, notably property (land and buildings), and the book value as recorded in company balance sheets. His particular skill appeared to be checking the saleability and value of assets on company balance sheets.

The acquisition of Mills and Allen was quickly completed. Most members of the Mills & Allen board were fairly quickly disposed of, and within a few weeks of completion, I was interviewed by the new managing director, who explained that for Barclay Securities three weeks was a long time, never mind the three years it took to complete a degree. I was offered the chance of working during the summer vacation in the Bristol branch of Mills & Allen, loading their accounts onto the Barclay Securities' computer systems. My future with the company would then be given due consideration.

I declined the offer and was terminated forthwith. By various means, including living in my new wife's district nurse/midwife's house, and receiving a local authority grant, I was enabled to complete the Management Sciences degree.

XXII The asset stripping game

As well as completing the degree, I was also concerned to learn more about the financial operations of companies like Barclay Securities.

The argument was widely made that companies such as Barclay were important, in order to ensure management of companies such as Mills & Allen maintained efficiency and did not just lapse into mediocrity.

I was not convinced. *My experience with M&R had been demanding, but it had been a terrific learning experience. I had been able to trust the people I had worked for and with. But the media treated the financial sector figures, such as John Bentley, as glamorous, even heroic. It was not till much later that I recognised the media as an important constituent of the organised money establishment, supporting the work of people like Jim Slater and John Bentley. In my experience of them, they were far from glamorous or heroic. So far as I could see, Bentley, driven solely by money, appeared prepared to do any amount of damage, purely for the benefit of his own bank balance.*

I set out to learn more about the activities of companies such as Slater Walker and Barclay Securities and that generation of asset strippers. It was a period of rapid property price inflation which made asset stripping a simple and financially rewarding operation.

Even though a company is well managed and profitable and with no known problem, it may still get into a serious assets position – when the market value of its assets is substantially higher than reported on the balance sheet and reflected in the share price. They may then be vulnerable to the likes of Slater Walker and its satellites.

The process has no positive gain for the overall economy, and generally results in substantial loss in terms of productive capability and employment. Nevertheless, some companies existed then and still exist today for no other purpose than to profit from such opportunistic dealing.

Slater Walker Securities had been set up by chartered accountant Jim Slater and politician Peter Walker and was the prime mover with a number of satellite corporate raiders which identified and attacked companies which appeared vulnerable.

The asset stripping process took advantage of professional accountancy which was committed to certain principles, two of which were prudence and conservatism. That meant that if there were two acceptable alternatives for reporting an item, the accountant should choose the one which indicated the lower income and/or asset value; likely losses were to be anticipated and reported, but potential gains never to be anticipated. The aim, in this uncertain world, was not to mislead potential investors into thinking a position is better than it really is.

In the case of the valuation of fixed assets reported in a company's balance sheet, accountants report the value of, for example, land and buildings, as at the last professional valuation, possibly less some depreciation. During a period of rapidly rising property prices this means the value of property included on company balance sheets will invariably be understated. The extent of that undervaluation will depend on how frequently the assets are revalued.

Professional revaluation is a costly process, so companies were reluctant to undertake it frequently, since it had no benefit for the company operations. The difference between the reported book value of property assets and their current market value could therefore become substantial. An indication of how substantial was provided by knowledge of when they were last revalued, which information was included in notes supporting the published balance sheet. Further evidence might be acquired by knowledge of relevant property values.

Another acquisition by Barclay Securities was Dorland's advertising agency, which owned a property in the City that was scheduled as being of historic interest. Barclay had the property revalued on the basis of its development potential, ignoring its scheduled status. That enabled them to claim a huge surplus on the deal. The initiative for this acquisition came from Slater Walker. Since Walker was the minister responsible for historic buildings, the impression was given that the rules were being ignored for the benefit of his business connections. Certainly, justice was not being seen to be done.

The required skill set for asset strippers such as Slater Walker and its satellites amounted to some diligence in collecting information about potential victim companies and their property values. It was a skill set certainly not as impressive as that required of billposting.

XXIII A further step to corruption

Another Slater Walker satellite, led by Christopher Selmes, was involved in a hostile takeover of Franco Signs, a company which had long associations with M&R. Selmes and colleagues were reported as devising a form of loan stock to raise the necessary funds to complete the takeover. The stock was to pay a relatively low fixed interest return but to be convertible in some proportion into voting and non-voting equity at some time in the future. Selmes had proposed a long and complicated descriptive title for the stock and was challenged by a colleague that people would not understand what it meant. Selmes had agreed. That was the point. *The only thing investors would have to go on was the name of the bidding company and its outstanding growth record so far. There would be no information regarding any specific assets to which the stock was related. Investors would be betting on the company's continued progression and returns to shareholders. It was a simple form of what became known as junk bonds.*

There were many involved in such financialised business, focused on acquisition and asset stripping. They sought to justify their activities by claiming that they turned around underperforming businesses and made them profitable. That was clearly untrue; their effect was more or less entirely negative. The false argument was that, not only was there a positive effect on the acquired business, but also there was a more general positive impact, keeping company managements on their toes, ensuring they made the most of the opportunities open to them.

The means of achieving the 'turn around' was extremely simple and generally involved mass redundancies and business closures. If property prices are rising faster than share prices, asset strippers are in heaven. But their lack of anything more substantial than opportunistic aggression is revealed when the tide turns.

Jim Slater, after his several years as the doyen of financial entrepreneurs (if that isn't a contradiction in terms), bankrupted his company, which was taken over by the Bank of England, reputedly leaving Slater with £2 million of assets and £3 million of debts, declaring himself 'a minus millionaire'.

Bentley's Barclay Securities was taken over by J.H. Vavasseur less than two years after the Mills & Allen acquisition, but in the interim had caused enormous damage. It was surprising to me at the time that there was so little apparent interest in their activities. When Barclay Securities announced they were closing down three factories at Redcar, Erith and Harborne, throwing 750 people out of work, *Bentley was quoted in* The Times *as saying 'the theory of what we are doing is to release half the cash, half the assets and half the number of people employed'. No critique of the 'theory' was offered.*

Selmes was later instrumental in the failure of the Keyser Ullman merchant bank which had, under Edward Du Cann's incompetent chairmanship, lent £17 million to Selmes, secured on a valueless guarantee. Selmes later fled the country, leaving debts of more than £20 million.

These and other financialised businesses prospered and did great damage to the UK's real economy, before being wiped out of existence.

Such hostile takeovers and mergers, based mostly on asset stripping, resulted in increased unemployment, a less equal distribution of income and wealth, reduced overall investment and therefore a negative impact on the economy as a whole. The fruits of stripping were real enough for the individual company. Barclay's profits in the year after acquiring Mills & Allen increased by about 170 per cent over the previous year. The dividend for the year was up 50 per cent. The share price went from a low of 69p to a high of 227p. At the cost of a few hundred jobs, the Barclay chairman and major shareholder had become a multi-millionaire.

The strippers aim was, naturally enough, to gain control of a victim company as cheaply as possible. A widely adopted approach was by a stock market raid, gaining control of a sufficient proportion of shares to enforce the deal before the victim company management had time to mount an effective defence.

Following acquisition, the stripping begins and the half of value that was 'released' found its way ultimately into the shareholders' pockets. The process was a fairly cynical exploitation of the country's resources. Factories which were making a worthwhile contribution to the economy could be closed down merely to satisfy the cash needs of the stripper. These needs were excessive because the stripper was caught in a perpetual cycle of acquire, strip, acquire. Should the process cease or slowdown, the growth momentum would be lost and the company risked sliding into oblivion, which was the inevitable end result.

Victim companies were analyzed in the light of their short-term contribution to group cash flow. Any acquisition requiring substantial investment in the future would not be retained in operation. But the economy depends on substantial long-term investments being made. If every company looked merely to maximise short-term profits, the economy would rapidly grind to a halt. Thus fundamentally, the stripper was riding on the back of the rest of industry; and those companies that made long-term investment would risk exposing themselves to being acquired and stripped.

The basic philosophy had been succinctly stated by Jim Slater: 'We're not interested in making things, but money.' The distinction was between the real economy and the financialised economy – which accommodated the asset strippers. For them, it made no sense to invest £1 million on a project whose return was uncertain but expected to be around 5–10 per cent per annum, when they could acquire a company for the same amount, strip out £0.75 million, and then show a return of 25 per cent or more on the remaining investment. The second choice was almost self-financing and provided funds for the next asset stripping move almost immediately. At this abstracted level, the idea of overall economic and social costs, never mind issues such as environmental stewardship, were totally irrelevant.

Unfortunately, it is still impossible to measure social costs. The psychological damage of unemployment is immeasurable, and people retained in victim companies, such as the Mills and Allen subsidiaries as outlined previously, are also damaged. They previously understood and were engaged with the existential purpose of their employing organisation. Now, suddenly that employing organisation has been transformed into an apparently predatory, quasi-criminal organisation seeking to smash anything in order to maximise shareholder gains. Human motivation of system members is completely lost, and the negative impact of the takeover is further multiplied.

Similar predatory processes still work in 2020, with slightly different technological mechanisms but similar detrimental effects. The silence of the press is not surprising, given they are mostly owned by the organised money that is still the prime beneficiary of that process.

XIV Joining a 'blue chip' corporate

Had I remained with Mills & Allen, it was the intention to set up a corporate planning section. On graduation I was offered a similar role as Company Planning Specialist with TAC Building Materials Limited, TAC standing for Turners Asbestos Cement. It was part of Turner & Newall Ltd, a major UK company, included in the FT30 index.

Never having done a company plan previously, I was looking forward to being a planning specialist. I was curious to know what it would be like joining the Turner & Newall Group (T&N), then a highly regarded 'blue chip' corporate despite its asbestos involvement.

T&N had been formed in the 1920s by the merger of four companies all engaged in the processing of various grades of asbestos, a naturally occurring mineral that was widely applied for its heat resistance, tensile strength and insulating properties. It was used for a wide variety of products from fireproof vests to home and commercial construction, high pressure water pipes and electrical insulation papers. It was woven into fabric, and mixed with cement. The unique mix of characteristics gave asbestos remarkable potential for making things better in many applications.

However, it was a toxic fibre, presenting severe health risks. Some understanding of that problem was known about as early as the 1920s, but it was still not fully understood. Blue asbestos had already been outlawed in Scandinavia and T&N had also ceased using it. The health standards applicable in UK factories and used by the Factory Inspectorate, measured in parts per million of asbestos fibre in the factory atmosphere, were based on T&N's research.

The dangers asbestos posed were only slowly being understood, partly because its toxic effects could take many years of exposure to develop, and then only slowly. But its effects could be catastrophic, causing lung diseases, mesothelioma, cancer and asbestosis.

Bans on the use of asbestos had started to be imposed in the 1970s. Today it is totally banned in more than 50 countries (not including the US), and its use has been dramatically restricted in most others.

TAC's production processes were all wet, including asbestos cement products, insulation board and papers. Being wet processes, they did not produce much asbestos 'dust', and were all therefore relatively safe production processes. Their various applications in building products, pipes, fire protection, and heat and electrical insulation still appeared to justify the carefully controlled production using asbestos fibre. Such denial appears to be a human characteristic currently being applied to the climate crisis.

XXV Company planning specialist

TAC had five factories, the largest being at Trafford Park, Manchester, which also accommodated the Head Office, where I was to be based. Part of my introduction to TAC was to be taken round the factories and shown the various processes in producing corrugated asbestos cement roofing sheet, insulation board, pressure water pipes, high pressure and high temperature gaskets and different grades of insulation papers.

Though there was a general confidence in TAC that the health risks were under control, they nevertheless presented the company with a very real challenge, to reduce reliance on asbestos fibre. That could be achieved both by substituting alternative fibres in existing products and introducing new non-asbestos products. That was the main reason TAC's corporate planning department had been established: to plan the long-term elimination of reliance on asbestos fibre.

The department comprised three sections: New Products Investigation, Market Research and Company Planning. There were three new products investigators, a physicist with some experience of fibrous reinforcement who could provide specialist knowledge to new product and process development, and two chemical engineers with a variety of specialist knowledge including some of paper and board manufacture. There were three market researchers with qualifications and experience in the practicalities of marketing research. I was a section all on my own. We all reported to a head of department who was an economist.

The New Products section spent much time investigating the replication of asbestos cement corrugated sheets with similar profile products but with different fibre reinforcements. They also investigated other construction materials, notably including the acquisition of a calcium silicate brick manufacturer, the appraisal of which was my first of several acquisition proposals I was responsible for assessing and presenting for board approval.

The Market Research section was coordinated with New Products Investigation to produce market assessments of any proposed new developments. *Departmental meetings were held monthly to report and discuss progress on all these projects, as well as to discuss what further initiatives the department should consider proposing to the TAC board of directors. Those departmental meetings were significant reminders of the organisational system within which we worked and a perpetual reminder of the fundamental purpose to which we contributed.*

Those departmental meetings also reviewed TAC's monthly management accounts and how they related to progress with the five-year corporate plan. That was deemed to be my responsibility as Company Planning Specialist. Compared to the very real and important progress with realigning TAC's product portfolio, this review of management accounts seemed of almost trivial significance. The company plan comprised what was really no more than an annual budget projected for five years. It included cash flow and capital expenditure forecasts.

My first experience, soon after arrival at TAC, was with that process of five-year budgeting, generating the whole budget for presentation to the TAC board of directors. The realignment of TAC's product portfolio, though clearly of the greatest importance to the company's long-term future, hardly seemed to figure. The TAC directors' main concerns appeared to be with the credibility and acceptability of their five-year submission to the T&N parent board, which had the job of agreeing a group budget. That was a fully integrated combination of all subsidiary company budgets, parts of which might be made public for the benefit of investors.

My first involvement in preparing a five-year submission was an interesting process. The original draft 'plan' was presented by the Corporate Planning Manager to the TAC board at a Friday board meeting. During their discussion it was decided that the cash flow projections might not be acceptable to the parent board and so would need to be amended. Ways of achieving this were discussed and it was agreed to increase the year-on-year sales revenue growth rates by 1 per cent each year. It was also felt that the levels of capital expenditure might be thought excessive. The proposed capital expenditures were therefore reconsidered at length and it was eventually agreed to postpone a major proposed investment in one of the main asbestos cement replacement products. All of which required the accounts to be recalculated.

In my time at TAC, I became increasingly aware of the tension between the very real and important innovative role of the New Products Investigation and Market Research people and the more politically sensitive role that I had been drafted into as Company Planning Specialist. The plans themselves were more of an in-company political document, identifying what was thought of as likely to be acceptable at the higher level, rather than a real declaration of intent to achieve the strategic aims of developing TAC's business.

XXVI Boston box for real

T&N's Head Office had a small Strategic Planning Department which had hired BCG to advise on the processes of corporate planning for a multi-business company such as T&N. BCG was at that time the leading international consultancy specialising in strategic management. One of the consultants spent a short period at TAC, pretending interest in how we did strategic planning, and later instructed us regarding BCG's approach based simply on assessments of cumulative market share and market growth.

BCG had developed the 'box' of cash based 'strategic' prescriptions as follows:

- Stars (High share of a high growth market): Invest to maintain market share. Keep prices up only reducing them in order to maintain market share.
- Cash Cows (High share of a low growth market): Strictly ration new investments. Keep prices up but ensure no new entrants enter the market.
- Problem Children (Low share of high growth market): Invest to convert into Stars, or withdraw on most advantageous terms by progressively pricing out of the market.
- Dogs (Low share of a low growth market): Manage tightly for cash and withdraw.

By following the prescribed 'strategic' moves, it was intended to achieve a balanced portfolio of businesses with a selection of problem children to groom into stars, an adequate succession of stars ready to take over from today's cash cows and a sufficient level of cash cow business to fund the future.

T&N's original business, including the whole of TAC's products, were almost all mature and low growth. They were therefore designated as either Cash Cows or Dogs, either to be milked or divested. BCG offered little guidance regarding the real strategic problems facing T&N around the asbestos issue.

The framework had been adopted by leading multi-business companies across the globe, providing corporate headquarters the illusion of controlling the strategic development of all their subsidiaries with very little requirement for detailed knowledge and understanding of those businesses. In T&N's case, it was a means of avoiding the real strategic problem.

XXVII The view from corporate headquarters

In due course I moved from TAC to T&N's Head Office where I became involved in the Strategic Planning Department's coordination of the various subsidiary company contributions and knitting them together into a coherent whole which was submitted to the parent board for amendment and approval. My initial role was to liaise with subsidiary companies and tutor them in submitting five-year corporate plans in the required BCG format.

The department also vetted major proposed developments emanating from subsidiary units, and provided an authorised version of the broad economic forecast against which subsidiary company strategic plans should be constructed.

T&N's activities were spread across the globe excepting mainland Europe where it was said agreement had been reached with Eternit, the European asbestos company, not to trespass. In Africa the involvement was primarily asbestos mining in Swaziland, and manufacture in South Africa and Nigeria where one of my first roles at Head Office was to assist subsidiaries with their corporate planning submissions.

T&N's corporate strategy should, obviously, have been to sort out the asbestos problem. Corporate planning should have been focused on the search for a solution to those real inherited problems, but instead carried on regardless, applying the then fashionable management gizmo to pretend adoption of a coherent and relevant strategy. I proposed an alternative way forward, but my plan and I were rejected.

XXVIII A company in context

I was then offered employment as director of administration at Clay Cross (Iron & Foundries Ltd), the main operating arm of the Clay Cross Company (hereafter CXC). It was a business first established by George Stevenson, the railway king, who in digging the rail tunnel under Clay Cross in Derbyshire had discovered deposits of both coal and iron ore and established the company to take advantage of that happy coincidence.

The town of Clay Cross was mostly based around CXC. Its inhabitants were originally the families of company workers in the coal mines, iron foundries, gas works and quarries. Vestiges of that close town and company relationship were still apparent when I joined the company. There was a massive bonfire and firework occasion laid on by the company for employee families each 5 November, and a Christmas party for employees' children, as well as an annual lunch for company pensioners.

Even so, being situated on the Nottinghamshire–Derbyshire coalfield with a historical involvement in its activities and formerly with wide membership of the National Union of Mineworkers, the company had a lively, and sometimes combative, industrial relations culture.

When coal was nationalised after WW2, six coal mines owned by the company were taken over and the compensation was invested in a sand and gravel quarry at Croxden in Staffordshire. It was said to be the largest sand and gravel reserve in the whole of Europe. That was what made CXC attractive to Ready Mixed Concrete Ltd (RMC) of Australia, who had taken it over in the 1970s. RMC had plans to increase their UK operations, which were anticipated to involve some further acquisition activity.

The main activity of the company was the production of ductile iron spun pressure pipes for the gas and water supply industries. Ancillary to the main foundry operations was a small, quarry owned by the company at nearby Milltown. This produced fluorspar which was used as fluxing agent in the iron smelting process, and barytes which, as the North Sea oil industry became established, found its main application as a weighting lubricating agent in deep sea drilling muds.

CXC had around 20 per cent of the UK ductile iron pipe market, 80 per cent being supplied by the Stanton & Staveley Company, part of the nationalised British Steel. CXC involvement maintained an element of competition in the industry, which would perhaps have limited the extent to which British Steel could exploit its market power.

As well as pipes and pipe fittings and junctions, CXC also produced high quality engineering castings. RMC was investing in the latest high pressure moulding technology to enable the production of high quality ductile and spheroidal graphite engineering castings. That enabled the company to diversify its activities into different industries such as automotive.

XXIX Personnel and industrial relations

My responsibilities included accounting, IT and computerisation, buying, personnel and industrial relations. Computerisation of order processing, production control and accounting was being supervised by external consultants based on new integrated software systems accessible by various shop floor stations. It was an innovative approach which sounds sophisticated considering the primitive and expensive hardware then available.

Buying provided some enlightening experiences with the chief buyer reported as having been on the receiving end of various illicit payments from grateful suppliers. He left the company rather abruptly a couple of months before Christmas and I was then deluged with seasonal gifts intended for that individual, which were then raffled off for charity at an employee's Christmas party.

My most interesting responsibility was in personnel and industrial relations. I was first taken round the CXC foundry by Terry Hunt, the personnel manager, and introduced to the various department supervisors and some of the leading union people including the works convenor, who was the top union representative. I was told about the numerous different bonus schemes in existence at the plant, which were used as the basis for periodic disagreement over pay and conditions.

Industrial relations on the Notts-Derbys coalfield were in a sensitive state, which apparently necessitated periodic visits to CXC by people from the 'Special Branch', whatever that was. They came to enquire after the activities of certain named individuals.

Terry Hunt had been a union representative himself and had been funded to do a degree at Ruskin College, Oxford, after which he admitted to having 'turned gamekeeper'. The Ruskin website reports that the college's 'founders understood that education is power ... aimed to provide university-standard education for working class people to empower them to act more effectively on behalf of working class communities and organisations such as trade unions, political parties, co-operative societies and working men's institutes'.[7]

I started *a monthly Communication and Consultation meeting with union reps and shop floor supervisors, to which I presented a monthly management account, showing all the sources of cash coming into the company and all its applications. At that time, it included quite a lot of additional spending on capital projects. Initially, Communication and Consultation appeared to be welcomed and formed the basis of genuine discussion and exchange of views. It was initiated on the basis of a Deming type understanding of the operation of organisational systems. It was unique in CXC, in being a routine formal contact between management and union reps without being centred on some point of disagreement, as was the norm for exchanges between those two parties.*

After a while, however, it appeared to be less welcome to the union people, who stopped expressing any views or interest in the company's progression and development. In the end they made a formal request that I stop providing them with that information. The reason, as explained to me, was that knowledge of such accounting information might have the effect of inhibiting workers when making their case for improved pay and conditions. The information continued to be circulated but was no longer included in the Communication and Consultation meetings.

Because of the sensitive industrial culture across the coal field, people working at CXC were frequently on the verge of disagreement with management. On one occasion, there was a declaration of a 'work to rule' resulting from a patently false claim about some action taken by the works director. A meeting was held with the union reps, the matter was shown to be falsely based and the air was cleared. On the way out of the meeting I asked the works convenor what it had been all about, since he knew the allegation was false. His answer was one word: 'politics'.

It was an interesting confirmation of the politicising of relationships within organisational systems.

XXX The Bullock Report

The 1970s had been a period when politics-driven industrial relations was causing much damage to UK industry – the real economy. The Labour government established an enquiry into industrial democracy in 1975, as an attempt to harmonise worker participation in company management.

The resulting Bullock Report of 1977 recommended that companies employing 2000 or more people should have employee representatives on the board of directors. The proposal was that the number of directors representing employees should equal the number representing shareholder interests. A third group of co-opted directors must not exceed the number of employee or shareholder directors. Representation was to be on the existing British unitary board system, with no two-tier boards. Employee directors were to be chosen solely through trade union machinery, with only unionised employees influencing the choice of employee directors. That was to operate exclusively through a Joint Representation Committee, representing the unions in the company, and not directly representing all employees whether union members or not.

The Bullock Report met with a mixed response. One view from the employers' perspective argued that the more people were able to influence decisions which closely affect their work, the greater their commitment to the company's objectives, which would ultimately benefit the community as a whole. That was getting close to a systems analysis of the situation, a point frequently made in interviews with the media.

Direct participation was nevertheless rejected by members of the Confederation of British Industry (CBI), who recommended employee directors, not union representatives, should serve on a supervisory board of a two-tier system, rather than on a unitary board. They also proclaimed shareholders as the 'owners' of companies who should retain the ultimate authority and control in general meeting.

Ironically, the unions also found the Bullock recommendations problematic. As with the CXC Communication and Consultation meetings, they had been opposed to having any involvement with company management. Their representatives should be accountable solely to union members on whose behalf they conducted 'free collective bargaining'. Anything which might compromise or weaken the collective bargaining strength of the unions was to be rejected. In the end it was the unions themselves that turned down the proposals for industrial democracy in Britain. *Bullock was consigned to history.*

It was an opportunity missed for the UK to achieve some degree of industrial democracy which could have provided defence against the abuse of industry by the predatory finance sector, such as Slater Walker, Barclay Securities and their 21st century successors.

Employee representation on the supervisory board of a two-tier system has been required by German law since 1870. The two-tier system establishes a management board with responsibility for day-to-day running of the enterprise, and the supervisory board with various legally defined responsibilities including the appointment of management board members, approving their remuneration and sometime dismissal, as well as major strategic decisions, notably including those involving M&A.

Implementing the Bullock recommendations could have provided these various protections for real UK business against the predatory financial sector.

XXXI Preparing for M&A

M&A activity is a global phenomenon and while I was at CXC, the joint venture partners who owned RMC of Australia decided to split up. They therefore agreed to divide the RMC assets between them and CXC became a wholly owned subsidiary of Blue Metal Industries. The new owners took a different view of their UK holdings. As a consequence, the Croxden Gravel business was to be put up for sale.

I was to prepare the sale document for the disposal of Croxden Gravel. It was to be presented to N M Rothschild & Sons, merchant bank, who would be handling the sale.

The value of the business would depend on a number of factors. The published accounts were obviously an important part of the sale document, providing details of the assets included in the sale. The book value of the company's assets was one input to its valuation, though a view had to be taken as to how that last professional valuation differed from the current market value. The history of Croxden's profits and cash flows were used as the basis for five-year projected accounts, with suitable supporting explanations and justification. So much was fairly straightforward. From those projections, and taking account of quoted companies in the sand and gravel quarrying business, it was possible to forecast a likely valuation that might be achievable for the business sale.

The ratio of share price to earnings which generally applied in the sector could be applied to Croxden's earnings. The share price thus derived, plus the typical premium over normal quoted prices when a sector takeover is announced, was then applied. Thus a second assessment of Croxden's probable market valuation could be derived. I also included this alternative valuation in my paper.

However, the main asset which made the business so interesting to potential purchasers, just as it had been to Clay Cross Co, was the enormous sand and gravel reserves. They covered a large land area with agricultural working on the surface. But their main attraction was in providing absolute security of supply for many decades ahead. In fact, at the then current rate of usage, it was estimated there would be over 150 years of supplies. But it was not clear what the value today of a tonne of sand would be, if it wasn't to be used for 150 years. Clearly, on any known mode of valuation, its current value would not be very much.

The method of calculating such items is fairly straightforward. Clearly, the sooner Croxden's sand and gravel reserves could be extracted and sold, the greater their value and the higher the price that might be payable for acquiring the Croxden Gravel business.

Sand and gravel are fairly low value commodities and are heavy and bulky and therefore costly to transport. A crude rule of thumb that was commonly used was that the effective distance it could be profitable to transport was around 50 miles. Therefore, the speed with which the reserves could be used, and therefore their present value maximised, depended on the amount of product that would be consumed within a 50-mile radius of the Croxden quarry. It was therefore vitally important to identify that consumption level. This was done by looking at the normal annual consumption rate and then identifying any major projects, over and above the norm, that were forecast to take place. These included a number of major new residential developments on the north side of Birmingham and some to the south of Manchester, plus some new motorway developments.

All these calculations were included in the sale document, which was presented to the Rothschild's people. Three very different indicative prices were included in the paper, based on market prices of quoted companies in the same sector, book value of assets and the present value of the reserves.

XXXII Inputs from the City of London

The first time I went down to the Rothschild premises in St Swithin's Lane, I was shown round some of the public area with various historic features including paintings and ancient furniture being revealed with the historic Rothschild connections explained as though to impress me with what an ancient and honourable organisation it was.

Rothschild people were extremely courteous but appeared unwilling to comment on my alternative valuations. It was as though they were careful to avoid making any such qualification in case they might be later accused of responsibility for wrongly influencing the price of the deal. When asked, they made no significant comment to me on the sale document.

They introduced me to senior individuals in various bodies in the City of London, including the OFT, which it was thought might possibly object to the sale being made to an existing big supplier of sand and gravel in the Staffordshire area. For similar reasons I was also introduced to some members of the M&MC, and provided with high quality working lunches.

I think the only contribution the Rothschild bank made of any significance was to make contact on CXC behalf with senior members of the Tarmac company that was the eventual acquirer. It was a contact we would have been perfectly capable of making ourselves. I could only imagine that the service provided by Rothschilds was a typical demonstration of merchant banking prowess at the time, based not on what you know, but who you know.

The logic and mathematics of calculating the present value of Croxden Gravel's reserves were flawless. By that impeccable process, the calculated value of that piece of earth was reduced to pennies. By similar logic, the value of earth itself could be reduced to something not worth spending serious money on its long-term protection. That is the mathematical logic which underpins the dominant economic theory which treats investment in environmental stewardship as calculably not worthwhile.

But planet Earth is different from Croxden Gravel. It has to be treated as just as valuable in a hundred years, or even a thousand, as it is today, and therefore to be assessed without any discounting. That is the only way it can be protected for the benefit of our successor generations. The impeccable logic has to be made subservient to a value system in order to ensure the human species survives.

XXXIII Researching industrial innovation

In due course, my employment at CXC became sufficiently uncomfortable for fellow directors that my contract was terminated with due compensation. It enabled me to contemplate a full-time research project funded on reasonable terms, which had been advertised at Manchester Business School. It involved completion of a PhD which I proposed focusing on technological innovation and what made some companies good at it and others less so.

T&N had clearly needed to be highly innovative in order, as a minimum requirement, to modify its raw material usage and its main product ranges. Some of the subsidiary business units, notably in Engineering Components Ltd and British Industrial Plastics Ltd, were highly successful innovators. Other units, in essentially similar circumstances, had been much less successful. What was the reason for that difference?

That was the basic question posed in the PhD proposal which was accepted and in due course completed under the title 'Innovation in a Mature Industry', with a version later published by McGraw-Hill as *The Competitive Organisation: Managing for Organisational Excellence.*[8]

Stage one of any research is to gain familiarity with the state of knowledge and understanding which the research is based on and seeks to develop further. In the case of technological innovation, that literature already extended to over 3,000 publications, the majority of which were empirical studies of innovation diffusion.[9] Such a well-researched subject area should provide a good understanding of the overall causes and effects of innovation as well as its operation in more local contexts, such as the T&N situation I had experienced. There was also a substantial historical literature relating to innovation.

My project identified effective innovation as depending on systemic characteristics related to strategy and culture. The strategy dimension involved identifying a clear strategic direction and communicating it to all those involved. That direction was necessarily focused on the user/consumer, oriented to the long term and aimed at developing and exploiting distinctive competences, aligned with the purpose for which the organisational system existed to serve. The culture dimension involved building corporate integrity, empowering people and involving them in the project's key decision-making processes. These two dimensions defined a competitive matrix, positioning on which suggested the necessary actions to achieve effectiveness as innovators.

XXXIV Joining academia

Before completing the PhD, I engaged in some teaching and consultancy roles in the areas of strategic management and business ethics notably with the West Midlands Regional Management Centre at Staffordshire Polytechnic. The Management Centre brought together an interesting and highly practical group of people with experience in a lot of different industries, some with technical backgrounds, others primarily general management. The staff members of the Management Centre were not focused on developing academic careers but provided excellent practical business training and education.

Not long after I completed my PhD, the polytechnics converted into universities. That led, in the area of business and management, to some refocusing away from practical teaching and consultancy to the long pursuit of academic credentials, focused mainly on publication as evidence of research. That raised the question which has been addressed many times as to the purpose of a university. The question of the purpose of polytechnics seems not to have been raised, the assumption seeming to be that they were simply second division universities. That was clearly not the case: polytechnics had a valuable and highly practical role to play in the coordination of organisational systems.

In due course I joined Keele University's Department of Management. *Keele's approach to higher education might have been fashioned by a systems practitioner, based on the interconnectedness of different fields of knowledge and education, rather than specialising in different separated subject areas. That was achieved by requiring students to attend a foundation year which comprised components from natural sciences, humanities and social sciences, plus the subsequent three-year degree course comprising 45 per cent each from two of those academic fields and 10 per cent from the third. It was what might be called a heterodox approach to higher education. It had long roots back to the work of R.H. Tawney and the Workers Education Association.*

I joined the Management Department when it was first established as an independent unit, newly separated from the Economics Department, with which it retained close relations.

Working in a university department was obviously different from anything I had previously been associated with. *But the entirely surprising discovery was how similar working in a university department was to all the other jobs I had previously engaged in.*

The department was a separate entity, an organisational system, with all the system characteristics: an existential purpose – to develop its distinctive teaching and research programmes, and to teach those attending our degree courses, and publish the research contributions, and in so doing achieve a satisfactory overall financial outcome for items within the department's control, satisfactory being as agreed with the university HQ. That needed to be understood by all department members as well as their role in its fulfilment. Also it was vital for a university department, as with any other organisational system, for that purpose to be compatible with, and supportive of, the macro-systems with which it interacts. The main macro system was Keele University, a distinctive entity with a unique position within the UK higher education sector.

Regular departmental meetings were held which encouraged members to collaborate, and invariably included discussion and amendment of a 'Draft Long Term Departmental Development Plan' to which all members of the department were invited to contribute. A précis of that draft plan was submitted to the university at the end of each academic year.

I was reminded of the CXC Communications and Consultation meetings, which, despite involving two competing constituents within the CXC organisation, fulfilled much the same function as the departmental meetings at Keele.

Collaborative working in private for-profit and public not-for-profit organisations was surprisingly similar. Both were organisational systems and both needed all their members to know and understand the existential purpose to which they contributed, and both needed to be compatible with and supportive of the macro-systems within which they operated.

Whatever that purpose is, the motivation must be to survive in the short term and grow and prosper in the long term, facilitating organisational system members to achieve. It also, of course, requires full consideration of the democratic commitments outlined in the main text.

XXXV The academic industry

The similarities of private for-profit and public organisations do not end there. Domination by neoclassical dogma promoted by organised money has afflicted the university sector just as it has the rest of the real economy.

To survive, a university needs to attract students. To attract students, it needs to achieve a reputation and standing in the various subject areas it pursues. The relevant key performance indicator that has been agreed within the academic industry relates to the quantity and quality of publications its academic faculty achieve. Such performance indicators are easy to measure and establish relevant league tables.

Quality is assessed by the journals in which articles are published, that quality being decided by the journal position on published league tables. Access to those journals is controlled by editorial boards, which may be guided by a particular academic position, theory or ideology. Membership of those editorial boards is self-controlled.

So universities are persuaded to regard themselves as businesses, necessarily competing with other like businesses, for an increasing share of the market, both home and abroad, and to do so through quality and quantity of publication by its academic faculty. The result of this established process has been an explosion in publication and in academic journals.

> No one knows how many scientific journals there are, but several estimates point to around 30,000, with close to two million articles published each year. … There is too much being published because the academic system encourages unnecessary publication.[10]

However, *universities are not businesses. Their real purpose is to serve the common good by teaching and learning so as to contribute to the advancement of knowledge and understanding in their many forms, including in particular the development of the necessary sustainability revolution. In so doing, they are 'guardian[s] of reason, inquiry and philosophical openness, preserving pure inquiry from dominant public opinions'.*[11]

XXXVI Practitioner conclusions

These notes relate to the period during which neoclassical capitalism and the power of organised money re-emerged, having been temporarily defeated by the social democracy of Roosevelt and Keynesian economics. *There are lessons of relevance to the 2020s. The 'tech titans', the platform organisations such as Airbnb and Uber that enable escape from normal employer responsibilities, and their Chinese equivalents and competitors who are 'challenging the world by innovating faster, working harder and going global' will surely dominate the economic future.*[12]

They are certainly very different from the organisational systems such as M&R, T&N and CXC. But there are a lot of similarities too. Real human beings have not changed. As Adam Smith indicated in the opening sentence of The Theory of Moral Sentiments, *though people may be assumed to be only self-interested, 'there are evidently some principles in their nature which interest them in the fortune of others'. Knowing what we know now, those 'others' include the whole human race and all succeeding generations.*

There are also still the Jack Clydes of this world, concerned with providing real value and assisting their clients, rather than simply exploiting them to maximise their own take. And there are still many soundly based M&Rs, concerned for the welfare and development of their employees as well as their customers and other stakeholders, and also concerned for the global future.

There are also, of course, still the crooks and vagabonds masquerading as wealthy gentlemen. My experience with the asset stripping fraternity of Jim Slater, John Bentley et al, is repeated many times over by much of the activity of today's self-perpetuating organised money establishment, focused simply on MST from the real economy. Some things never change.

But it is also no doubt true that most individuals working within the organised money establishment work with perfectly reasonable intentions and are becoming increasingly aware of the predatory ill effects of financial sector activities. They might have the power to achieve positive change. Maybe some will be constrained by their personal responsibilities to focus on earning more, but it seems inevitable that at some stage they will contribute to reversing the current direction and momentum of finance. The question is whether it will be soon enough and forceful enough.

Many leading economists today are hugely critical of today's neoclassical version of microeconomics. Like Sumantra Ghoshal a generation ago, they may advocate it being removed in its entirety from the taught curriculum. Remaking the real economy will not be achieved otherwise, and if the real economy continues to be driven simply to make as much money as possible for stockholders, then destruction awaits us all.

That is how it looks from the top of a billposter's ladder. Bear in mind, the average billposter probably has as much intelligence as the average banker or hedge fund trader, not to mention 'businessman', and also has to demonstrate a whole load more personal courage. So it may take members of the organised money establishment some time to catch up, but hopefully not too long.

A final reflection on that practitioner experience goes right back to the beginning of my working career in the RAF. That experience brought people of all backgrounds together in circumstances where their interdependence was clearly apparent. That involuntary experience was lost for subsequent generations. That is apparent among ranks of politicians, in the contrast between those who were conscripted to serve, especially in wartime, and the current generation of politicians who lack that experience of close proximity with all ranks of their fellow human beings. Such profoundly humanising experience might be gained by working on projects such as those offered by the VSO[13] or by such service being made mandatory for a period on a national basis. A timely reminder of our real interdependence is currently being provided by the COVID-19 pandemic.

References

Preface

1 Wells, S. (2010) *Pandora's Seed: the Unforeseen Cost of Civilisation,* London: Penguin Allen Lane.

2 United Nations Department of Economic and Social Affairs (2019) 'World Population Prospects', https://population.un.org/wpp/

3 Roser, M. (2019) 'Economic growth', Our World in Data, https://ourworldindata.org/economic-growth

4 Pearson, G. (1990) *Strategic Thinking,* Hemel Hempstead: Prentice Hall International.

5 Deming, W.E. (1982) *Out of the Crisis,* Cambridge MA: MIT Center for Advanced Educational Services.

6 Juran, J.M. (1970) *Quality Planning and Analysis,* New York: McGraw-Hill.

7 Crosby, P.B. (1979) *Quality is Free: The Art of Making Quality Certain,* New York: McGraw-Hill.

8 Business Roundtable (2020) https://opportunity.businessroundtable.org/wp-content/uploads/2020/04/BRT-Statement-on-the-Purpose-of-a-Corporation-with-Signatures-Updated-April-2020.pdf

9 https://aboutus.ft.com/en-gb/new-agenda/

Part I

1 Wallace-Wells, D. (2019) *The Uninhabitable Earth: A Story of the Future,* London: Penguin Books.

Chapter 1

1 Smith, A. (1993 [1776]) *An Inquiry into the Nature and Causes of the Wealth of Nations,* Oxford: Oxford University Press.

2 Ricardo, D. (1911 [1817]) *The Principles of Political Economy and Taxation,* New York: Dover Publications.

3 Marx, K. (1979 [1859]) *A Contribution to the Critique of Political Economy,* London: Lawrence and Wishart.

4 Smith (1993 [1776]).

5 Smith (1993 [1776]).

6 Khurana, R. (2007) *From Higher Aims to Hired Hands: The Social Transformation of American Business Schools and the Unfulfilled Promise of Management as a Profession,* Princeton NJ: Princeton University Press.

7 Drucker, P.F. (1993) *Post-Capitalist Society,* Oxford: Butterworth-Heinemann.

8 Pitt, W., the Younger (1792) 'Budget speech', in Rae, J. (1895) *Life of Adam Smith,* London: Macmillan, pp 290–91.

9 Pearson, G. (2009) *The Rise and Fall of Management: A Brief History of Practice, Theory and Context,* Farnham: Gower Publishing.

10 Marx, K. (1867) *Das Capital,* Vol I. Vols II and III were posthumously published in 1885 and 1894 respectively, edited by Engels. *Capital: A New Abridgement* is published by Oxford University Press as an Oxford World's Classic.

11 Engels, F. (1844) *The Condition of the Working Class in England.*

12 Ruskin J. (1862) 'The roots of honour', in *Unto this Last*, London: Penguin Books.

13 Marshall, A. (1922) *Principles of Economics* (8th edn), London: Macmillan, pp 762–3.

14 Lucas, R.E. (1996) 'Nobel lecture – Monetary neutrality', *The Journal of Political Economy*, 104(4).

15 Lucas, R.E. (2013) *Collected Papers on Monetary Neutrality* (ed M. Gilman), Cambridge, MA: Harvard University Press, p 384.

16 Routh, G. (1975) *The Origin of Economic Ideas*, London: Macmillan.

17 Galbraith, J.K. (1989) 'In pursuit of the simple truth', commencement address to women graduates of Smith College, Northampton, Massachusetts.

18 Ghoshal, S. (2005) 'Bad management theories are destroying good management practices', *Academy of Management Learning and Education,* 4(1).

19 Friedman, M. (1976) 'The road to economic freedom: the steps from here to there', address to the Institute of Economic Affairs, https://iea.org.uk/wp-content/uploads/2016/07/From%20Galbraith%20to%20Economic%20Freedom.pdf

20 Piatier, A. (1984) *Barriers to Innovation*, London: Francis Pinter.

21 Mont Pelerin Society, www.montpelerin.org/

22 von Mises, L. (1962) *The Free and Prosperous Commonwealth* (trans R. Raico; ed A. Goddard), New York: Van Nostrand Co.

23 Van Offelen, J. (2004) Preface to the Mont Pèlerin Society's *Inventory of the General Meeting Files (1947–1998)*, http://rybn.org/thegreatoffshore/THE%20GREAT%20OFFSHORE/1.ENCYCLOPEDIA/MONT%20PELERIN%20SOCIETY,%201947/DOCS/Inventory%20of%20the%20General%20Meeting%20Files%20(1947-1998).pdf

24 Hayek, F.A. (1944) *The Road to Serfdom*, London: Routledge.

25 Hayek (1944).

26 Hayek, F.A. (1988) *The Fatal Conceit: The Errors of Socialism,* London: Routledge.

27 von Mises, L. (1951 [1922]) *Socialism: An Economic and Sociological Analysis* (translated by J. Kahane), New Haven CT: Yale University Press.

28 von Mises (1962).

29 Friedman, M. (2003) Interviews with Joel Bakan for the documentary film 'The Corporation', www.youtube.com/watch?v=Y888wVY5hzw

30 Blyth, M. (2015) *Austerity: The History of a Dangerous Idea*, Oxford: Oxford University Press.

31 Martin, F. (2014) *Money: the Unauthorised Biography,* London: Vintage Random House.

32 Smith (1993 [1776]).

33 Friedman (1976).

34 Friedman (2003).

35 Friedman (2003).

36 Friedman, L.M. (1973) *A History of American Law*, New York: Simon & Schuster Touchstone.

37 Maier, P. (1993) 'The revolutionary origins of the American corporation', *William and Mary Quarterly*, 3rd Series.

38 Levy, A.B. (1950) *Private Corporations and their Control*, London: Routledge & Kegan Paul.

39 Friedman, M. (1962) *Capitalism and Freedom*, Chicago, IL: Chicago University Press.

40 Fox, J. and Lorsch, J.W. (2012), 'What good are shareholders?', *Harvard Business Review*, 90(7/8): 48–57.

41 Alchian, A.A. and Demsetz, H. (1972) 'Production, information costs, and economic organisation', *American Economic Review*, 62: 778.

[42] Jensen, M.C. and Meckling, W.H. (1976) 'Theory of the firm: managerial behaviour, agency costs and ownership structure', *Journal of Financial Economics*, 3: 305–60.

[43] Khurana (2007).

[44] Lan, L.L. and Heracleous, L. (2010) 'Rethinking agency theory: the view from law', *Academy of Management Review*, 35(2): 299.

[45] Ghoshal (2005).

[46] Trebeck, K. and Williams, J. (2019) *The Economics of Arrival: Ideas for a Grown Up Economy*, Bristol: Policy Press.

[47] Krekel, C., Ward, G. and De Neve, J-E. (2019) 'Employee wellbeing, productivity and firm performance', CEP Discussion Paper No 1605, Centre for Economic Performance, London School of Economics and Political Science.

[48] Krier, D. (2009) 'Speculative profit fetishism in the age of finance capital', *Critical Sociology*, 21 September, https://journals.sagepub.com/doi/10.1177/0896920509337613

[49] Krugman, P. (2007) 'Who was Milton Friedman?', *New York Review of Books*, 17 February.

[50] Piketty, T. (2014) *Capital in the Twenty-First Century*, Cambridge, MA: Belknap Press of Harvard University Press.

Chapter 2

[1] Roosevelt, F.D. (1936), Address at Madison Square Garden, New York, 31 October. Original text held by Franklin D. Roosevelt Presidential Library and Museum, *Franklin D. Roosevelt – 'The Great Communicator': The Master Speech Files, 1898, 1910–1945, Series 2: 'You have nothing to fear but fear itself'*: FDR and the New Deal, p 5, http://www.fdrlibrary.marist.edu/_resources/images/msf/msf01033

[2] Rogers, P. (2017) *Irregular War: the New Threat from the Margins*, London: I.B Taurus & Co, p 5.

[3] Ghoshal (2005).

[4] Kindleberger, P.C. (1997) *Manias, Panics and Crashes: A History of Financial Crises*, New York: John Wiley and Sons.

[5] Minsky, H. (1986) *Stabilizing an Unstable Market*, New Haven, CT: Yale University Press.

[6] Morrison, A.D. and Wilhelm, W.J. Jr. (2007) *Investment Banking: Institutions, Politics and Law*, Oxford: Oxford University Press.

[7] Shaxson, N. (2011) *Treasure Islands: Tax Havens and the Men who Stole the World*, London: Bodley Head.

[8] *New York Times* (1975) 'Obituary: Sir Denys Lowson, British Financier', 12 September, www.nytimes.com/1975/09/12/archives/sir-denys-lowson-british-financier-exlondon-lord-mayor-hit-by.html

[9] Martin (2014).

[10] Shaxson (2011).

[11] Henry, J.S. (2005) *The Blood Bankers: Tales from the Global Underground Economy*, New York: Basic Books.

[12] Fletcher, L. (2010) 'Start-ups fuel growth in super-fast trading', Reuters.com, 7 April, www.reuters.com/article/idUSTRE6363VE20100407

[13] Lewis, M. (2014) *Flash Boys: Cracking the Money Code*, London: Penguin Allen Lane.

[14] Lanchester, J. (2010) *Whoops! Why Everyone Owes Everyone and No One Can Pay*, London: Penguin Allen Lane.

[15] Henwood, D. (1997) *Wall Street: How It Works and for Whom*, London: Verso Books.

16 Corporate Finance Institute (2020) 'What is Repo 105?', https://corporatefinanceinstitute.com/resources/knowledge/accounting/repo-105/

17 Chandler, A. (1977) *The Visible Hand: The Managerial Revolution in American Business*, Cambridge MA: Belknap Press of Harvard University Press.

18 Blonigen, B.A. and Pierce, J.R. (2016) 'Mergers may be profitable, but are they good for the economy?', *Harvard Business Review*, November.

19 Institute of Directors (1991) *Guidelines for Directors* (5th edn), London: Director Publications.

20 Faroohar, R. (2019) *Don't be Evil – The Case Against Big Tech*, London: Penguin Allen Lane.

21 Faroohar (2019).

22 Khurana, R. (2007) *From Higher Aims to Hired Hands: The Social Transformation of American Business Schools and the Unfulfilled Promise of Management as a Profession*, Princeton NJ: Princeton University Press.

23 Murray, S. (2013) 'MBA teaching urged to move away from focus on shareholder primacy model', *Financial Times*, 7 July.

24 Smith, J. (ed) (2019) 'Top UK business schools', *Prospects*, October, www.prospects.ac.uk/jobs-and-work-experience/job-sectors/business-consulting-and-management/top-uk-business-schools

25 Ghoshal (2005).

26 Earle, J., Moran, C. and Ward-Perkins, Z. (2017) *The Econocracy: On the Perils of Leaving Economics to the Experts*, London: Penguin Random House.

27 Routh (1975).

28 Khurana (2007).

29 Faroohar (2019).

30 Mulgan, G. (2017) 'Truth and the media: a modest proposal', NESTA (National Endowment for Science, Technology and the Arts) blog, 6 January, www.nesta.org.uk/blog/truth-and-the-media-a-modest-proposal/

31 Lewis, M. (2018) *The Fifth Risk: Undoing Democracy*, London: Penguin Random House.

32 Lewis (2018).

Chapter 3

1 Judt, T. (2010) *Ill Fares the Land*, London: Penguin Allen Lane.

2 Malthus, T.R. (2008 [1798]) *An Essay on the Principle of Population*, Oxford: Oxford University Press.

3 Pimm, S.L., Russell, G.J., Gittleman, J.L. and Brooks, T.M. (1995) 'The future of biodiversity', *Science*, 269: 47–50.

4 *The Economist* (2012) 'The Libor Affair – Banksters', 7 July, www.economist.com/node/21558260

5 Ridley, K. (2015) 'In FX rigging: "if you ain't cheating, you ain't trying"', Reuters.com, 20 May, www.reuters.com/article/banks-forex-settlement-traders/in-fx-rigging-if-you-aint-cheating-you-aint-trying-idUSL5N0YB3Q820150520

6 Intergovernmental Panel on Climate Change (2018) 'Summary for Policymakers of IPCC Special Report on Global Warming of 1.5°C approved by governments', 8 October, www.ipcc.ch/pdf/session48/pr_181008_P48_spm_en.pdf

7 Faroohar, R. (2016) *Makers and Takers: How Wall Street Destroyed Main Street*, New York: Crown Business.

8   Corporate Reform Collective (2014) *Fighting Corporate Abuse: Beyond Predatory Capitalism*, London: Pluto Press.

9   Krier, D. (2009) 'Speculative profit fetishism in the age of finance capital', *Critical Sociology*, 21 September, https://journals.sagepub.com/doi/10.1177/0896920509337613

10   House of Commons Home Affairs Committee (2012), *Olympics Security*, 18 September, https://publications.parliament.uk/pa/cm201213/cmselect/cmhaff/531/531.pdf

11   Ghoshal (2005).

12   Mazzucato, M. (2018) *The Value of Everything: Making and Taking in the Global Economy*, London: Penguin Allen Lane.

13   Shaxson, N. (2018) *The Finance Curse: How Global Finance is Making us All Poorer*, London: Vintage.

14   Mendick, R. (2013) 'Buckingham Palace 'hired out' for bank dinner', *The Telegraph*, 24 November, www.telegraph.co.uk/news/uknews/theroyalfamily/10470458/Buckingham-Palace-hired-out-for-bank-dinner.html

15   Tett, G. (2015) 'Penalise the banks but use the money well', *Financial Times*, 14 January.

16   Tett (2015).

17   Ridley (2015).

18   Shubber, K. (2018) 'Barclays to pay $2bn to settle US mortgage mis-selling probe', *Financial Times*, 29 March, www.ft.com/content/9ff69988-3352-11e8-ac48-10c6fdc22f03

19   Heffernan, M. (2011) *Wilful Blindness: Why we Ignore the Obvious at our Peril*, London: Simon & Schuster.

20   Kalantarnia, M., Kahn, F. and Hawboldt, K. (2010) 'Modelling of BP Texas City refinery accident using dynamic risk assessment approach', *Process Safety and Environmental Protection*, 88(3): 191–99.

21   House of Commons Public Accounts Committee (2014) *Contracting our Public Services to the Private Sector*, 26 February, https://publications.parliament.uk/pa/cm201314/cmselect/cmpubacc/777/777.pdf

22   Wilkinson, R. and Pickett, K. (2009) *The Spirit Level: Why More Equal Societies Almost Always do Better*, London: Penguin Allen Lane.

23   ICIJ (International Consortium of Investigative Journalists) (2016) *The Panama Papers: Exposing the Rogue Offshore Finance Industry*, www.icij.org/investigations/panama-papers/

24   Anti-Slavery International (2020) 'For a world free from slavery for everyone, everywhere, always', www.antislavery.org/slavery-today/slavery-uk/

25   Standing, G. (2017) *The Corruption of Capitalism: Why Rentiers Thrive and Work Does Not Pay*, London: Biteback Publishing.

26   Beatty, J. (1998) *The World According to Drucker*, London: Orion Publishing Group.

27   House of Commons Hansard (2019) 'FTSE Company pay ratios', 23 January, Volume 653, https://hansard.parliament.uk/Commons/2019-01-23/debates/7CD70CBB-2798-4871-B9B4-63C48007AC84/FTSE100CompanyPayRatios

28   Coffey C., Espinoza Revolto, P., Harvey, R., Lawson, M., Parvez Butt, A., Piaget, K., Sarosi, D. and Thekkudan, J. (2020) 'Time to Care: unpaid and underpaid care work and the global inequality crisis', Oxfam Briefing Paper, https://policy-practice.oxfam.org.uk/publications/time-to-care-unpaid-and-underpaid-care-work-and-the-global-inequality-crisis-620928

29   Oxfam: quote is from a media briefing of 18 January 2013 (ref 02/2012) titled *The Cost of Inequality: How Wealth and Incomes Extremes Hurt Us All*.

30 Credit Suisse (2019) *Global Wealth Report 2019*, www.credit-suisse.com/about-us/en/reports-research/global-wealth-report.html

31 Rogers (2017), p 5.

32 World Bank (2014) 'Chapter 3: Youth activity and unemployment', *Breaking the Barriers to Youth Inclusion*, www.worldbank.org/content/dam/Worldbank/document/MNA/tunisia/breaking_the_barriers_to_youth_inclusion_eng_chap3.pdf

33 Piketty (2014).

34 Nature Conservancy, 'Our priorities: a future where people and nature thrive', www.nature.org/en-us/what-we-do/our-priorities/

35 IPCC Synthesis Report on Climate Change 2014 Summary for Policymakers, https://www.ipcc.ch/site/assets/uploads/2018/02/AR5_SYR_FINAL_SPM.pdf

36 Attenborough, D. (2018) 'Collapse of civilisation is on the horizon', *The Guardian*, 3 December, www.theguardian.com/environment/2018/dec/03/david-attenborough-collapse-civilisation-on-horizon-un-climate-summit

37 Rogers (2017).

38 Sweney, M. (2018) 'Disney raises offer to $71bn in bidding war for Murdoch's 21st Century Fox', *The Guardian*, 21 June, p 41.

Chapter 4

1 Lawance, M.I. Jr (ed) (2018) *House Divided: The Antebellum Slavery Debates in America, 1776–1865*, Princeton NJ: Princeton University Press, p 445.

2 Hall, C., Draper, N. and McClelland, K. (eds) (2016) *Legacies of British Slave-Ownership: Colonial Slavery and the Formation of Victorian Britain*, Cambridge: Cambridge University Press.

3 AAAS (2014) *What We Know: The Reality, Risks and Response to Climate Change*, https://whatweknow.aaas.org/wp-content/uploads/2014/07/whatweknow_website.pdf

4 Klein, N. (2014) *This Changes Everything*, London: Simon & Schuster.

5 United Nations (2019) 'Sustainable Development Goals', www.un.org/sustainabledevelopment/sustainable-development-goals/

6 Engels, F. (1844) *The Condition of the Working Class in England*.

7 UNESCO (United Nations Education, Science and Cultural Organisation) (2017) '6 out of 10 children and adolescents are not learning a minimum in reading and math', 21 September, http://uis.unesco.org/en/news/6-out-10-children-and-adolescents-are-not-learning-minimum-reading-and-math

8 United Nations (2019) 'The Ten Principles of the UN Global Compact. Principle Seven: Environment', www.unglobalcompact.org/what-is-gc/mission/principles/principle-7

9 Tawney, R.H. (1931) *Equality*, London: Allen & Unwin.

10 Galbraith, J.K. (1958) *The Affluent Society*, London: Hamish Hamilton.

11 Galbraith (1958).

12 Galbraith, J.K. (1958) *The Affluent Society*, London: Hamish Hamilton.

13 United Nations Human Settlement Programme (2003) 'The challenge of slums: global report on human settlements 2003', www.un.org/ruleoflaw/files/Challenge%20of%20Slums.pdf

14 Lewis, M. (1989) *Liar's Poker*, London: Hodder & Stoughton; Lanchester (2010); Tett, G. (2010) *Fool's Gold: How Unrestrained Greed Corrupted a Dream, Shattered*

Global Markets and Unleashed a Catastrophe, London: Abacus Little Brown Book Group.

[15] Raworth, K. (2017) *Doughnut Economics: Seven Ways to Think Like a 21st Century Economist*, London: Penguin Random House.

[16] Froud J. and Williams, K. (eds) (2018) *Foundational Economy: The Infrastructure of Everyday Life*, Manchester: Manchester University Press.

[17] Heidarzadeh, M. (2019) 'Whaley Bridge dam collapse is a wake-up call: concrete infrastructure will not last forever without care', The Conversation, 5 August, https://theconversation.com/whaley-bridge-dam-collapse-is-a-wake-up-call-concrete-infrastructure-will-not-last-forever-without-care-121423

[18] Bowman, A., Erturk, I., Froud, J., Haslam, C., Johal, S., Leaver, A., Moran, M. and Williams, K. (2015) *What a Waste: Outsourcing and How it Goes Wrong*, Manchester: Manchester University Press.

[19] Mazzucato, M. (2013) *The Entrepreneurial State: Debunking Public vs. Private Sector Myths*, London: Anthem Press.

[20] Lewis (2018).

[21] Coyle, D. (2011) *The Economics of Enough: How to Run the Economy as if the Future Matters*, Oxford: Princeton University Press.

[22] Trebeck and Williams (2019).

Part III

[1] Deming, W.E. (2000) *The New Economics for Industry, Government, Education* (2nd edn), Cambridge, MA: MIT Press.

Chapter 5

[1] Smith, A. (2006 [1759]) *The Theory of Moral Sentiments*, New York: Dover Publications.

[2] Smith (2006 [1759]).

[3] Smith (1776).

[4] Maslow, A.H. (1943) 'A theory of human motivation', *Psychological Review*, 50: 370–96.

[5] Alderfer, C.P. (1972) *Existence, Relatedness and Growth*, London: Free Press.

[6] Herzberg, F. (1966) *Work and the Nature of Man*, Cleveland, OH: World Publishing.

[7] Gruenfeld, L.W. and Foltman, F.F. (1967) 'Relationship among supervisors' integration, satisfaction, and acceptance of technological change', *Journal of Applied Psychology*, 51(1): 74–77.

[8] Frey, B.S. (1997) *Not Just for the Money: An Economic Theory of Personal Motivation*, Cheltenham: Edward Elgar.

[9] Veblen, T. (1899) *The Theory of the Leisure Class: An Economic Study in the Evolution of Institutions*, New York: Macmillan.

[10] Taylor, F.W. (1911) *The Principles of Scientific Management*, New York: Harper.

[11] Kanigel, R. (1997) *The One Best Way: Frederick Winslow Taylor and the Enigma of Efficiency*, London: Little, Brown & Company.

[12] Barnard, C. (1948) *Organization and Management*, Cambridge, MA: Harvard University Press.

[13] Mayo, E. (1933) *The Human Problems of an Industrial Civilization*, New York: Macmillan.

[14] Mayo, E. (1949) *The Social Problems of an Industrial Civilisation*, London: Routledge.

15 McGregor, D. (1969) *The Human Side of Enterprise*, New York: McGraw-Hill.

16 Ghoshal (2005).

17 Ghoshal (2005).

18 Lipman-Blumen, J. (2010) *A Pox on Charisma*, in Pearce, C.L., Maciariello, J. and Yamawaki, H. (eds) *The Drucker Difference: What the World's Greatest Management Thinker Means to Today's Business Leaders*, Chichester: McGraw-Hill.

19 Cable, D.M. (2018) *Alive at Work: The Neuroscience of Helping your People Love What they do*, Cambridge MA: Harvard Business Review Press.

20 Ridley, M. (1996) *The Origins of Virtue*, London: Viking Penguin.

21 Seabright, P. (2004) *The Company of Strangers: The Natural History of Economic Life*, Princeton, NJ: Princeton University Press.

22 Caulkin, S. (2009) 'Individuality can banish the downturn blues,' *The Observer*, 24 May, Business & Media, p 6.

23 Beatty (1998).

24 Seddon, J. et al (2019) *Beyond Command and Control*, Buckingham: Vanguard Consulting.

25 Shaxson (2018).

26 Brown, W. (1962) *Piecework Abandoned: The Effect of Wage Incentive Schemes on Managerial Authority*, London: Heinemann.

27 Di Muzio, T. (2015) *The 1% and the Rest of Us: A Political Economy of Dominant Ownership*, London: Zed Books.

Chapter 6

1 Deming, W.E. (2000 [1994]), *The New Economics for Industry, Government, Education*, Cambridge, MA: MIT Center for Advanced Educational Services.

2 Farroohar (2016).

3 Lewis, M. (2011) *The Big Short*, London: Penguin Books.

4 Deming (2000).

5 Deming (1982).

6 Koehler, W. (1938) *The Place of Values in a World of Fact*, New York: Liveright.

7 Mitra, S. (2013) 'How to reduce infant entrepreneur mortality', *Harvard Business Review*, June.

8 Otar, C. (2018) 'What percentage of small businesses fail and how can you avoid being one of them?', Forbes Finance Council, Forbes, 15 October, www.forbes.com/sites/forbesfinancecouncil/2018/10/25/what-percentage-of-small-businesses-fail-and-how-can-you-avoid-being-one-of-them/#234c7eb543b5

9 Pearson, G. (1999) *Strategy in Action: Strategic Thinking, Understanding and Practice*, Harlow: FT Prentice Hall.

10 Business Strategy Hub (2019) 'SWOT analysis of Apple', https://bstrategyhub.com/swot-analysis-of-apple-apple-swot-2018/

11 Seddon, J. (2014) *The Whitehall Effect: How Whitehall Became the Enemy of Great Public Service and What We Can Do About It*, Axminster: Triarchy Press.

12 Kotabe, M., Mol, M.J. and Ketkar, S. (2008) 'An evolutionary stage model of outsourcing and competence destruction: a Triad comparison of the consumer electronics industry', *Management International Review*, 48(1): 65–94.

13 von Mises (1962).

14 Smith (1993 [1776]).

15 Deming (2000 [1982]).

16 Dorling, D. (2015) *Inequality and the 1%*, London: Verso.

17 McGregor (1969).
18 Smith (1993), p 129.
19 Deming (2000 [1994]).
20 Deming (2000 [1994]).
21 House of Commons, Health and Social Care Select Committee (2019) *Collaboration, Not Competition is the Key to Solving Health Care Challenges*, committee report on the NHS long term plan, 24 June, https://www.parliament.uk/business/committees/committees-a-z/commons-select/health-and-social-care-committee/news/nhs-legislative-proposals-report-published-17–19/

Chapter 7

1 Froud and Williams (2018).
2 Lewis (2018).
3 Pierson, B. (2017) 'Martin Shkreli, who raised drug prices 5000% heads into fraud trial', *Scientific American,* 26 June, www.scientificamerican.com/article/martin-shkreli-who-raised-drug-prices-5-000-percent-heads-into-fraud-trial/
4 Solomon, J. (2007) *Corporate Governance and Accountability* (2nd edn), Chichester: John Wiley & Sons.
5 Pearson, G. (2012) *The Road to Co-operation: Escaping the Bottom Line*, Farnham: Gower Publishing.
6 López-Espinosa, G., Maddocks, J. and Polo-Garrido, F. (2009) 'Equity-liabilities distinction: the case for co-operatives', *Journal of International Financial Management & Accounting*, 20(3): 283–84.
7 Scott Bader, 'About us', www.scottbader.com/about-us/
8 Owen, R. (1970 [1814]) *A New View of Society and Report to the County of Lanark*, London: Penguin Pelican Books.
9 Simms, A., Boyle, D. and Robins, N. (2010) *Eminent Corporations: The Rise and Fall of the Great British Corporation*, London: Constable.
10 Erdal, D. (2011) *Beyond the Corporation: Humanity Working*, London: Bodley Head.
11 Erdal (2011).
12 Mazzucato (2013).
13 Lewis (2018).
14 Pearson, G. (1992) *The Competitive Organisation: Managing for Organisational Excellence*, Maidenhead: McGraw-Hill.
15 Pearson, G. (1995) *Integrity in Organisations: An Alternative Business Ethic*, Maidenhead: McGraw-Hill.
16 Kondratiev, N.D. (1935) 'The long waves in economic life', *The Review of Economic Statistics*, November.
17 Schumpeter, J.A. (1939) *Business Cycles: A Theoretical, Historical and Statistical Analysis of the Capitalist Process*, New York: McGraw-Hill.
18 Piatier (1984).
19 Castells, M. (2000) *The Rise of the Network Society: The Information Age: Economy, Society and Culture*, London: John Wiley & Sons.
20 'Engage with graphene', www.graphene.manchester.ac.uk
21 Slade, G. (2007) *Made to Break Technology and Obsolescence in America*, Cambridge, MA: Harvard University Press.
22 Cadwalladr, C. (2019) 'Cambridge Analytica a year on: "a lesson in institutional failure"', *The Guardian*, 17 March, www.theguardian.com/uk-news/2019/mar/17/cambridge-analytica-year-on-lesson-in-institutional-failure-christopher-wylie

23 Panuk, H. (2018) 'Trump targets pair of Obama-era green rules to boost oil and coal industries', Reuters.com, 6 December, https://uk.reuters.com/article/us-usa-energy-trump/trump-targets-pair-of-obama-era-green-rules-to-boost-oil-coal-idUKKBN1O52L7
24 Chang, H-J. (2014) *Economics: The User's Guide*, London: Penguin Pelican.
25 Chang, H-J. (2010) *23 Things they Don't Tell you about Capitalism*, London: Penguin Allen Lane.

Chapter 8

1 Piatier (1984).
2 Wolfers, J. (2014) 'The Fed has not stopped trying to stimulate the economy', *New York Times*, 29 October.
3 Martin (2014).
4 Shaxson (2011).
5 Routh (1975).
6 Kenner, D. (2015) *Inequality of Overconsumption: The Ecological Footprint of the Richest*, GSI Working Paper 2015/2, Cambridge: Global Sustainability Institute, Anglia Ruskin University.
7 Froud and Williams (2018).
8 BBC News (2016) 'Libraries lose a quarter of staff as hundreds close', 29 March, www.bbc.co.uk/news/uk-england-35707956
9 BBC News (2019) 'UK government cancels Brexit ferry deals', 1 May, www.bbc.co.uk/news/business-48117366
10 See https://www.gov.uk/government/news/10-000-extra-prison-places-to-keep-the-public-safe
11 See https://www.nao.org.uk/wp-content/uploads/2020/01/High-Speed-Two-A-progress-update.pdf
12 Heidarzadeh (2019).
13 The details of 'fit for purpose' in the different contexts depend on specialist knowledge and understanding of such things as the supply of clean water, adequate public sanitation, defence capability and the requirement to be able to participate appropriately in wider defence or regulation of international coordination by such as NATO or the EU.
14 Roosevelt (1936).
15 Chandler (1977).
16 Faroohar (2019).
17 Lewis (2018).
18 Mazzucato (2018).
19 Shaxson (2018).
20 World Bank (2019) 'Understanding poverty: overview', www.worldbank.org/en/topic/poverty/overview
21 Shaxson (2018).
22 Friedman (2003).
23 Ghoshal (2005).
24 Shaxson (2011).
25 Bullough, O. (2018) *Money Land: Why Thieves and Crooks Now Rule the World and How to Take it Back*, London: Profile Books.
26 Friedman (1953).
27 Hayek (1989).

[28] Keynes, J.M. (1936) *The General Theory of Employment, Interest and Money*, Macmillan, Chapter 24, Section V.

[29] Earle et al (2017).

[30] Ghoshal (2005).

[31] Raworth (2017).

[32] Deming (2000).

Chapter 9

[1] Piatier (1984).

[2] Save the Children (2019) 'Yemen: the challenges for children in Yemen', www.savethechildren.org/us/what-we-do/where-we-work/greater-middle-east-eurasia/yemen

[3] Stiglitz, J.E. (2012) *The Price of Inequality*, London: Penguin Allen Lane.

[4] Keynes (1936).

[5] Keynes, J.M. (1940) *How to Pay for the War*, Basingstoke: Macmillan & Co.

[6] Coyle, D. (2014) *GDP: A Brief but Affectionate History*, Oxford: Princeton University Press.

[7] Chang (2014).

[8] Fioramonti, L. (2013) *Gross Domestic Problem: The Politics Behind the World's Most Powerful Number (Economic Controversies)*, London: Zed Books.

[9] Jackson, T. (2017) *Prosperity without Growth: Foundations for the Economy of Tomorrow*, London: Routledge.

[10] Pilling, D. (2018) *The Growth Delusion: The Wealth and Well-Being of Nations*, London: Bloomsbury.

[11] Stiglitz, J.E., Sen, A. and Fitoussi, J-P. (2010) *Mismeasuring Our Lives: Why GDP Doesn't Add Up*, New York: New Press.

[12] Raworth (2017).

[13] Mazzucato, M. (2018) *The Value of Everything: Making and Taking in the Global Economy*, London: Penguin Random House.

[14] Stiglitz (2012).

[15] United Nations (2000) 'Millennium development goals and beyond 2015', www.un.org/millenniumgoals/

[16] United Nations (2000).

[17] United Nations (2000).

[18] United Nations (2019) 'Sustainable Development Goals', https://unstats.un.org/sdgs/report/2019/#:~:text=This%20report%20therefore%20highlights%20areas,greater%20focus%20on%20digital%20transformation

[19] United Nations (2019) 'Ten Principles', https://www.unglobalcompact.org/what-is-gc/mission/principles

[20] UK Government (2019) 'Implementing the sustainable development goals', 5 July, www.gov.uk/government/publications/implementing-the-sustainable-development-goals/implementing-the-sustainable-development-goals--2

[21] Lewis (2018).

[22] Friedman (2003).

[23] Ghoshal (2005).

[24] Krekel et al (2019); Krier (2009).

[25] Appelbaum, B. (2019) *The Economists' Hour: How the False Prophets of Free Markets Fractured Our Society*, London: Picador.

26 *The Economist* (2019) 'When economists ruled the world', 31 August, https://www.economist.com/books-and-arts/2019/08/31/when-economists-ruled-the-world
27 Applebaum (2019).
28 *Financial Times*, 'New Agenda', https://aboutus.ft.com/en-gb/new-agenda/
29 Tett, G. (2019) 'Does capitalism need saving from itself?', *Financial Times*, 7 September, www.ft.com/content/b35342fe-cda4-11e9-99a4-b5ded7a7fe3f?segmentId=9d8c66e5-f845-1254-610a-f597ecc6b8b8
30 Business Roundtable (2020).
31 CECP: Chief Executives for Corporate Purpose, https://cecp.co/
32 Klein, N. (2019) *On Fire: The (Burning) Case for a Green New Deal*, London: Simon and Schuster.
33 Klein, N. (2019) 'The Green New Deal: A Fight for Our Lives', *New York Review of Books*, 17 September.

Practitioner notes on real organisational systems

1 www.ashridge.org.uk/
2 www.ipa.co.uk/
3 www.showcaseoutdoor.co.uk/useful-info/billposting/
4 Brown (1962).
5 The GMAT exam, www.mba.com/global/the-gmat-exam.aspx
6 Mayo, E. (1933) *The Human Problems of an Industrial Civilisation*, New York: Macmillan, and, Mayo, E. (1949) *The Social Problems of an Industrial Civilisation*, London: Penguin.
7 www.ruskin.ac.uk/about/history/
8 Pearson, G. (1992) *The Competitive Organisation: Managing for Organisational Excellence,* Maidenhead: McGraw-Hill.
9 Rogers, E.M. (2003) *Diffusion of Innovations* (5th edn), New York: Free Press Simon & Schuster.
10 Altbach, P.G. and de Witt, H. (2018) 'Too much academic research is being published', *University World News,* 7 September, www.universityworldnews.com/post.php?story=20180905095203579
11 Pearson UK (2018) 'What is the purpose of a university?', 20 April, www.pearson.com/uk/educators/higher-education-educators/course-development-blog/2018/04/what-is-the-purpose-of-a-university-.html
12 Fannin, R.A. (2019) *Tech Titans of China: How China's Tech Sector is Challenging the World by Innovating Faster, Working Harder, and Going Global*, Boston, MA: Nicholas Brealey Publishing.
13 VSO, 'Volunteer with VSO', www.vsointernational.org/volunteering

Index

A

academia 33–5, 140, 202–4
academic-bureaucratic complex 24
Act of Parliament, 1766 15
Adam Smith Institute 37
Africa 65, 138
agency staff 104
agency theory 17
agriculture 15
air 67, 70, 128
Airbnb 32, 118
Alderfer, C.P. 81
Amazon 31, 32, 36, 95, 117–18, 133
Amazonian rainforest burning 53
America *see* United States
Anglo Irish Bank 54
anti-trust law 102
Appelbaum 159–60
Apple 32, 72, 95, 113, 117
Arkwright, Richard 3
Arthur Anderson 43
artificial intelligence 79, 117
artisans 110–11
asset stripping 30, 101, 112, 185–7
Atos 45, 49, 128
Attenborough, Sir David 53
Attlee, Clement 85
auditory consultancies 43, 48, 132–3, 135, 137
austerity 12, 13, 135
Austrian School 12

B

balance and the real economy 70–3
banking 13, 23, 27, 133, 141–2
Bank of England 27
Barclays Bank 35, 42, 49
BBC 36, 154
Becker, G. 144
Beijing 67
Bentham, Jeremy 7
best interests 18, 31
Beveridge, William 62, 63, 64, 70, 109, 155
'big bang,' 1986 26, 27, 31, 35, 131

'big data' 32, 119
Big Tech 31–3, 89, 95, 113, 117, 119, 136
  and regulation 133–4
billposting 168–9
biotechnology 118
'blue chip' corporations 190–1
Boots the Chemist 112
Boston box 193–4
BP 49
Bretton Woods settlement 23
British Airways 134
broadcast media 36
Brown, Wilfred 87, 88
bubble *see* speculation
Buckingham Palace 48
Bullock Report 197–8
business management education 33, 34, 144
  see also academia

C

Cambridge Analytica 119
Capita 45, 49, 54, 128
capitalism 11
Carillion 45, 129
Carnegie Foundation 33
cartels 5, 21, 102, 131
  see also monopolies
Centre for Policy Studies 37
Chandler, A. 29
Chang, Ha-Joon 73, 120
charisma 85
checks and balances 37–8, 141
Chief Executives for Corporate Purpose (CECP) 160
chief executive's pay 51, 86
China 67, 149
City of London 17, 26, 137, 141, 200–1
civil service 157
classical economics 7
climate change 54, 61, 120, 153, 162
closed shop cartels 26
coal 15, 119, 132, 152
collaboration 89, 91, 104

see also cooperation and cooperatives
'command and control' 86
common good 7, 25, 35, 39, 139
'commons' 69, 108, 128
communism 11, 21, 125
companies 15, 16, 18, 194–5
Companies Acts UK 31, 38
company planning 191–3
competition 5, 7, 11, 44, 131, 135, 156
   protecting 101–3
computerisation 28, 117
computerised modelling *see*
   mathematical modelling
conflicts of interest 156
contractual systems 49
cooperation and cooperatives 85–6, 91,
   110, 112
coordination, external and
   internal 97–8
corporate headquarters 194
corporate planning 182
corporate purpose 159–61
corruption 26, 50, 187–90
costs, minimising 8
council housing 143
Coyle, D. 74, 151
Crash 2008 8, 12, 13, 25, 27, 117, 135
credit rating agencies 28–9
Credit Suisse Global Wealth Report 51
criminality 27, 42, 50, 68, 107, 138–9,
   141, 158
customer needs 92, 94

D

dams 71, 129
Debenhams 112
debt 48
deception 48
Deepwater Horizon 49
Defense Advanced Research Project
   Agency (DARPA) 72
Deloitte 43
Deming, W.E. 91–3, 101, 103, 115,
   119, 145, 159
democracy 11, 21–3, 38, 74, 75,
   99, 136
   protection of 156–7
   and sustainable progression 59–65
deregulation 14, 26, 27, 28, 29, 35
Diamond, Bob 49

dictatorships 11, 27
Dimon, Jamie 48, 160
directors 17, 31
discrimination 65–6
distribution 178–9
diversification 30, 44
Dodge v Ford Motor Co. 18
dot.com bubble 25
Drucker, P.F. 6, 51, 85, 86, 115, 161
drugs 27, 45, 73, 113
Duke of York 48

E

Earle, J. 144
ecological destructions and impacts 20,
   24, 53–4
econocracy 35, 144
economic growth 11, 23
economic progression 59
economics as science 8
'economics of arrival' 74
Economist, The 41, 159–61
economy *see* real economy
education 5, 63, 153
efficient market hypothesis (EMH) 8
Eisenhower, President 23
elections 60, 157
elites 21
employee ownership 112
energy 69, 108, 117, 119, 136, 150
energy companies (UK) 46–7
Engels, F. 7
engines of enterprise 78, 79–85
Enron 27, 29, 43, 49
environmental destructions 42, 45, 49
environmental stewardship 60–2, 127–
   8, 137, 149, 155
equality 11, 64–6, 74, 150
   see also inequalities
European Union 73, 134, 146
exchange-rate stability 23
extraction industries 15
   see also fossil fuels
extreme weather 53
EY 43

F

Facebook 32, 36, 43, 95, 117–18, 134
Factory Acts 6
fake news 36, 135, 157

Faroohar, R. 33, 92
ferries 129
finance, predatory 24–9
financial derivatives 48
financialised business 29–33,
    45–50, 185
financialising the real economy 42–5
financial sector 13, 139–40, 143
Financial Times 48, 160–1
financial transactions tax 142
fines 42, 48
Fitch 29
flooding 129
food and food banks 41, 51
    see also hunger and starvation
Ford Foundation 33
foreign financial operators 151
Forex trading scandal 42, 48
fossil fuels 137, 150
    see also coal, oil
foundational economy 71
France 60
frauds 26–8, 41–5, 48–50, 107,
    123, 136
freedom 11, 12
free markets 5, 11, 13, 20, 21, 33,
    35, 101
Friedman, Milton 10–15, 17–18, 46,
    51, 87, 92, 143, 146, 158
Froud, J. 71

G

G4S 45, 49, 128
Galbraith, J.K. 10, 66–9, 107, 121
GDP growth metrics 150–2
Germany 16, 60, 111
Gettysburg address 59–60
Ghoshal, S. 19, 22, 24, 35, 46,
    85, 144–5
giant evils 62, 70
gig economy 89
Glacier Project 87, 88
Glencore 132
global warming 53, 162
Goldman Sachs 117
goods and services 25
Google 31, 32, 36, 95, 117–18, 134
Gore-Tex 86
government role 5, 12, 20, 22,
    141, 157

GPS 136
graphene 73, 118
Great Depression 8, 11, 12, 13, 135
green GDP 152
Green New Deal (US) 120, 162
green technologies 73, 108, 137, 158
Grenfell Tower fire 51

H

Harmsworth 35
'Hawthorne effect' 83–4
Hayek, F.A. 11, 12, 143
health and social care 108, 128, 153
Heffernan, M. 49
hierarchies of human need 80–2, 162
high speed rail 129
high street retailers 32
Holiday, Billie 64
homelessness 51
Hoover, President 23
housing 128, 143
human need and relations 79, 80–5
human rights 62–4, 123, 150, 153
Human Rights Act (UK) 1998 64
hunger and starvation 63, 150

I

income 50–2, 153
    see also pay
industrial innovation 201
industrial relations 195–7
industrial revolution (4IR) 117, 136
industrial revolution and
    industrialistion 3–4, 11, 15, 25,
    62, 149
inequalities 19, 21, 42, 50–2, 51, 87,
    123, 127, 136, 153, 161
inflation 11
Information Commissioner's Office
    (ICO) 134
information technology 117
infrastructure 71, 108
Initial Public Offerings (IPOs) 17
innovation 108, 114, 116
Instagram 36, 43
Institute of Directors (UK) 18, 31
Institute of Economic Affairs
    (UK) 14, 37
*Institut Européen d'Administration des
    Affaires* 34

'institutional truths' 3, 10, 15–19, 47
insurance 15, 26
integrity 7
intellectual capital 134
International Monetary Foundation
    (IMF) 23, 73, 146
internet search and provision 43
investment 14, 15
investment banking 25, 26
Iraq 54

J

Japan 16, 41, 92, 111, 149
job creation 12
Joint Stock Companies Act, 1844 15
journals 34
JP Morgan 48
Judt, Tony 41
junior management practice 172
Juran, J.M. 92, 159
justice 37, 66, 68, 108

K

Keynesian economics 10–12, 23,
    144–5, 151
Khurana, R. 33, 35
King, Martin Luther 64
Klein, N. 162
Koehler, W. 94
Kondratiev, N.D. 116
KPMG 43
Krugman, Paul 19, 73

L

labour 4, 7, 8
laissez faire 12
Lan, L.L. 18
Lanchester, J 28
land tax 138
Lay 49
leadership 85–6, 115
legal non-compliance 45
Lehman Brothers 13, 29
Lewis, M. 37, 38, 114
Libor index rigging 48, 49
libraries 128
life-cycle 149
'light touch' 29, 136
limited liability 15, 16
Lincoln, President 59

LinkedIn 36
living standards 5
lobbyists 24, 36, 142, 143, 157
London Olympics 45
Long-Term Capital Management
    (LTCM) 8
long-term interests 14, 23, 34, 61, 75,
    113, 137
Los Angeles 67
low-cost finance 23
Lucas, Robert 9

M

macroeconomic theory 7
Madoff, Bernie 27
majority shareholding 16
'makers' 92
Malthus, Thomas 41
management 6, 171–2
management sciences 83–5, 183–4
management trainee 167
Mandela, Nelson 65
manufacturing 14, 15, 172–3, 178
market forces 4–5
Marx, Karl and Marxism 4, 7, 11
Massachusetts Institute of Technology
    (MIT) 28
mathematical modelling 7, 9, 117
mature industries 30, 42, 131
maximising shareholder take (MST) 19,
    20, 27, 28, 31, 33
Mayo, Elton 83–4
Mazzucato, M. 47, 72, 73, 113,
    136, 152
McGregor, D. 84, 101, 115
measurements/targets 103–4
media, the 24, 28, 35–6, 140
'mental mutilation' 5, 159
merchant banking *see* investment
    banking
mergers and acquisitions 30–3, 44, 101,
    132, 182–3, 198–200
microeconomic theory 7
Middle East 11, 24, 54
migration 41, 53
military-industrial complex 23
Mill, J.S. 7
mills 3, 63, 112
minerals 132, 138
Ministry of Justice, UK 45

molecular engineering 118
money 12, 80, 84, 86–9
money laundering 48
monopolies 21, 23, 32, 42–4, 131
Monopolies and Mergers
    Commission 32, 102
Mont Pelerin Society 10–15, 23, 103
Moody 29
moral values 7, 20, 27, 35, 51,
    151, 162
mortgage mis-selling 49
motivations 13, 79, 80–3, 89, 98, 115,
    144, 161
Murdoch family 35, 36, 54

N

NASA 72
National Health Service (NHS) 47, 63,
    73, 88, 103
nationalisation 12
National Nanotechnology Inititative
    (US) 113
Nazism 60
neoclassical belief 3–10, 19–20, 42, 74,
    123, 128
    displacing 73–5, 143–5, 158–9
neoliberal economics 15
Netflix 36
'New Agenda' 160
New Deal 12, 13, 23
new technology 43, 72, 117, 121,
    123, 157
    and employment 133
Nightingale, Florence 61
Nobel Prize 8, 9, 19, 143
non-domiciled status 141

O

observation 3–6, 121, 136
Office of Fair Trading (OFT) 32, 102
offshore tax 15
oil 11, 49, 116, 117, 119, 135, 152
online technology 43, 133, 152
organisational systems 91–8, 99–101
    and the real economy 107–13
Organisation of Petroleum Exporting
    Countries (OPEC) 11
organised money 13, 23–9,
    121, 138–43
    restraint of 157–8

organising for growth 179–80
Orphan Drugs Act (US) 113
outsourcing and privatisations 14,
    45–7, 49, 71, 99–100, 103, 109,
    143, 151
    and progression 129–30
Owen, Robert 112
ownership 99, 104–5
Oxfam 51

P

Panama Papers 50
pandemic 13, 110, 145, 205
Paradise Papers 50
parks 128
Parks, Rosa 64
patents 135
pay and payment systems 8, 21, 51,
    86–9, 98, 115, 177
pension funds 26
people 68, 77, 79–85
personal data see user data
personnel 173–4, 195–7
pharmaceuticals 42, 72, 109
phone hacking 36
Piatier, A. 11, 116, 117
Piketty, T. 21, 51, 74
Pitt, W. 6
planned economy 11
political-economics 6, 20, 37, 41, 74,
    121, 135, 143
political text (online) 135
politicians and the political sector
    36–8, 99, 140, 157
pollutions 45, 53
poor, the see poverty
population 24, 41, 75, 119, 121, 149
Posner, Richard 159
post-war reconstruction 23, 63,
    109, 116
poverty 12, 14, 19, 51, 64, 67, 121,
    153, 154
practitioner notes and
    conclusions 165, 204–5
predatory finance 24–9
prices 12, 30, 101–2
prisons 45, 129
private sector 11, 12, 100
privatisation see outsourcing and
    privatisations

production 4, 7, 91, 92–4
production control 174–6
productivity 19, 84
product range 31, 181
professional services 43
profits, maximising 7, 11, 16–19, 23
progression 59–66
  action for 125–30, 135–42
  measures of 149–57
  of the real economy 155–6
progressive-competitive economy
  72–3, 110–13, 130–5
progressive culture 108, 115
progressive taxation 137–8, 161
property rights 12
Public Accounts Committee (UK) 49
public assets 51
publications record 34
public companies 17
publicly funded technology 113, 136
public service operators 128
public services/provisions 45–6, 50, 66,
  67, 109, 129
public spending 12
PwC 43

Q

quality control 177–8
quantitative easing (QE) 13
quantity theory of money 12
Quiggin, J. 74

R

racial prejudice and discrimination 65
railways 15
Raworth, K. 70, 74, 145, 152
real competition 101–3
real economy 3, 15, 25, 31, 70–3,
  108, 135
  organisations 42–5, 47
  progression 155–6
  remaking the 139–43
reality 10
real people 79–85, 98
real progression 149–57
real world 9, 21
rebuilding 128–30
recipients of returns 21
regulation 5, 24, 26, 36, 46, 72,
  101, 156

and monopolies 132–5
and new technology 43
renewable energy *see* energy
rentiers 21
Repo 105–29, 48
retail 178–9
retail banking 26–7, 43
Reuters 27
revolving doors 24
Ricardo, David 4, 7
rich, the *see* wealthy, the
Rochdale Pioneers 112
Rogers, Paul 54
Roosevelt, President 12, 23, 24, 157
Routh, G. 10, 35
Royal Air Force 165–6
Ruskin, John 8, 9
Russia 11, 36

S

salesmen 181–2
Say, Jean-Baptiste 3, 7
Schumpeter, J.A. 116
Scott Bader Commonwealth
  Limited 112
sea level rises 53
Second World War (WW2) 12, 23
  see also post-war reconstruction
Seddon, J. 86
self-interest 7, 10, 13, 20, 37, 39, 80
Serco 45, 49, 128
shadow banking 26
shareholder primacy 15–19, 20,
  31, 144
shares and bonds 15, 25
Shaxson, N. 27, 47, 74, 136, 137–8
Sherman anti-trust law, 1890 102
Shkreli, Martin 109
short-term 17, 44
'simple truth' 10
site getting 170–1
Skilling, J. 49
Sky News 36
slavery 59–60, 65
small and medium sized enterprises
  (SMEs) 17, 44, 110–11
Small Business Innovation Research
  (US) 113
Smith, Adam 3–7, 13–14, 21, 42, 80,
  91, 102, 127

Smith, Craig 34
Smith College, Massachusetts 10
social balance 66–70, 107, 123, 153
social dysfunction 68
social effects 7, 20
social-infrastructural economy 71–3, 108–10, 120, 128–30
socialism 7, 11, 12, 20, 21, 24, 39
social justice 11, 22
social media 24, 43, 135, 157
social sustainability 156, 157
social unrest 42, 51, 127, 157
South Sea Bubble 25
space selling 170–1
speculation 23, 25, 26, 28
'stagflation' 11, 135
Standard and Poor 29
standard costing 176–7
start-ups 95, 110–11
starvation *see* hunger and starvation
state owned enterprises 92
Stiglitz, J.E. 74, 152
stock markets 28
strategy and innovation 114–15
sub-prime securities 13, 29
supply and demand 4, 8
Supreme Court of Michigan 18
sustainable development 72, 119–20, 123, 152–5
sustainable progression 59–65
swaps and derivatives 28
system components 97–9
systems approach 131, 135
systems innovation 114–16

T
'takers' 92
Tawney, R.H. 66
taxation 6, 12, 14, 20, 127, 158
progressive 137–8
tax avoidance and evasion 14–15, 26, 48–50, 87, 107, 112
and M. Friedman 51, 158
preventing 127, 137–8, 141–2
Taylor, Fred 83
technological-revolutionary economy 73, 113–14, 136–7
technological revolutions 116–19
technology 24, 32
telecoms/broadband 69

Tett, G. 49, 160
Texas City Refinery 49
Theories X and Y 84–5, 115
think tanks 24, 37, 143
third world tyrants 27
trade unions 83, 117
trading systems 28
transactions 12
transport infrastructure 3, 15, 25, 128
Trebeck, K. 74
'trickle down' 14, 21, 70
Truman, President 85
trustworthiness 14, 26, 74, 115
truth 36, 37
Tulip mania 25
Turing Pharmaceuticals 109
Twitter 36
two-tier boards 142

U
Uber 32, 89, 95, 118, 133
UK constitution 59
understanding by observation 4–6
unemployment 51, 63
United Nations 64, 66, 73, 146, 150
Development Goals 61, 63, 74, 153–5
Panel on Climate Change 42, 53, 162
United States 17, 29, 59, 72, 113, 120, 162
business 6, 18, 33
civil rights 64
and democracy 37, 38, 108, 157
see also New Deal
user information 32, 134
utilities 69

V
value, the nature of 6
value extraction 21, 45–50, 161
VAT 138
von Mises, L. 11, 12, 102

W
Wall Street Crash, 1929 8, 11, 23, 25
war 23, 54, 65
warehousing 181–2
waste collection 67
water systems 46, 50, 68, 70, 71, 108, 128, 153

wealth 21, 33, 138
wealth and income 50–2
wealthy, the 5, 14, 19, 51, 154, 160
welfare payments 63
wellbeing 159
WhatsApp 43, 134
'wilful blindness' 49
Williams, K 74
'witchcraft' 3, 8, 42, 47
women 10, 153

work and workers 5, 23, 32, 51, 83, 118, 159
working class 7, 196
work measurement 176–7
World Bank 23, 51, 73, 138, 146
Worldcom 27
wrongs 41–4, 48–55

Y
Yemen 150
YouTube 36